"This is an extraordinary book. Spiro has provided a feisty account of a spiritual journey that raises a host of fascinating issues. He clearly articulates in a refreshing manner his own hard-won efforts to answer the big questions of theology and philosophy. At one level, Spiro moves beyond the current temptation to settle for a thin dispute between theists and atheists. At another level, he shows theologians how things appear to an intelligent layperson who takes seriously the task of theology. For either theologians or laypeople to ignore this vista would be a failure of intelligence and love in relating to our sophisticated neighbors."
—WILLIAM J. ABRAHAM, ALBERT COOK OUTLER PROFESSOR OF WESLEY STUDIES, PERKINS SCHOOL OF THEOLOGY, SOUTHERN METHODIST UNIVERSITY

"Dan Spiro challenges both the religious skeptics and the fundamentalists of all faiths. His ability to clarify how a person can meaningfully occupy a middle ground between those positions is a welcome addition to growing literature on spirituality. Most importantly, the book helps us understand the power of multi-faith engagement. Each of us can become better human beings if we are faithful to our respective religious heritages even as we explore, ally with and learn from people of other faiths. Only then can religion help us chart a course to a more peaceful and just world."
—RABBI SID SCHWARZ, SENIOR FELLOW, THE NATIONAL JEWISH CENTER FOR LEARNING AND LEADERSHIP; AUTHOR OF JUDAISM AND JUSTICE: THE JEWISH PASSION TO REPAIR THE WORLD

"Daniel Spiro is fascinated by the subject of God and if you join him on his quest, you will soon be too. For the veteran seeker or the merely curious, this book invites you on an intellectual and spiritual journey you will not soon forget. With passion, clarity and humility, Spiro introduces the joys of theological speculation while mounting a powerful argument for interfaith engagement as the great religious adventure of our time."
—RABBI NANCY FUCHS KREIMER, DIRECTOR, MULTIFAITH STUDIES AND INITIATIVES, RECONSTRUCTIONIST RABBINICAL COLLEGE

"This is a delightful book by a self-thinking mind inspired by the bold philosophy of Spinoza. The Talmud tells us that the Torah can function either as an elixir or as poison. Here is a remarkable attempt to spell out a religion free from the poison of contemporary fundamentalism."
—YITZHAK MELAMED, PROFESSOR OF PHILOSOPHY, JOHNS HOPKINS UNIVERSITY, AUTHOR, SPINOZA'S METAPHYSICS: SUBSTANCE AND THOUGHT.

"Daniel Spiro's Liberating the Holy Name is indeed a liberating work. I love the way in which he wrestles with a very touchy subject and the respect he gives to the range of believers and non-believers. He provides needed insight into the evolution of God-thought and composes a philosophy of religion that all can benefit from. In a world torn apart by competing needs and spiritual insecurity, Daniel Spiro offers us a Light."
—RABBI DAVID SHNEYER, SPIRITUAL LEADER OF THE AM KOLEL JEWISH RENEWAL COMMUNITY AND THE KEHILA CHADASHA HAVURAH AND PAST PRESIDENT OF OHALAH, THE ASSOCIATION OF RABBIS AND CANTORS FOR JEWISH RENEWAL

"In this lucid and engaging book, author Daniel Spiro makes the case for God and challenges God's 'cultured despisers' (like new-atheist Richard Dawkins) who have monopolized the American God-conversation for too long. Spiro demonstrates that intellectual honesty can co-exist with the God-smitten heart of a mystic as he invites readers to 'fall in love with God' without compromising their integrity. A Jewish advocate of interfaith dialogue, Spiro systematically develops his arguments in conversation with philosophers like Nietzsche and Spinoza and finds wisdom in the Torah and the Trinity, the Qur'an and Kabbalah."

—PROFESSOR MARY JOAN WINN LEITH, CHAIR, DEPARTMENT OF RELIGIOUS STUDIES, STONEHILL COLLEGE

"*Liberating the Holy Name* is an extraordinary book, a rare undertaking that succeeds in filling the immense gap between the negativism of the flaming atheists and the intransigent fundamentalists. Spiro writes as one who has spent the better part of five decades asking the deep questions of life that we all ask, and now puts it all together in a philosophical approach that embraces the uncertainty that both Socrates and Spinoza would applaud. It is an inquiry with all of the intellectual tools at our disposal, and a celebration of the journey that honors the best in contemporary thinking. How can reading a book with a new question for every answer be such an intellectual joy? You have to try it and discover for yourself."

—REV. E. MAYNARD MOORE, PH.D., PRESIDENT, WESLEYNEXUS

LIBERATING THE HOLY NAME

Liberating the
HOLY NAME

A Free-Thinker Grapples
with the Meaning of Divinity

DANIEL SPIRO

 CASCADE *Books* · Eugene, Oregon

LIBERATING THE HOLY NAME
A Free-Thinker Grapples with the Meaning of Divinity

Cascade Books
An Imprint of Wipf and Stock Publishers
199 W. 8th Av.e, Suite 3
Eugene, OR 97401

ISBN 13: 978-1-62564-630-9

Cataloging-in-Publication data:

Spiro, Daniel, 1960–.

Liberating the holy name : a free-thinker grapples with the meaning of divinity / Daniel Spiro.

x + 236 p. ; 23 cm. Includes bibliographical references and indexes.

ISBN 13: 978-1-62564-630-9

1. Faith and Reason. 2. Religion—Philosophy. 3. God. I. Title.

BL51 S758 2014

For all who wage war against both religious apathy and fanaticism.

Table of Contents

PART III—GOD IN THE FIRST PERSON 161

Acknowledgments

As an attorney with a full-time practice, I could never have written this book without the help of a wide range of individuals and institutions who have encouraged my philosophical and religious pursuits. I wish to thank the Goethe-Institut Washington and the members of the Washington Spinoza Society. Since 2001, the presentations and discussions at this society have continued to enrich my life as a student and teacher of philosophy. Even more importantly, this society has been a source of wonderful friends. None of this would have been possible without the Goethe-Institut's generous support over the years. Long live that Society and that Institute!

In 2009, I was blessed to co-found another organization that would come to play a major role in my life, the Jewish-Islamic Dialogue Society of Washington, or JIDS. I wish to express my thanks to Haytham Younis, Ira Weiss, Sabir Rahman, Andra Baylus, Kay Halpern, Kamal Mustafa, Sahara Khamis, and the other dedicated members of the JIDS community. They continue to inspire me with their faith, patience, intellectuality, and commitment to the interfaith movement, and that inspiration has paid dividends in this book. Perhaps the greatest tribute to their work is that so many *non*-Jews or Muslims have chosen to become a part of this group. The fact that they have created such a loving environment is precisely why our dialogues can be so provocative and stimulating.

I wish to express special gratitude to Tim Beardsley, Alexander Patico, and Elizabeth Thede, who provided invaluable edits to an early version of the manuscript for this work. I know for a fact that reading an early draft of a book can be a painful experience, but somehow those three individuals were able to ignore the bumps in the road and lead me to where I needed to go. They are all dear friends, and I cannot thank them enough for their service to this book.

I am also grateful to those individuals from the publishing industry who have opened their minds to the theological and philosophical musings of a lawyer. I will always appreciate the assistance of John McGraw, whose press published my first two books. And I must additionally thank Robin Parry, who spearheaded Cascade Books' decision to publish this work and has served as its editor.

As for my family, my mother Evelyn Spiro, daughters, Hannah and Rebecca, and wife Kathleen all took the time to read early drafts of this book and improve it. It is surely my greatest blessing as an individual to be part of such a close family. I am truly humbled to be associated with each of these amazing people.

Finally, last, but hardly least, thank you, God—for literally everything.

Introduction

"I know that I have no wisdom, great or small."

—Socrates (from Plato's *Apology*)[1]

"Whereof one cannot speak, thereof one must be silent."

—Ludwig Wittgenstein (from the *Tractatus Logico-Philosophicus*)[2]

TRADITIONALLY, GOD'S SERVANTS HAVE been people of faith. I pride myself in being a person of doubt. I doubt our ability to predict the future or to answer definitively the questions of religious philosophy. And while I accept that we can make theological arguments in which the conclusions follow perfectly from the premises, I doubt our ability to gain certainty about which of those premises are right and which are wrong. But I can live with that skeptical attitude. Combine it with a dose of curiosity, a twist of awe, and a heaping of gratitude, and we people of doubt can still find our way back to God. While it is certainly more circuitous than the traditional route, which begins and ends with faith, people of doubt must face the fact that we never do well with straight paths.

In the more cosmopolitan parts of the world, skepticism is king these days when it comes to matters of religion. God is no longer a given,

1. Plato, *Selected Dialogues*, 288.
2. Kenny, *Wittgenstein Reader*, 30.

1

and neither is atheism. As for that all-so-chic label known as "agnosticism," that's just a distraction. On the most superficial level possible, all people of doubt are agnostics. Webster defines the word as "a person who believes that the human mind cannot know whether there is a God or an ultimate cause, or anything beyond material phenomena."[3] It's just another way of saying that when it comes to the ultimate religious questions, agnostics are people of doubt. But that's only a starting place, isn't it? The real questions begin once we acknowledge our doubt and ask ourselves, now what? Do we opt to "believe" or not to believe? And precisely what belief is it that we're thinking about adopting? A belief in the God of Sinai? In a world soul? In the great, interconnected web of existence? In the "eternal Thou"?

Choosing a worldview used to be simple. You took what your parents believed, which happened to be what the leaders in your community believed, and you either adopted it yourself or moved to another community. Today, however, we have options, and I'm afraid that "agnosticism" *in practice* is usually just another word for saying that you'd rather not bother to confront those options or even think about the whole topic of religion. You'd rather focus on other things.

If you're of that mindset, this probably isn't the book for you. But if you enjoy thinking about God across religious traditions *and heresies*, then welcome! You're in the right place.

⊷

I first read the above quotation from Socrates in a college philosophy class and became enthralled with the idea that the world's greatest philosopher is precisely the person who is most willing to accept his own ignorance. Of course, Socrates wasn't professing a complete lack of knowledge, but only a lack of *wisdom*. He must have realized what every schoolchild knows today—that there indeed are statements we can make with utter confidence. Statements about the meaning of words or the basic principles of mathematics fall into that category. We know that the sum of three angles of a triangle is the sum of two right angles. We know that all bachelors are unmarried. What we can't be sure about is what most interested Socrates, and that includes the subject of this book.

---

3. "Agnostic," *Webster's New World College Dictionary*, 27.

Socrates, the gadfly, buzzed about at a time when philosophy and the natural sciences were only beginning to be addressed as disciplines. All the pre-Socratic philosophers worth their salt couldn't help but be struck by the primitive level of our knowledge. In asserting his ultimate skepticism, Socrates was putting down a marker for the idea that even such self-evident propositions as geocentrism might ultimately prove to be false. History, as we know, has proven him to be prophetic. And now, nearly all philosophers can declare themselves to be disciples of Socrates and people of doubt.

A lot has transpired during the twenty-four centuries since Socrates drank his hemlock. To name just a few highlights, Columbus sailed the ocean blue, Galileo confirmed the truth of Copernicus' heresy, and Darwin showed that Genesis lacks a monopoly on how to account for intelligent life. These twenty-four centuries, however, have not exactly been dominated by great explorers and geniuses. The powers-that-be have been pedestrian monarchs, courtiers, and clerics who have accepted their era's conventional wisdom as if it were ordained from above. It is they, rather than the disciples of Socrates, who have controlled the agenda about what we mean by "God."

What's notable, though, is that if you look at the greatest figures of religious history, many of them were the heretics of their day. Each of the founders of the great Western faiths revolted against the religions of their elders. Whether you believe that Abraham, Jesus, and Muhammad were inspired by their own thoughts or by supernatural intervention, the outcome is undeniable: they refused to accept conventional religious wisdom on faith. It is only their so-called "followers" who assert that wisdom consists in following a carefully trod path that has been set forth by others, rather than a path that individual seekers set out for themselves.

This book, by contrast, is the product of a contemporary American mind. For better or worse, I approach the big questions not so much as a member of an insular community of faith but rather as an individual who freely chooses what to believe and why. Sometimes, those choices are clear. For most of us, the decisions not to kill, steal, or humiliate others become second nature at an early age. But the same cannot necessarily be said for our choice of religious beliefs. There, it strikes me that the only prudent American option is to embark on a lifelong search for truth and meaning that never really ends, because we can never know what religious beliefs are "true" or even which ones will add the most meaning to our lives in five, ten, or twenty years.

It was my love of philosophy that taught me to adopt that perspective, but I don't think you have to be philosophically minded to find it appealing. All you have to be is a skeptic who respects his or her ancestors. Historically, the domain of religion was seen as second to none in importance, both to one's education and to one's orientation in life. So if I am correct that the great religious questions are impossible to answer definitively, but our ancestors are correct that these questions need to be taken with the utmost seriousness, we are obliged to grapple with them as a lifelong adventure.

What follows is an attempt to set forth the results to date of my lifelong search for wisdom concerning God. I hope to inspire you to embark on your own search or to further the journey that you have already begun. Candidly, though, I also hope to engage you as social activists by enlisting you in a specific fight. I will try to demonstrate that whatever your religious views may be, as long as you are a lover of freedom, you should be offended by what is happening today to the Word of Words (God). This attack is being perpetrated by the strangest of bedfellows: religious fundamentalists and outspoken atheists. At least in this one respect, these two groups are moving the world in the same direction. And given how difficult it is to fight a two-front war, the rest of us have our work cut out for us if we'd like to return the divine name to anywhere near the status it once held.

⇝

Just as it is bad for our economy when a corporation is able to monopolize an industry, our spirituality is sapped by any successful monopoly over the meaning of "God." In both of these domains, prosperity depends upon our respect for the value of diversity and competition.

If this book is an argument against one idea, it is the notion that the divine name can only mean what it has traditionally meant for centuries, and any alternative conception is illegitimate. I've heard this claim from some of the most strident pro-religion voices and *all* of the unabashedly anti-religious people who I've encountered. The funny thing is, while the anti-religious folks probably realize that they're getting help from their God-fearing counterparts, I don't think the latter have a clue that they're playing right into their opponents' hands.

Stated simply, many members of both groups share an interest in strait-jacketing the debate. They want to keep our choices simple when it comes to religion: accept "God" or reject religion altogether. *What* God you ask? Please, you know the conception I'm talking about. "He" is an omnipotent, omnibenevolent, eternal being who has created the universe and all of its contents in accordance with his own inscrutable will, and who has revealed his existence to human beings known as prophets. Am I arguing here that such a God cannot possibly exist? Not at all. What I would say, however, is that people can modify that conception of God and still be every bit as spiritual and religious as any traditional minister, rabbi, or imam. In fact, the more we treat such alternative conceptions of God as illegitimate, the more we marginalize the entire religious enterprise within contemporary society. Atheists understand that, and it makes them happy. Traditionalists? They may be even more offended by "heresy" than non-belief, and they're certainly not likely to encourage it, even if that means chasing progressive thinkers away from religion altogether.

One aim of this book is to broaden our understanding of the Word of Words by relating it back to its simple essence. To me, "God" has both a common connotation, which is narrow and often parochial, and a denotation, which is both more general and more profound. What it connotes, typically, is the biblical God of Abraham—at least that's the conventional Western meaning. By contrast, what the word denotes is the *Ultimate*. That is the one meaning that seems to be adopted by nearly everyone who embraces the word, whether they are traditional or "progressive" in their religious philosophies. This is illustrated by the use of the term "false god," which suggests a deity that someone might take to be the "ultimate" (say, money or power) but that does not, in truth, possess that status.

When progressive theologians talk about God in non-biblical terms, they point to what for them is not only more ultimate than any biblical character but also deeply transcendent of anything as limited as money or power. This is why enlightened traditionalists, though they may have in their minds a different conception of God, will at least recognize the progressive theologian as a fellow "believer." In both cases, they are searching for God based on the essence of the term, which is the *Ultimate*, as opposed to any form God would take as a character in a book or as the object of our prayers.

The orthodox followers of the Abrahamic faiths recognize that the standard of ultimacy is decisive as to what turns a "god" (with a small

g) into the one true God. They would simply maintain that the God of their Scriptures satisfies this standard. As for those believers who see themselves as religious progressives, they may assert that the scriptural deity is a fiction, but most would still adopt the idea that there truly is an *Ultimate*. Whether they think of this *Ultimate* as a process, a being, or as Being itself, it is to that notion of ultimacy that they assign *The Name*. Of course, they might emphasize that they are attempting to honor the real God and not the Lord of man's making, yet that may not stop them from praising, or otherwise encountering, the Divine in recognizably religious ways. To deny their belief in God would thus seem arbitrary, if not downright obnoxious.

People who would resist the idea that "God" refers to what is truly the *Ultimate* often see themselves as anti-religious. As far as they are concerned, we should keep the definition of God narrow enough so that it refers only to the Lord of Scripture, regardless of whether that Lord satisfies the criterion of ultimacy. Armed with this position, these anti-religious forces hope to persuade more and more people that "God" does not exist. For example, they might say to the religious progressive, "We understand that you claim to believe in 'God,' but that word is already taken by the traditionalists; you'll need to find another word to refer to whatever you view as the *Ultimate*."

Personally, I don't think we should allow those who deny the existence of God to define what is meant by that word. It must be understood broadly so that it respects all who embrace its potential power, and so that it demonstrates our own humility. Who are we to say that some people believe in "God" and others don't simply because their view of the *Ultimate* differs from our own? Moreover, while we're remembering the importance of humility, let us not think that simply because we can name God, we can truly understand God. When I refer to *The Name* (or put "God" in quotation marks), I am speaking of a man-made tool—a piece of language that we create and endow with meaning. By contrast, God, or the Divine, is ultimately shrouded in mystery. That point must not be forgotten, especially when embarking on a journey to explore the meaning of divinity.

Nevertheless, in referring to either *The Name* or *The Ultimate*, I will generally do so in italics in order to emphasize that while the meanings they convey to us are merely human constructs, what they point to is none other than the Most High. The mysterious nature of divinity need not preclude us from celebrating the utter holiness in honoring the

Divine by referring to God as *The Name* or by recalling that our search for God is identical to our search for *The Ultimate*.

⊸

Why do I care so much about the straightjacketing of debate on the meaning of a word? Because I see this development as helping to replace our spirituality with apathy, and I'm not a big fan of religious apathy.

Many other skeptics, however, feel differently. And they have found solace in statements like the words of Wittgenstein quoted at the start of this chapter. When he wrote that "whereof one cannot speak, thereof one must be silent," he unwittingly spoke for millions who would like to marginalize the topic of God in our society and turn religious philosophy into a solitary and esoteric discipline.

In certain circles, *The Name* comes up with regularity. For example, when Muslims say that they plan on doing something at a particular time, they typically add the word "insha'Allah,"—meaning "if God wills it." ("Are you coming to the meeting Sunday night?" "I'll be there by six thirty, insha'Allah.") Outside of a few subcultures, however, you can easily live your life in cities like Paris, Moscow, or Washington and rarely hear the word "God" come up in conversation. What is rarer still is when educated people use the word in a way that suggests that God is an important figure in their lives.

The truth is that with few exceptions, God has become an unspeakable topic outside of traditional religious communities, and this is largely due to how alienated many people feel from the Lord of Scripture. We live in a transitional phase, a time when we are only beginning to challenge the hegemony that the priests have held over *The Name*. When it comes to the public sphere, that challenge is muted at best, reflecting the small number of "believers" who are motivated to fight over the meaning of the Word of Words. Once you remove from the arena all the traditionalists, everyone who is religiously apathetic, and all who are antagonistic to the whole religious project, you've crossed off most of the population. What's more, the bulk of the candidates who might otherwise issue the challenge sadly recognize that their thoughts about God are vague and incoherent. For such people, it can be comforting to remind themselves that "whereof one cannot speak, thereof one must be silent," and then get back to discussions on more solid ground, like those involving politics, the arts, or the world of business.

Not surprisingly, given how little is said today about God in the public domain, when the topic does come up, the discussion generally takes place at a frustratingly low level—much more superficially, say, than when people talk about sports. This discourse about God is dominated by fundamentalists of different stripes, some of whom claim to speak on behalf of religion and others whose anti-religious passion is equally grounded in dogma—they are no less fundamentalist than the religious people they claim to oppose. At the risk of sounding certain about anything involving this topic and thereby contradicting Socrates, we can do better. It is our job to convert *The Name* from one of social divisiveness to one of social unity while we still have the chance.

Nature, after all, abhors a vacuum. And if religious fundamentalism comes to dominate the discussion, is there any doubt why it has garnered such power in the contemporary world? In *The Case for God*, Karen Armstrong makes an especially powerful argument against fundamentalism. She laments the failure of modern society to accept scriptural stories *as myth*, which she claims was their original purpose. "Today," she says, "because the modern West is a society of *logos*, some people read the Bible literally, assuming that its intention is to give us the kind of accurate information that we expect from any other supposedly historical text and that this is the way these stories have always been understood."[4] In fact, adds Armstrong, "until well into the modern period, Jews and Christians both insisted that it was neither possible nor desirable to read the Bible in this way, that it gives us no single, orthodox message and demands constant reinterpretation."[5]

Armstrong is undeniably correct that ours is a society of *logos* in which people thirst for the reasonable, the intelligible, the measurable, the orderly. Now, more than ever, we have become an information-worshiping society, one that extols cold, hard facts, and devalues philosophical speculation and the exploration of myths. As Armstrong points out, this love of the *logos* has led some to read the Bible as literally as they read any other book that purports to describe human history. But for others, the idea of a Supreme Being who has tampered with our beloved laws of nature smacks of the height of folly. That's certainly how Jefferson and his

4. Armstrong, *Case for God*, 28.
5. Ibid.

fellow Deists would have perceived the notion that Moses literally parted the Sea of Reeds, or that Jesus literally walked on water. As products of the Enlightenment, they couldn't bring themselves to accept statements so antithetical to the teachings of modern science.

Biblical literalism, then, is not likely to be the option of choice for most of the educated, affluent citizens of today's world. And given the paucity of public discourse about viable alternatives, is it surprising that religion is losing its importance? Just consider a survey that was taken in both developed and developing nations near the dawn of this new millennium. In a 2002 worldwide poll conducted by the Pew Research Center, 38,000 people in forty-four countries were questioned about the importance of religion in their lives.[6] Sure enough, the survey found a sharply negative correlation between a country's per capita income and the percentage of its citizens who believe that religion is "very important" to their lives. The United States stood out among highly affluent societies in affirming the continuing relevance of religion. Whereas 59 percent of Americans stated that religion was very important to them, the analogous numbers in Europe and Japan were far lower (e.g., France 11 percent, Japan 12 percent, Russia 14 percent, Germany 21 percent, Italy 27 percent, Great Britain 33 percent). By contrast, in poorer countries like Senegal, Nigeria, Indonesia, India, and the Ivory Coast, more than 90 percent of the respondents answered the question in the affirmative.

Here in the United States, God is clearly a more frequent dinner table companion in some parts of the country than others. The southeastern and south-central portions of the country have been termed the "Bible Belt," but they could just as well have been called the "Outliers," because relative to the rest of the developed world, these regions stand alone for their embrace of religion and God.

Will southern Americans remain outliers? That I can't answer. What can be said is that there are plenty of Americans in the south and otherwise who couldn't care less about the topic of God, and plenty of others who would sorely welcome religion's demise. Then there are folks like me who would view that development as no less tragic than if we were to witness the death of music, art, or literature. I could live without any of the above, but my life wouldn't be nearly as rich or meaningful. And that is especially true when it comes to my embrace of *The Name*. For while I recognize that God may never literally have appeared to Moses in the

6. The Pew Global Attitudes Project, "Among Wealthy Nations," table.

form of a burning bush, God *does* appear to me in the form of a burning heart, a withered face, or a rainbow. I could no more abandon that God than I could worship the cosmic magician of the traditionalists.

❧

My guess is that if Socrates were alive today he would acknowledge that there are some areas in which we can go about our lives with considerable confidence and others in which we are destined to poke around in the dark, and that first among the latter category is theology. It is precisely because of that point that we need to open our minds to many different religious traditions and teachers. If we find inspiration from reading heretics like Spinoza or Nietzsche, so much the better. And that can also be said for the traditional texts, such as the Talmud, the Gospels, or the Upanishads. We cannot afford to ignore any source of spiritual insights, given the paucity of wisdom available to us relative to the infinite depths of our theological ignorance.

In other words, we must respect Ken Wilber's admonition to "give to Caesar what is Caesar's, to Einstein what is Einstein's, to Picasso what is Picasso's, to Kant what is Kant's, and to Christ what is Christ's."[7] Let me add that we also need to give to ourselves what is ours. In the domain of religion this means that we must recognize that our religious views inescapably reveal our own backgrounds as unique individuals, as the offspring of particular parents, and as members of a limited number of societal sub-cultures. Stated differently, we should accept that in tackling a subject like God, to be human is to be influenced by personal biases, which will become every bit as important to our journey as our command of logic. Armed with these influences, we can hopefully select a sensible, inspiring religious philosophy, and perhaps even find common ground with others who live in distant places and times. What we can't do is attain absolute objectivity. Nor can we provide proofs that pass the laugh test or justify suppressing dissent.

For better or worse, when either writing or reading a book about God, we must cloak the project in humility and realize that despite our best efforts, the primary subject of the book will be ourselves, not God. No matter how far you open your eyes, this book has more to teach you about your own unique passions and needs than about the Infinite.

---

7. Wilber, *Integral Spirituality*, 194.

One advantage I have in writing this book is my profession. I make my living as an attorney who specializes in investigating and litigating against corporate fraud. That's another way of saying that I am *not* in the "God business," either as a cleric, an academic, or a self-proclaimed guru, so perhaps my readers can better relate to my own life than to the lives of many who write about this topic. In any event, I hope we can agree that no matter how we ply our trade, where we live, or the extent of our education, each of us has the power to grow immensely from closely examining our thoughts on God. Speaking for myself, I know of no topic over the past few decades that has fascinated me more.

⊷

The title of this book, *Liberating the Holy Name*, identifies my fundamental objective. I aim to remove the straightjacket that atheists and religious fundamentalists alike have placed around the name of God when they deny the authenticity of any non-traditional interpretation of divinity. If I am correct that divinity refers to *the Ultimate*, and that the Scriptural figure who goes by the name of "God" is simply one of the many ways that people may choose to portray the concept of ultimacy, we need to fundamentally revisit the way we think about the Divine. The "question of God" becomes a mystery that we embrace, rather than an opportunity to express our faith or lack thereof. It leads to deeper inquiries like "What is your view of *the Ultimate*?" or "How can human beings, who are tiny specks on a tiny planet, ask such a question without losing our humility in the process?" Once *The Name* has been liberated to embrace its roots in the concept of ultimacy, we will stop asking ourselves whether to believe in God, and begin asking how we have come to view *The Ultimate* and how we have allowed this view to affect our life. This book reflects my best efforts to answer those questions.

Candidly, it was not until my manuscript for this work was virtually finished that it received its present title. The original one, the title I expected to use throughout the drafting process, was *God in Three Voices*. That notion continues to form the central idea for the book's structure.

The concept of God *in three voices* has nothing to do with what some people refer to as relationships within the Divine. I am using the term "three voices" in the same sense that it is used in a middle school foreign language class. Part I of this work will analyze God in the third person (so to speak, as a "he"). Part II will address God in the second person (as a "Thou"). And Part III will contemplate the prospects for individual human beings or humankind generally to view God in the first person (as an "I" or "We").

My decision to use those three voices in reflecting on God originated with a statement I heard several years ago in a Unitarian-Universalist church. I had recently finished giving a lecture on my favorite philosopher, Baruch Spinoza—whose theology may glibly be summarized by the pantheist notion that God and nature are one—when a member of the church approached me with a lesson of his own. "The best conceptions of the divine," he said, provocatively, "must enable us to address God in the first person, the second person, and the third person. You need all three."

I felt those words like a blast of cold wind in the face. It was a blunt reminder that for all the time that I had spent thinking about or praying to God, I was really just beginning my journey. The churchgoer forced me to consider that my pantheism may have successfully removed some of the impurities from the "old-time religion," but what kind of depth does it offer? How can it possibly satisfy the heart of a spiritual seeker? Sure, it is great to be able to praise the *Ultimate* without buying into fundamentalist myths—the kind of myths that have done so much to fuel atheism. And yes, it is a blessing when we can toast the Divine as being inside of us and speak of ourselves as being inside of the Divine. Yet the Jew in me demanded more. For when you have over-intellectualized your relationship to God to the point where you have lost sight of God as a Thou—in other words, when you have lost your ability to address the Divine as Abraham, Moses, or Isaiah addressed the Divine—haven't you sapped some of the life and breath out of your spirituality?

My greatest challenge as a student of philosophy generally, and Spinoza in particular, was to encounter God in the second person. But what I found so compelling about the statement by my Unitarian-Universalist interlocutor is that it would likely present equally potent problems for others whose perspectives on God are different from my own. To traditional theologians who view God as the cosmic "other" in heaven who created this world, their greatest challenge might be to encounter God in the first person (as an "I" or a "we"). To practitioners of New Age mysticism who worship the goodness in us all and in nature, their greatest challenge might be to talk about God in the third person without sounding Pollyannaish one moment and logically challenged the next. And to followers of the great Jewish philosopher, Martin Buber, it might be a challenge to talk about God in either the first or the third person—for Buber's God can only be known through the I-Thou encounter.

Any way you slice it, my interlocutor at that UU church set a high bar for us all. And if a philosophical pantheist cannot cross it, I reasoned, nobody can. Being a lover of philosophy, I should be equipped to communicate clearly and consistently about God in the third person. Being a *pan*theist—one who doesn't fundamentally separate God from ourselves or the rest of our world—I should be equipped to speak about God in the first person. And being a pan*theist*, I had better be able to address God as a Thou—or else we are dealing with something that is way too dull and irrelevant to be worthy of the Word of Words. So, God in three voices, here we come.

By the time this work is completed, it is my hope: (a) to identify a conception of God in the third person that is logically coherent, satisfies the demands of modern philosophical thought, and is worthy of the ultimacy inherent in the divine name; (b) to demonstrate that even though we have stripped from the Divine those characteristics that make "him" sound like a cosmic Superman, we can still enter into a rich, relationship with God as an Eternal Thou; and (c) to see ourselves as important manifestations of the Divine who have been inspired by this awareness to live in a way that honors God, honors one another, and nurtures the only world we can begin to comprehend. Yet in offering this alternative conception of God, I do not wish simply to replace one parochial view with another. However we as individuals come to conceive of God—however we choose to put flesh on the bones of the Holy Name—we must remember that despite our longing to portray God in understandable terms, the divine cloak of mystery can never be lifted. "God" denotes ultimacy, and *the Ultimate* shall always remain beyond our ken.

Why then seek *the Ultimate* if we can never find precisely what we're looking for? Because there is immeasurable joy and enlightenment in the search itself, as well as in the relationships that flow from it.

Bless you for joining me on the voyage.

PART I

GOD IN THE THIRD PERSON

"So, do you believe in God?" It's been a long time since someone asked me that question, yet it came up often when I was a teenager. Back then, I assume the expected response was one of two words, which in my case would have been "no." When adults ask the question today, they would probably expect a more nuanced response. "That depends on how you define the term," is a likely candidate. Or alternatively, "How would I know if there's a God? What's for lunch?"

At the risk of seeming unsophisticated, if asked today whether I believe in God, I might respond with two words: "Hell yes!" To me, the question isn't about whether we think that everything that traditionally has been said of God is literally true. It's whether we have made room in our lives for a belief in *divinity*—in other words, the *Ultimate*—however we choose to define those terms.

Part I of this book will examine many conceptions of divinity. Frequently, they will be expressed in terms of the various roles that God is deemed to play in the lives of contemporary believers. Make no mistake, it is easy to dismiss several of these conceptions simply as antiquated. But that would be a missed opportunity. No journey to better understand God can go far if we ignore the signposts that others have planted.

I intend to analyze different conceptions of the Divine that have been presented through Western Scriptures and through the writings of eminent philosophers and theologians. But I will also draw heavily on my personal story. Indeed, my standard for deciding whether to discuss the ideas of a particular thinker or system of faith is rather simple: did they have a profound and indelible influence on my own personal philosophy? If so, I'll be talking about them; if not, I won't.

In the course of this discussion, you will find references to several of the world's great religions, and especially the three Abrahamic faiths. I must ask your indulgence regarding these references, which may at times suggest that each of these faiths is monolithic. Even among traditionalists of a single faith, there are important, if subtle, differences in beliefs, as well as rituals. And while it is beyond the scope of this book to examine all of these differences, I wish at least to acknowledge that they exist. (It is especially vital to note that the references to Christianity pertain to *Western* Christian traditions, rather than to Eastern Orthodox Christianity, which I have only recently begun to study.) My general view is that all of the great faiths of both the West and the East are fertile enough to give rise to either enlightened doctrines or dangerous falsehoods, depending upon who is doing the interpreting.

The goal of this part of the book is to set forth a framework for how God may be conceived. It is hoped that this framework will be satisfying to the heart without being an affront to our voice of reason. The framework that emerges from Part I will form the foundation of what follows. This will be the "God" to whom I will address Part II of the book. It will also be the "God" that, in Part III, will serve as the inspiration for how we can legitimately appreciate each other as fellow expressions of a divine "We" and use this knowledge to heal and unify our planet. Notably, however, any conception we could possibly enunciate can at best be a temporary resting place on a never-ending road. Truth seekers who are aware of their limitations must never get too enamored of any one resting place.

As the Coordinator and a Cofounder of the Jewish-Islamic Dialogue Society of Washington, or JIDS, I have learned a lot these last several years about both the underlying similarities and the profound differences between those two faiths. But one of the most notable pieces of information I've learned at JIDS is that arguably the most controversial symbols in these faiths—"jihad" and "Israel"—are actually synonyms. The central meaning of "jihad," the so-called "greater Jihad," is not a war of violence but a spiritual struggle to better oneself. Similarly, the word "Israel" comes from the name Jacob received when he wrestled all night with an angel of God and somehow held his own. Each of the Abrahamic faiths requires us to struggle continually with our understanding of the meaning and glory of divinity. And for me, that struggle has always involved a fascination with the widely divergent ways in which sages over the millennia have spoken about God. All my life, I have presumed that each such approach has more than a grain of truth. It is now time to explain how I have gathered some of those grains together in an attempt to harvest as compelling a philosophy of God as possible.

CHAPTER 1

God the Nurturer

"[Judah ben Tema] used to say: At five years the age is reached for the study of the Bible, at ten for the study of the Mishnah, at thirteen for the fulfillment of the commandments, at fifteen for the study of Talmud, at eighteen for marriage, at twenty for seeking a livelihood, at thirty for full strength, at forty for understanding, at fifty for giving counsel; at sixty a man attains old age, at seventy white old age, at eighty rare old age; at ninety he is bending over the grave; at a hundred he is as if he were already dead and had passed away from the world."

—From *Ethics of the Fathers*, chapter 5[1]

"All I really need to know I learned in kindergarten."

—Title of a best-selling book by Robert Fulghum

RELIGIOUS HYPOCRISY. THERE'S NO type of hypocrisy quite like it, is there? And if you want to search for the foundation of religious hypocrisy, go no further than the whole idea that the most religious people are the most humble.

1. *The Ethics of the Fathers* is a tractate of the Talmud that exclusively addresses moral principles. The translation used above is from Birnbaum, *Daily Prayer Book*, 522.

Just consider the phrase "human, all too human," and reflect on what it indicates. Human beings, as the Talmud points out, arise from a putrid drop and are destined to a place of dust and maggots. During the interim, we alternatively succeed and fail at a series of tasks that may seem momentous to us, but barely scratch the surface of the cosmos, let alone what lies beyond. And yet, somehow, despite the fact that we are smaller relative to the cosmos than those maggots are relative to us, we have the temerity to pontificate about God. I don't call that humility; I call it chutzpah.

So where do we get the gall to speculate about the ultimate truths of existence? From our elders, of course. Traditionally, we learn at an early age that it is our birthright to think about those truths. They don't come to us in the form of philosophical questions. They don't come to us in the form of questions at all. They come in the form of stories. And what five-year-old doesn't love a good story, whether it's about dragons, super-heroes, or the Creator of the universe.

One of the things I love about little children is that if you ask them if they believe in God, they'd never ask you first to define the term. They'd give you a response from the heart. And you'd know exactly what concep-tion of God they'd be referring to; it's the same one to which children in the Western world have been exposed for century after century.

Looking back to my own childhood, I remember two books that stand out in shaping my spirituality. One was written for adults, and I will discuss it in a later chapter. The other is a classic children's book. Published in 1954 by Ktav Publishing House, it is entitled *Bible Stories for Jewish Children*. So yes, it was intended exclusively for Jewish kids, but that is of little moment. Hundreds, if not thousands, of similar books have been given over the years to Christian and Muslim children to intro-duce them to the Holy Scriptures and to the character in those Scriptures known by the names of God, Lord, Adonai, or Allah. Those words may have somewhat different connotations to adults. Yet for the young chil-dren who have been entranced by such books, the God-character nearly always plays the same role.

The other day, I opened up my copy of *Bible Stories for Jewish Chil-dren* and was faced with an inscription: "To Danny, Love Aunt Helen and Uncle Ray." Immediately, I recognized the context in which I first saw the book. This was given to a young boy by loving members of his family. And indeed, their goal was to present him with his precious birthrights— a relationship with God, a membership in a people, and a path to virtue.

My aunt and uncle's book contained an unforgettable set of stories that would confer on me at an early age my sense of identity as a member of the Jewish people and the Jewish faith. At the heart of that faith is an array of values with an underlying message. And when I began re-reading the book, that message quickly became apparent: if you love and obey God, He will always take care of you. (You will forgive my use of gendered language, but the God of children's literature, or for that matter, the God of Scripture generally, is almost always a "he.")

From this comforting message, all the other lessons flow. One can see, for example, that even though bad things might happen to anyone, good people ultimately will find their reward. Indeed, we learn that the greatest among us are sometimes called upon to withstand torment so that the rest of us can be uplifted. This was illustrated by the story of Joseph, who came to love the very brothers who sold him into slavery. I read that when Joseph saw his brothers, he said "Do not fear. I shall not punish you for your sin against me. Don't you see, it was God's will that I come here to Egypt and store up corn so that we all might eat in the time of the famine."[2]

To be sure, children also learn from their Bible stories that consequences abound for those who disobey. They even learn that any act of disobedience, even if there is no "witness," is subject to punishment, since God sees all. (Just ask Adam, Eve, or their fratricidal son, Cain.) Still, you can bet that in the context of a children's book, even when God is dispensing punishment, he is depicted in the most nurturing light possible. Take, for example, the way my book told the story of Noah, the man who had to bear witness to the deaths of nearly every man, woman, child, and animal of his generation, but at least was able to save his immediate family. If any of us today found ourselves in Noah's position, we would be none too pleased with God. But my children's book told me that Noah, rather than lamenting God's cruelty, said that "We must thank God for being so good."[3] So Noah prayed to God, God "was pleased with Noah," and as a reward, God presented Noah with the vision of a beautiful rainbow and a promise "that I will never send a flood again to cover the earth. . . . Then, God said: 'Whenever you see a rainbow in the sky, remember that I am here. I will always take care of you and all My children.'"[4] That's what I call putting the best face on the slaughter-to-end-all-slaughters.

2. Samuels, *Bible Stories*, 46.
3. Ibid., 10.
4. Ibid.

Whereas the Bible contains plenty of examples of impatience or idolatry on the part of the Jewish people, the merciful God depicted in my children's book continued to keep his promises to them and shower them with miracles. In one case, however, God did appear to treat a Jew unduly harshly. Simply because he struck a rock with anger and disobeyed God's command not to speak to the rock, Moses was prevented from entering the Promised Land with his people and was left to die alone on the wrong side of the River Jordan. But even in the sad story of Moses' death, this children's book made an inspiring point: that God expects the most from those who are most exalted, and no person is more exalted than Moses. Here is how the book ended: "Moses died somewhere in the Land of Moab. No man has ever seen his grave. But no man has ever forgotten his name. He was the greatest of all prophets."[5]

Intellectually, of course, it is silly to assert that Moses is the "greatest of all prophets," and thereby contrast his greatness to that of Jesus and Muhammad, to name just two obvious alternatives. Yet to a child, this is not an intellectual matter. The objective magnitude of Moses' greatness is beside the point. What makes Moses the greatest of prophets to a Jewish child is that he is the central human figure in *our* story. As we have seen, though, no single figure in that story is more central than our God.

It is tempting to say that the biblical God is yet another "human" character—a figure created in our own image, and not vice versa. That bit of supposed irony has certainly been pointed out by enough iconoclasts. I know; I'm one of them. In truth, however, if you skim any decent children's book on religion, you'll notice that even those books maintain some respect for divine ineffability. We are not given enough information about God's "personality" from which to paint a vivid portrait. There are enough apparent contradictions in God's conduct—such as his mercy toward the Jewish people juxtaposed against his harshness toward Moses, or for that matter, Lot's wife—that we understand, even as children, that "God works in mysterious ways."

While certain character traits have routinely been attributed to the biblical God, such as mercy or love, that God comes to be known less for what he is than for what he does. If you are "good," he protects and provides for you. If you are "sinful" and do not change your ways, he might show you some amount of mercy but reserves the right to punish if necessary, and do so with vigor. It's a simple equation, really, and most kids

5. Ibid., 72.

have an intuitive sense of what it means to behave and what it means to make trouble. God can then play his assigned role, and the children who read about him will not lose their faith in divine justice. Whether individuals have the strength of will necessary to honor the demands God places upon them is a different matter. If a person's will is weak enough, acting like a paragon of virtue would be more tormenting than any divinely-created hell. And since everyone has his share of weaknesses, those Bible stories can create some amount of cognitive dissonance for all of us. But that generally doesn't become intolerable until we approach adolescence. For small children who are exposed to books like the one my aunt and uncle gave me, God can become an irresistibly lovable figure.

⟿

The two quotes at the beginning of this chapter truly should be understood together, even though one was written nearly two thousand years after the other. It is common knowledge that to the Jewish people, the Tanakh—a.k.a the Bible—is our holiest book and the foundation of our collective wisdom. The first segment of the Hebrew Bible, known as the Torah or the Five Books of Moses, is especially revered among Jews. But as you can see from an explicit statement in the *Ethics of our Fathers*, Jews are considered ready to tackle the study of Torah at the ripe old age of five, the same age today's children begin kindergarten.

How is it that kindergarten-age children can come to appreciate the majesty of the transcendent when so many adults find the concept fictitious, even alienating? For that matter, how can these little children, who are hardly even able to understand much of the adult world, possibly be expected to understand the basis for believing in the God of all reality?

To answer these questions, we must start where we began this chapter: by pointing out the absurdity of religious faith. Of course small children can't understand the ultimate truths of the universe. Of course they can't understand where the world ends and the transcendent begins. And just as obviously, they could never be expected to understand why their own perspective on "God" makes any more or less sense than anyone else's. If adults can't answer these questions, how can we possibly expect answers from children? The beauty is, though, that some kids know not to *ask*—or at least not until after they fall in love with God and his lessons.

You see, the mere fact that a five-year-old is exposed sympathetically to a book about God from a close relative tells the kid volumes. Kids appreciate that many profound topics are over their heads. Clearly, their aunt and uncle wouldn't buy them a book about multivariable calculus or physical chemistry because they wouldn't understand a word of it. And yet somehow, books about God are different. I trusted my aunt and uncle, and they were telling me that I should feel free to read their book and let my heart take me wherever it wishes to go. So what message were they sending? That the essence of religious truth is its *simplicity*.

It's like that line that the catcher told the pitcher in the movie *Bull Durham*: "You just got lesson number one: don't think. It can only hurt the ball club." In that case, once the pitcher stopped thinking while he was winding up and started striking out batters, he didn't need to ask questions: he saw the results. And in the case of the child who is emotionally transfixed by the stories of Scripture, the lesson is much the same. When the stories present you with a Holy Beloved, a virtuous path, and a sense of purpose in life, you don't need to ask questions. You see the results.

The beauty of "lesson number one" in both cases is that it rings true. The pitcher in *Bull Durham* wasn't on the mound because of his IQ; he was there because of his arm. As for a five-year-old's introduction to *The Name*, if he has any brains at all, he'll realize that the whole idea of a King of the Universe is so far over our heads that it makes no difference if you're a kindergartener, a brain surgeon, or a rocket scientist—complex reasoning will get you nowhere. You're left with your gut. And your heart. In those regards, I suspect that kids don't feel any less worthy than the rest of us, especially once they are able to detect a feature of biblical stories that grabs hold of them and doesn't let them go. I'm referring to the picture of virtue that shines through the Torah's leading characters.

Judaism, Christianity, and Islam all trace their lineage back to a single monotheist, Abraham, and in my favorite children's book, Abraham's virtue is proudly on display. The book's cover depicts the bearded Abraham in a flowing yellow headdress adorning a purple robe. He is standing on a beach with a staff propped against his shoulder. His gaze is outward, toward a starry sky, and his hands are upraised, suggesting a man at prayer. The text of the book explains that Abraham is giving thanks to the Lord for this great land that has been promised to him and his descendants. But the picture tells a thousand words. Abraham isn't merely thankful; he is himself mesmerized by the beauty that he sees in nature, in life, and in God. Any child viewing this picture quickly realizes that Abraham's state is one of blessedness.

And he is hardly alone. The readers of these children's books see that sense of blessedness not only in those patriarchs who are being tangibly rewarded but also in the ones who appear, on the surface, to be cursed. Joseph, the great grandson of Abraham, wasn't given a beautiful view of the Land of Canaan; he was given a cell in a prison. But rather than losing hope, Joseph kept the faith and thanked God for every little gift he received, such as when he was named a prison guard. The rest, as they say, is legend—Joseph, still a prisoner, was blessed with the gift of prophesy, he went on to save his kingdom from famine, and ultimately he became an Egyptian lord. The lesson is clear—if you have faith in God, you will achieve a state of blessedness. The Nurturing God will never let you down.

It is precisely this sense of resiliency, of permanence, that gives blessedness its power. Young children experience their ups and downs like everyone else. They understand what it's like to enjoy the beauty of nature or to have a "good day" with family or friends. But they also understand that not every day can be spent on the beach looking up at a starry sky, and that is why the story of Joseph is so inspiring. Joseph teaches us that with devotion to God, we can feel thankful even in a prison. We can feel hopeful even when we're sold into slavery. And we can someday look back at the roller coaster of our life and feel enriched by every twist and turn. Such is the meaning of blessedness.

Still, even children understand that blessedness is not a stand-alone concept. It has what some might call an evil twin. What makes these patriarchs and prophets our honored fathers isn't so much that they are blessed, for that is merely a reward for their efforts. What makes these figures so great is that they feel *commanded*.

As a Jewish adult, I have plenty of difficulty with Abraham's binding of Isaac; I know for a fact that no alleged "God" could get me to murder one of my daughters. Little children aren't so troubled by that story, however, because they understand Abraham as the authors of the Bible intended him to be understood. This is a man who loves his God with all his heart, all his soul, and all his might, just as we are directed to do by Scripture. Somehow, he received a specific directive from up high to kill his son, and for Abraham, this was all that needed to be said. When God speaks, we obey. That is certainly how my traditional Muslim friends understand the point of the story, and it is absolutely central to their faith.

So, what starts with a sense of devotion and enchantment soon becomes associated with blessedness . . . but only if we are serious enough to respect our duties *as* commandments. And who is the figure that grounds and galvanizes each of these emotions? Who watches over us? Who protects the blessed among us? And who sometimes, but not always, punishes those who disregard his laws? To a young child, there is typically one answer: God the Nurturer. It is only with the passage of years that he might become mocked, as a figment of our imagination, or detested, as a noose around our freedom-loving necks.

ᴔ

The truth is that while I once believed in the Nurturing God, that phase lasted all too briefly. But believe me, that was my loss. If ever the words "age appropriate" apply, they apply to young children who are enchanted with their Bible stories.

Those kids who open their hearts to the Nurturing God are indeed the luckiest people in the world. The world becomes more magical; virtue more compelling; transcendence more imaginable.

To the children who feel cosmically nurtured, an entire door of meaning is thrown wide open. No longer do they look up and see just a starry night. Now they see the blessings of light and space. No longer do they look to their side and see just a human face. Now they see the blessings of companionship and cooperation. No longer do they listen to their teacher hand out an assignment and feel bored. Now they recognize a directive and a challenge. Why would we ever deny a child the opportunity to see the world in this way?

Yes, I know the common rebuke: "We don't want our kids to believe in B.S. If the world isn't the product of some Cosmic Santa Claus, why should we brainwash our children into believing it is?" The answer is that we don't have to brainwash our kids. Just expose them to the stories, tell them how deeply those stories have influenced their ancestors, and the stories' power will speak for themselves. This is why these tales have survived for centuries on end—they seize the human heart at a very critical stage in its development.

To be sure, children who fall head over heels in love with God the Nurturer may well grow up in ways that are less than healthy. If they take on the attitude that true piety involves always feeling blessed and enchanted, worshippers may acquire feelings of guilt or self-loathing simply because they experience normal human urges. Not everyone can have the faith of an Abraham or the patience of a Joseph, and once we start falling short of our standards, the danger exists that we'll lose our pride. Moreover, the Nurturing God is a source of *commands*, not merely moral suggestions, and the truth is that with respect to many moral dilemmas, it is far from clear what is demanded of us. The child who is overly steeped in the Nurturing God and his battles with good versus evil may later come to have lots of trouble dealing with moral ambiguity and begin a life of intolerance and dogmatism. We've all seen this outgrowth of organized religion. It's never pretty, and it sometimes can be quite horrific.

So, like anything else, exposing young children to the Nurturing God is a mixed bag. But for those of us who have been entranced and inspired, we would never deny our own children the joy we experienced. And more to the point, we ourselves can never fully outgrow that experience. You see, those basic emotional needs that we identify at five are still around at fifty-five. In choosing a religious philosophy, it behooves us to remember those emotional needs, rather than trying to repress them.

CHAPTER 2

God the Planner

"And so I brought what my parents had taught me and what Jesus had said and I put that to work in my NFL career. And God told me not to leave Washington D.C., so I was there for 20 years. That was during free agency time. Yes, I was a part of that. I was a part of that free agency. But God had a plan for me. I stayed the course. Not only did I stay the course on the field, I stayed the course faithfully to this woman for almost 24 years. Faithfully to my community. Faithfully to my pastor, Pastor Brett Fuller, and the Grace Covenant Church in Chantilly, Virginia, faithful to my community and the centers and the other works and faithful to the people. . . . And so as I prepare to close, folks, there's two things that I know: Number one, no matter how gifted you are, or how hard you work, if there's no one willing to give you an opportunity, it doesn't mean a thing. Secondly, I believe that this day is a part of the continuation of God's sovereign purpose and righteous destiny for my life. And that [destiny] being knowing Jesus, loving him, and making him known. I did that even as a professional football player everywhere I went. And that was done through the visibility, the influence, the access, all that God gives us, the Lord gives us, while we play a childhood game. Can I tell you today at the expense of sounding real self-righteous, I belong here. I belong here. I belong here. I belong here because I know what to do with it. I know what to do with God's fame, with God's dollars, with God's

visibility, God's influence and relationships. I know what to do with it. To Jesus be the glory. Thank you. Bless you."

—Darrell Green, from his 2008 induction speech
at the Pro Football Hall of Fame[1]

IF ONLY WE WERE all like Peter Pan, we would have no need to talk further about God than what was said in the previous chapter. To the person who never wants to grow up, God the Nurturer works just fine.

The problem for the rest of us is that we soon see that the abridged Bible stories we read as children don't exactly give the full picture. And not surprisingly, the God of the *real* Bible doesn't seem quite so nurturing. At one point, God leads his Chosen People to attack the towns of King Sihon, leaving no survivors (Deut 2:26–34). At another, God is directing his People to offer some fairly macho terms for peace when they enter the Promised Land: either submit to a life of slavery or prepare to die (Deut 20:10–14). Somehow, my children's book never talked about God being a "heads I win, tails you lose" kind of Lord. The real biblical God frequently sounds more like a Klingon than the Cosmic Santa Claus.

Of course, what most precludes us from a sense of feeling perpetually nurtured is simply living and learning. It soon becomes readily apparent that people are not rewarded, at least not in this life, based strictly on the power of their faith and the strength of their will. Here's how my father put it: "Danny, you often meet people who do bad things, and you keep thinking that eventually they're going to get what's coming to them. But sometimes they never do." What's more, we occasionally watch wonderful people become disabled or die young. And when we see our loved ones suffer in agony with cancer or ALS, it isn't easy keeping the faith that God will always take care of us and "all his children." You and I would never treat our children like that, so why would a Nurturing God?

Inevitably, other, more concrete questions arise: What kind of "Nurturing God" would allow the Nazis to kill six million Jews? Or bury well over a hundred thousand Haitians in an earthquake? Or send a bubonic plague to slaughter one-third of Europe? For some, the answer is clear: "Are you stupid? There is no God." For others, though, that response is not satisfactory. They might recognize that the Nurturing-God concept

1. Green, Enshrinement Speech, para. 29–30, 33–37.

is a little too simplistic, but they don't want to do away with divinity altogether. And so, they look for a deeper perspective.

Traditional Jews, Christians, and Muslims believe that they can
find such a perspective in the teachings of the ancient sages. Embrace
the mystery of mysteries, they are taught. Recognize that things always
happen for a reason, though that reason may be far beyond our ken. Have
faith in a Lord whose wisdom is so great that we can never possibly understand it.

The deity who emerges from this perspective can be called the Nurturing God All Grown Up . . . or the "Planning God" for short. To have
faith in such a God is to convince yourself that he has a plan and that
plan is good. God the Planner sees all, deliberates about what he sees, and
chooses this proper plan in accordance with his supreme wisdom. But
human adults also recognize that such a plan will never fully make sense
to us. Only God can appreciate why he does what he does. That is a point
on which Moses and Muhammad agree. Those who don't are viewed as
idolaters, and the "idol" in their case is their own exaggerated sense of
intelligence.

The quotation at the top of this chapter is full of irony. The speaker, Darrell Green, was once among the most beloved athletes in my city, Washington, D.C. Yet his comments are of the kind that are so often met with
ridicule in the more hoity-toity parts of the city. These days, there are few
things less respected among the intellectual elite than when an athlete or
some other entertainer gives thanks to God during an awards ceremony.
What could God possibly have to do with an Academy Award winning
performance or a Hall of Fame career? Yes, the "best and the brightest"
might read stories to their children about God watching over us, but do
you seriously think they believe those stories? Or that they assume that
God watches NFL football?

It bears pointing out, though, that if you read Green's statement
carefully, you'll note that he wasn't thanking God for allowing him to
defeat lesser competitors on the gridiron. He was thanking God for giving him a righteous sense of purpose in life. I would be hard pressed to
mock him for that. In fact, I feel that Green's statement merely reflects the
sincerity of his religiosity, which I find exemplary.

One facet of Green's statement that I appreciate is the value he emphasizes most: *loyalty*. The same steadfast faith that we saw in the biblical patriarchs is manifest in Darrell Green. And what is faith, if not loyalty? Green surely feels commanded to be steadfast in his devotion to God and in everything wholesome that he associates with the path that God has set out for him. What's more, Green is telling us that he has honored this commandment.

Green's pride in this accomplishment means more to him than any achievement on the football field. He wants us to know that he was loyal to his team, his community, his church, his pastor, his wife, and yes, his God. From Green's perspective, it is precisely because God's plan gives rise to so much suffering that loyalty to all things wholesome, and God in particular, becomes so critical. We need our faith in pure goodness, the argument goes, to keep our wits about us in the face of evil. This faith presumably is what sustained Joseph in his prison and Moses in his final, solitary days.

I also appreciate that on the proudest day of Green's life, Green models a sense of humility. Even as he asserts that he belongs in the Hall of Fame, Green shifts the credit from himself to his beloved God. He attributes his merit not to the way he played a "childhood game" but to his discipline in honoring the directions of God the Planner. God was the one who set forth a "sovereign purpose" and "righteous destiny" for Green's life: "knowing Jesus, loving Him, and making Him known." God is the one who provided Green with "fame . . . dollars . . . visibility . . . influence and relationships" so that Green can fulfill that purpose. All Green did was recognize his own part in the divine plan.

"God had a plan for me. I stayed the course." With luck, those words can someday be part of Darrell Green's epitaph. To a traditional theist, such an epitaph would be the greatest badge of honor imaginable, far greater than induction to any secular hall of fame.

But if that is the perspective of traditional theism, what can be said from the perspective of heresy? How should a product of the Enlightenment view Darrell Green's statement? With disdain? Ridicule? A condescending roll of the eyes? According to the sages of the Enlightenment, isn't Green simply reflecting the stupidity of believing that there exists a divine Superman who sets forth specific "plans" for individual human beings?

Not so fast, my cynical friends. Consider the words of my favorite philosopher, and one of the patron saints of modern heresy, Baruch

Spinoza. Spinoza's pantheistic teachings were viewed as such a threat by his seventeenth-century Jewish community in Amsterdam that the community excommunicated him at the age of twenty-three. Spinoza made no bones about it: philosophically, it is unreasonable to believe in a God who creates in accordance with a master plan, let alone one who does so with omnibenevolence. Still, Spinoza remained quite enamored with the Darrell Greens of the world.

During the last several years of his life, Spinoza lived in the Hague in a home owned by a traditional Lutheran couple. Not only did he occasionally attend their church, but, in reference to their pastor, he once told his landlord "not to miss any sermon of so excellent a preacher."[2] When his landlady asked him directly whether he thought she could be saved if she maintained her religious faith, he responded "Your religion is good, and you need not search for another one in order to be saved, as long as you apply yourself to a peaceful and pious life."[3]

So said the great heretical hero. For him, it is one thing to confront the limitations of biblical faith as a system of philosophy. It is something far different to deny the blessedness of one who sincerely and peacefully practices that faith. Only a pompous fool would do that, and Spinoza was perhaps the least foolish writer I've ever read.

Hundreds of years after Green's beloved Jesus Christ walked this earth, and a millennium after the Torah was completed, Muhammad founded a religion that would ultimately go on to attract over a billion adherents. This religion has come to take the place in my life that Christianity must have taken in the life of Spinoza: an honorable, and indeed invaluable, supplement to our own native Judaism. Indeed, it solidifies for me the power and the beauty of this deity to whom we have referred as the Planning God.

You can see in Spinoza's writings the veneration that he held for Jesus as a man who intuitively recognized the connection between earthly forms and the eternal God.[4] Spinoza didn't speak with anywhere near

2. Nadler, *Spinoza*, 290.

3. Ibid.

4. References in this book to earthly or concrete "forms" are not intended in the Platonic sense of that word but pertain instead to its more conventional usage,

this respect for the Jewish prophets, despite his Jewish lineage. As for me, while I would never put Muhammad on such a pedestal, neither would I deny him the same place that is assigned to our common father, Abraham. Both men displayed the most steadfast possible faith in God, and just as importantly, an equally passionate disdain for idolatry. Anyone can praise God, but it takes a mensch to confront publicly the idolatries of those in power. We owe what wisdom we have to those of our ancestors who mustered such courage.

Armed with his supreme devotion to God, Muhammad didn't simply found a religious movement. He also became a statesman and a soldier, and in those capacities he experienced no shortage of frustration. Far from acting like a "Nurturing God," Muhammad's Lord would reveal himself like the title character in a game of Whack a Mole. One moment, he'd be with you. The next moment, He'd be gone.

Given this reality, how then could Muhammad talk about God without sacrificing either his power or his love? This was Muhammad's predicament. The Qur'an was his response. It begins as follows:

> In the name of Allah, Most Gracious, Most Merciful. Praise be to Allah, the Cherisher and Sustainer of the Worlds; Most Gracious, Most Merciful; Master of the Day of Judgment. Thee do we worship, and Thine aid we seek. Show us the straight way, the way of those on whom Thou hast bestowed Thy Grace. Those whose (portion) is not wrath, and who go not astray. (Qur'an 1:1–7).

Any Jew or Christian should be able to recognize these concepts, if not those precise words. It is the faith of Moses and Jesus. But according to Muslim commentary, "in Muhammad's mission, these other characters were combined. Gentler than Jesus, he organized on a vaster scale than Moses."[5] And as the Qur'an points out, he needed to give his message because the followers of these other prophets had fought with one another and largely rejected the divine teachings. Of course, "if Allah had so willed, they would not have fought each other; but Allah fulfilleth His plan" (Qur'an 2:253). There you have it—a recognition that the world is hardly as we would like it to be, combined with an admonition not to attribute this to the impotence of Allah, for everything that occurs is in

---

which encompasses particular organisms, inanimate things, ideas, institutions, or any discrete parts of these entities.

5. Ali, *Meaning of the Holy Qur'an*, 104.

accordance with the divine plan. Such is one of the most critical concepts of Islam.

You will note from the Qur'anic introduction the need to drum in the notion of God's *goodness*. To his followers, the Muslim God is seen as nurturing—Allah is the most gracious and most merciful. But if you look for justice from him, you are advised to keep in mind the Day of Judgment. In order to maximize his followers' faith in God's supreme justice, Muhammad decided to emphasize the rewards and punishments of the afterlife much more than they are stressed in Judaism.

What's more, Muhammad's God isn't merely good, he is also *great*. And it is precisely the extent to which Islam stresses God's greatness—not his likeness to human beings—that gives this religion its unique place in the family of Abrahamic faiths. It is said that Allah's universe is composed of 18,000 worlds, of which our material universe is among the smallest, and resembles but a grain of sand in a desert when compared to the invisible domain. According to this metaphor, the invisible domain contains seven heavens and seven earths encompassed by the divine footstool, which is itself encompassed by the divine throne. You can envision these domains as concentric circles surrounding our universe. As stated in a hadith, which is a collection of the sayings and conduct attributed to Muhammad, "The seven heavens and the seven earths compared with the Footstool are no more than a ring cast in the wilderness; and the superiority of the Throne over the Footstool is again like that of the wilderness over the ring."[6]

Contemplate this metaphor, and you will see what Islam has done to make God the Planner come alive. When you consider the vastness of the Divine in relation to the size of our entire visible universe, let alone our own tiny brains, the job of second-guessing Allah's purpose emerges as the height of chutzpah. Similarly, a Muslim is taught not to second-guess the extent of God's presence in the world. Allah is not merely some remote deity. His reach is everywhere and anywhere. Allah, the Qur'an tells us, is "nearer to [man] than (his) jugular vein" (50:16). In other words, both his plan and his involvement in seeing this plan through are all-encompassing. With wisdom, Allah makes every leaf as unique as a human fingerprint. And just as we can't possibly conceive of why each leaf in the universe is made exactly as it is, nor can we approach the understanding necessary to figure out why a saint dies young while

6. Al-Badawi, *Man & The Universe*, 5.

a sinner lives long and appears to prosper. For it is not our place to solve the so-called "problem of evil." Our job is simply to pray for the ability to identify the straight and narrow path that God has thoughtfully created for us and then to follow it, with faith that we will receive our reward in heaven, if not on earth.

Sound familiar? I think Darrell Green would have made a fine Muslim.

⟡

As religious orthodoxies go, there is much in Islam that attracts me, despite the stench of Islamophobia that pervades American popular culture today. Yes, there are plenty of lunatics who preach violence in the name of Islam, but they are truly a very non-silent *minority*. For the most part, orthodox Islam promotes both a peaceful and a universalist philosophy. Also, by embracing the "prophets" of its cousin faiths, it creates a warm and more welcoming feel for all who seek virtue and truth. It surely is no coincidence that, on average, traditional Muslims are the most fraternal people I've met.

Fortunately, though, being an orthodox follower of any religion isn't our only option. We can be devoutly religious *and* progressive, or should I say, heretical. In fact, even a heretic can gain incredible inspiration from each of the Abrahamic faiths. Judaism in particular may be attractive in its *non*-orthodox forms, not only because they are relatively well established institutionally but also because of the emphasis Jewish tradition places on God-wrestling. Today, the Jewish people is as much a "people of doubt" as it is a "people of faith," and to heretics like me, that could be the perfect combination. We can feel the power of the God we hold so dear, but that doesn't stop us from constantly questioning our beliefs and doubting our ability to answer these questions with certainty. In other words, Judaism remains amenable to philosophical inquiry, even though an inherent conflict exists between the discipline of philosophy and the idea that the truth is grounded in a divinely-inspired book known as the Torah.

Momentarily, we will begin to leave the domain of traditional theology and head toward the philosophical realm. But before doing so, it is important to note what we are leaving behind. Philosophers don't spew their ideas in a vacuum. They write as human beings for human beings. If they hope to be influential, their arguments must resonate with the same basic values and emotional attitudes that we've been discussing at length.

In the last chapter, we noted that to establish any emotionally viable spiritual framework, it is invaluable to foster a sense of enchantment, blessedness, security, and duty. In this chapter, we have identified some of the elements of a mature religious faith: a deep loyalty to that which we honor above all else, a steadfast purpose that impassions us at work and play, the humility to recognize how little we know compared to what we don't, and a sense of awe for that which shall eternally remain mysterious. Once again, we have discussed those values in the context of traditional religion, but let us not confine their relevance to religious orthodoxy. Darrell Green is a deeply religious man who just happens to be traditional in his spirituality. If heretics like me refuse to learn from the Darrell Greens of the world, we deprive ourselves of valuable lessons about spirituality in *all* its forms.

CHAPTER 3

God the Interconnected
Web of All Existence

"[M]an conceives a human nature much stronger than his own, and sees no reason why he cannot acquire such a nature. . . . The supreme good is to arrive at the enjoyment of such a nature, together with other individuals, if possible. What that nature is we shall show in its proper place; namely, the knowledge of the union which the mind has with the whole of Nature. This, then, is the end for which I strive, to acquire the nature I have described and to endeavor that many should acquire it along with me."

—Baruch Spinoza, from
Treatise on the Emendation of the Intellect[1]

"Now let us imagine . . . a tiny worm living in the blood, capable of distinguishing by sight the particles of the blood—lymph, etc.—and of intelligently observing how each particle, on colliding with another, either rebounds or communicates some degree of its motion, and so forth. That worm would be living in the blood as we are living in our part of the universe, and it would regard each individual particle of the blood as a whole, not a part. . . . Now all the bodies in Nature can and should

1. Spinoza, "Treatise," 5–6.

be conceived in the same way as we have here conceived the blood; for
all bodies are surrounded by others and are reciprocally determined to
exist and to act in a fixed and determinate way. . . . Hence it follows that
every body . . . must be considered as a part of the whole universe, and
as agreeing with the whole and cohering with the other parts. Now since
the nature of the universe, unlike the nature of the blood, is not limited,
but is absolutely infinite, its parts are controlled by the nature of this
infinite potency in infinite ways, and are compelled to undergo infinite
variations."

—Baruch Spinoza, from his November 20, 1665
Letter to Henry Oldenberg[2]

THESE TWO QUOTATIONS DO not, in my view, convey Spinoza's profound-
est insights. They do, however, capture his point of embarkation. Each
quotation is saying something slightly different, but the general thrust is
the same. Spinoza taught the belief in *radical unity*. For him, the "knowledge of the union existing between the mind and the whole of nature"
was the foundation for his entire philosophy. And for me personally, that
principle has formed the beginning of a progression from an altogether
traditional conception of God to notions that seemed to resonate more
with modern sensibilities.

We will start with one of the "easy listening" approaches to spirituality. Call it pantheism, or the idea that the All is One and *the One* is
God. Derived from the Greek word *pan*, meaning "all," pantheism in its
most basic form is the equation of God with nature as a whole. For some,
simple pantheism is nothing more than a bridge between traditional theism and atheism. It is an orientation that, temporarily at least, may appeal
to a spiritual searcher who wants to *believe*, but can't bring himself to
worship the God of his young childhood or that of Darrell Green.

Spinoza is generally associated today with pantheism. Yet, at the
time of his death, he was widely viewed as an atheist, whereas over a
century later, he was famously pegged by a leading German Romantic
(Novalis) as a "God-intoxicated man."[3] Who was right? The answer rests
on how flexibly you allow the word "God" to be defined. In a later chapter,

2. Spinoza, "Letters," Letter 32, to Oldenburg, 849.
3. Moreau, "Spinoza's Reception," 421.

we will see what Spinoza meant by that term, which he wholeheartedly embraced. For now, we will stress only the basis for Spinoza's belief in God—his undying faith in the idea of an overarching cosmic unity.

Truth be told, Spinoza had every bit as much faith in the interconnectedness of all beings as Darrell Green has in Jesus Christ. This may be hard to believe, however, because Green's faith harmonizes with our image of him as a traditional Christian, whereas Spinoza's doesn't fit so neatly into the way he is commonly stereotyped. Wasn't Spinoza a philosopher's philosopher? A man who developed an extremely complex and coherent system of thought and explicated this system with rigorous logical analysis? How does such a thinker make room for something as unintellectual as "faith"?

The answer is that Spinoza must have considered, and rejected, the alternative—taking nothing at all on faith. As a metaphysician whose stock in trade was abstract reasoning, Spinoza would have known the dirty little secret about logic's limitations: your conclusions are only as true as your premises. Thus, even though he could easily enough proceed "geometrically" from multiple premises through logical syllogisms to "valid" conclusions, the soundness of those conclusions would remain questionable as long as his premises were questionable. This is why he felt the need to have such solid faith in those premises—once they are undermined, the entire edifice collapses like a house of cards. This also explains why Spinoza sought to avoid placing his faith in any principles that do not have tremendous intuitive appeal, both intellectually and emotionally. In the end, Spinoza ranked intuition even above reason as the highest form of knowledge.

When I think about the idea of intuitively-appealing principles, few are more obvious than that we all need to believe in *something* in order to orient ourselves in the world. Maybe that "something" can change over time. Indeed, maybe such changes are the healthy sign of an open mind. Yet at any given time, we need faith just as we would need a port in the storm—to avoid being at sea (in this case, in the spiritual, emotional, and intellectual senses of the term).

Spinoza clearly was searching for a faith in God. Why else would he use that term, if he could have simply referred to "Being," "Existence," or "Nature" instead? But in embarking on this search, Spinoza did not enjoy the same luxury as the writers of Scripture. They were able to convey their message through stories, which could be read either literally or allegorically. Spinoza, by contrast, couldn't hide behind so-called "hidden meanings" or the notion of beauty in ambiguity. He sought clear and distinct ideas—the truths that most appeal to the rational mind. And he chose to present these ideas via the "geometrical method" of a logician. Accordingly, Spinoza had to avoid adopting as principles of faith any premises that sounded essentially mythical in nature. Those premises smack of being the figment of our imaginations, which tend to produce streams of thought that are either horrifying or too-good-to-be-true. Such premises might be acceptable in the realm of literature (the realm in which the Scriptural writers dwelt), but they cannot form the basis of a modern system of philosophy. After all, how ridiculous would it seem to base hundreds of pages of rigorous logical analysis on principles that neither appeal to the intuition of the educated reader nor are verifiable by empirical observation?

Spinoza identified two central premises in traditional theology as being inherently unreasonable. First, he couldn't abide by the premise that a fundamental chasm exists between our world and God. Traditionally, God creates the world "outside" of Himself. Even those Kabbalistic tales about a God who intentionally contracts in order to form a space that can be filled by the world envision a fundamental separation between God (the Creator) and the world (the creation). Spinoza never saw anything in nature or in logic that would lead one to proclaim such a divide. Indeed, positing that break violates the philosophical principle of parsimony, or "Occam's Razor," which teaches us that "entities must not be multiplied unnecessarily." This is commonly known today as the KISS principle: "keep it simple, stupid."

Secondly, Spinoza had little tolerance for positing that all of reality is controlled by someone that resembles a human being. In other words, he had no stomach for theological anthropomorphism. Consider the following, from one of his many letters:

> "[W]hen you say that you do not see what sort of God I have if I deny in him the actions of seeing, hearing, attending, willing, etc., and that he possesses those faculties in an eminent degree, I suspect that you believe there is no greater perfection than can be explicated by the afore-mentioned attributes. I am not surprised, for I believe that a triangle, if it could speak, would likewise say that God is eminently triangular, and a circle that God's nature is eminently circular. In that way each would

ascribe to God its own attributes, assuming itself to be like God and regarding all else as ill-formed."[4]

In short, it is clear from all of his books that Spinoza sought to be a *believer*, but he needed to get there philosophically, not by simply positing a divine Superman who creates the world "outside" himself, like Michelangelo would create a sculpture. So how then does one get to God? You start by remembering the core truth of the Abrahamic faiths: that God is One. Now just modify that ever so slightly: God is One, and God is One with the World, but God is not a Man. Spinoza was uncompromising in the extent to which he honored those precepts. He wanted to begin his philosophical enterprise with an approach to the Divine that is pure, and he saw nothing but purity and truth in those ideas.

The belief that all beings are interconnected seemed as reasonable to Spinoza in the seventeenth century as it does to those modern physicists who are coming up with more and more interconnections every decade. This is not some belief that requires devotion to antiquated scriptural testimony. Nor does it suggest human fabrication. Rather, it comports with our common sense, particularly once we contemplate analogies like Spinoza's "worm in the bloodstream." Just as the various particles inside our blood are ultimately part of the same human body, the animals, vegetables, and minerals in our universe would appear to be part of the same overarching unity. The fact that the more evolved we become, the more interconnections we find, lends tremendous support to the view that ultimately, all is one.

Armed with this faith in total unity, Spinoza popularized the phrase "Deus Sive Natura," meaning "God, or in other words, Nature." Consider that phrase to be a bomb dropped squarely on the head of traditional theology. The point was unmistakable: no longer need we worry about questions like whether God exists, or why bad things happen to good people. Now, once we accept the existence and unity of nature—of *is-ness*—we can aptly say that we believe in God. After all, isn't God supposed to refer to the *Ultimate*? And if everything is interconnected, what can be more ultimate than all-encompassing Nature? Suddenly, God has morphed from Heavenly Father to Universal Mother.

The implications of what we have said so far are indeed radical. This road began with our basic emotional need for nurturing. Yet what has the greater potential for nurturing: the idea of an alien Super-Being who

4. Spinoza, "Letters," Letter 56, to Boxel, 904.

is separate from his creation and reserves the right to reward or punish as he sees fit, or the view that we are all intimately related to one another inside the womb of a single resplendent unity? At a minimum, I think it is safe to say, the God of pantheism holds her own in the nurturing department.

↢

The title of this chapter, "God the Interconnected Web of All Existence" takes its name from the Statement of Principles of the Unitarian Universalist Association of Congregations. Not too familiar with the UUs? You're not alone. They are so few in number that they've even started referring to themselves on their official website as "The Uncommon Denomination."[5] It's a rather odd approach to marketing, if you ask me, but at least it has the virtue of being true. UUs represent only a tiny fraction of 1 percent of the population of America or of the world.

So why hasn't the UU movement grown more in size? One reason may be its refusal to take a stand on the question of God. While the movement's official statement of "Sources" identifies both religious and secular influences, its seven official "Principles" are conspicuously silent on the existence or nature of divinity. Most of these Principles express ethical values, such as freedom, compassion, and tolerance, and yet one UU Principle does reach beyond the human condition and address the nature of reality as a whole. It calls for "Respect for the interdependent web of existence of which we are a part."

The eighteenth-century theologian, Friedrich Jacoby, anticipated the philosophical direction that an Enlightenment-inspired group like the UUs would take. In 1785, Jacoby found himself at the heart of a huge controversy among the intelligentsia in Germany over the "pantheism" of Spinoza—meaning the idea that God and nature are one and the same. As a traditional Christian, Jacoby despised pantheism, which he viewed as just another form of atheism. But more to the point, he believed that when Enlightenment-era seekers replace Scripture with the study of philosophy, pantheism is their likely destination. Accordingly, he saw pantheism as a threat to his beloved Christianity.

If Jacoby were alive today, he would view the UUs as a perfect example of what goes wrong when the closest thing we have to a "Scripture"

5. Unitarian Universalist, "Hospitality and Marketing."

is each individual's voice of reason. From that standpoint, Jacoby would acknowledge the Spinozist idea that "all is one" is the most sensible framework for a religious philosophy. And indeed, the UUs, who pride themselves on being intellectual and open-minded, came to the same conclusion reached by Spinoza's rigorous analysis: affirming the idea of a cosmic "interconnected web." Yet the problem for the UUs is that the "interconnected web" isn't exactly a notion that is going to tug at anyone's heart. Moreover, the UU movement has stopped short of doing what Spinoza did—referring to the interconnected web of all existence as "God." In short, Unitarian Universalism has replaced God the Nurturer and God the Planner with what we may paraphrase as "The Interconnected Web of All Existence, Which May or May Not Be Called God Depending on Your Personal Preference."

Like I said—they're the "Uncommon Denomination." And they're proud of it.

⊖

To the philosophical mind, what matters most is whether one's beliefs are intellectually satisfying, whereas to the religious mind, what matters most is whether one's beliefs are emotionally powerful. When it comes to popularity, religion will always win that battle.

The fact is that some words have power and others don't. "God" evokes feelings about ultimacy, unity, blessedness, and meaning. The "Interconnected Web" evokes feelings about spiders. As a religious philosophy, I would argue, if pantheism has a chance to captivate the hearts of the masses, it needs to be expressed in terms of pan-*theism*, and not as something that sounds thoroughly secular and academic.

Still, even if you add the name of God to the idea of the interconnected web, it still doesn't answer another fundamental question: how emotionally powerful can pantheism be if it has stripped God of his human qualities? After all, many would say, isn't the term "God of the philosophers" an oxymoron?

In large part, this book is a response to those questions. But precisely because they are such central inquiries in this journey, I will leave them unanswered for now.

CHAPTER 4

God the Strawman

"Haven't you heard of that madman who in the bright morning lit a lantern and ran around the marketplace crying incessantly: 'I am looking for God! I am looking for God!' Since many of those who did not believe in God were standing around together just then, he caused great laughter. . . . 'Where is God?' he cried. 'I'll tell you. We have killed him—you and I. We are all his murderers. . . . God is dead! God remains dead! And we have killed him! How can we console ourselves, the murderers of all murderers? . . . [W]ho will wipe this blood off us? . . . What festivals of atonement, what holy games will we have to invent for ourselves? Is the magnitude of this deed not too great for us? Do we not ourselves have to become gods merely to appear worthy of it? There has never been a greater deed; and whoever is born after us will on account of this deed belong to a higher history than all history up to now!'"

—Friedrich Nietzsche, *The Gay Science*[1]

"A spirit thus emancipated stands in the midst of the universe with a joyful and trusting fatalism, in the faith that only what is separate and individual may be rejected, that in the totality everything is redeemed

1. Nietzsche, *Gay Science*, 119–20.

44

and affirmed—he no longer denies. . . . [S]uch a faith is the highest of
all possible faiths."

—Friedrich Nietzsche, *Twilight of the Idols*[2]

"There exists nothing which could judge, measure, compare [or] con-
demn our being, for that would be to judge, measure, compare [or] con-
demn the whole. . . . But nothing exists apart from the whole!"

—Friedrich Nietzsche, *Twilight of the Idols*[3]

THERE ARE TWO KINDS of people who read Nietzsche for the first time:
those who have a sophisticated understanding of pantheism and those
who don't. I fell squarely within the second, and larger, category when
I devoured his books in college. The gusto with which he savaged organized religion and proclaimed himself to be a deicide liberated me, for I
had essentially been an atheist since I was about eight years old. What I
didn't realize at the time was that Nietzsche's intense and yet subtle pantheism, some of which is evident in the two last quotations above, was
actually making me increasingly amenable to accepting a belief in cosmic
unity and the value of spirituality. It sounds insane to admit it, but if I
had to credit one writer for causing me to accept God in my adult life, it
would be the madman who popularized the phrase "God is Dead."

In some respects, Nietzsche saw himself as a modern-day Abraham.
Abraham founded a new philosophy based on the love for the one God
and for God's majestic creation. Nietzsche, his semi-disciple, was attempting to found a new philosophy based on jettisoning certain aspects
of the "Old God" (Nietzsche's term) but retaining others. He wanted to be
every bit as transfixed as Abraham was when he stood in front of pristine
nature and contemplated the sky above or the valley below. Nietzsche
took what he observed to be unified and wanted to feel that there is something about the unity of nature that is greater than the sum of the parts. In
other words, while he did not accept the biblical miracles, he very much
accepted the notion of *transcendence*; he simply chose to view the source

2. Nietzsche, *Twilight*, 103.

3. Ibid., 54.

of that transcendence as within nature and not above it. No less than Father Abraham, Nietzsche strove to be able to behold the majestic unity of the world in all its manifoldness and proclaim that it is good.

In the case of Father Abraham, the world's goodness stemmed from its being the product of an omnibenevolent, omnipotent will. By contrast, in Nietzsche's case, the world was "good" only in the sense that he willed to love it. More specifically, he willed to lovingly accept that the nature of the universe is to exist, necessarily, in just the way it exists, and that we can acknowledge this truth without sacrificing our freedom. In fact, our great freedom, according to Nietzsche, lies in the ability to revel in the grandeur of nature taken as a totality.

Here are his words from *The Gay Science*, the same book that contained such a lengthy discussion for why he and others killed God: "I want to learn more and more how to see what is necessary in things as what is beautiful in them—thus I will be one of those who make things beautiful. *Amor fati.* [Love of fate]: let that be my love from now on! I do not want to wage war against ugliness. I do not want to accuse; I do not even want to accuse the accusers. Let *looking away* be my only negation! And, all in all and on the whole: some day I want only to be a Yes-sayer!"[4]

In hindsight, the world should be delighted that Nietzsche didn't always avoid waging war against what is ugly, because he had so much to teach when he took up arms. Still, what is clear is that in slaying "God," Nietzsche was not attempting to destroy all possible deities. He was thinking of only one in particular. Call him the Lawmaker, the Judge, the Commander. They all mean the same thing to Nietzsche. As much as Nietzsche loved being free to exalt in the transcendent unity of Being, that's how much he hated servitude. And for him, Abraham's God, for all his virtues, was a leading cause of human servitude. The Old God had killed human autonomy from the moment he declared what can and can't be done in the Garden of Eden. Consequently, he himself had to be killed. There was no other way to free ourselves and our descendants so that we may live according to our own volition.

For those of us who love *The Name*, it is sad that the modern atheist movement did not develop with Nietzsche as its standard bearer. As a spiritual man, Nietzsche appreciated the power of *The Name*. In the ideal world, perhaps he would have used *The Name* to refer to Being itself taken as a unity, and that would have inspired people to feel blessed

4. Nietzsche, *Gay Science*, 157.

whenever they are breathing "God's" air. Unfortunately, from Nietzsche's standpoint, other religions beat him to the punch when it comes to interpreting the meaning of divinity. He was especially distraught that the Christians summoned *The Name* and linked it to an emaciated man on a cross. As a result, Nietzsche contended, they were able to completely transform morality, so that rather than exalting life in general and the ancient Greek and Roman virtues in particular, the "herd animals" who came to dominate the Western world exalted weakness, suffering, and other attributes that Nietzsche associated with the masses rather than the rulers of society.

Nietzsche wasn't a Godless man by nature. But as a freedom fighter, he felt compelled to destroy the creature(s) that had assumed the mantle of divinity. So he constructed God the Strawman (the "Old God," expressed unsympathetically) and proceeded to slay him with gusto. As you read above in this chapter's initial quotation, Nietzsche viewed this murder as the most momentous of all possible acts, so momentous in fact that human beings would have to rise up and "become gods" (i.e., supreme creators of meaning) simply to justify what we've done.

⊕

Nietzsche was a genius, but he was also crazy. If that wasn't clear enough from his writings up to the year 1889, it was certainly reinforced by the fact that he spent the next and final eleven years of his life in a mental and physical paralysis brought on by an earlier bout with syphilis. I hardly agree with everything he wrote, especially his more militaristic or unegalitarian musings, and yet, from the minute I first laid eyes on *Beyond Good and Evil*, I've always loved Nietzsche. The same cannot be said for my feelings about Karl Marx.

It was Father Marx, not Brother Nietzsche, who became the true patriarch of modern atheism, and the result has indeed been devastating, not only for organized religion, but for spirituality in general. As a deicide, Marx owed much of his success to the fact that he inspired a totalitarian movement that was explicitly anti-religious (in the traditional sense of that word) and that would soon enough seize power over much of the world. His treatment of religion did more damage to our appreciation for the transcendent than Nietzsche would have ever contemplated doing, even if he could have matched Marx's success in the political realm.

Marx executed the Old God by building a system in which religion (like all other interests aside from economics) wasn't so much reviled as trivialized. This is illustrated by his references to religion as the "opium of the people," which "requires illusions."[5] You may also recognize the latter term from Freud, who wrote his own book about religion entitled *The Future of an Illusion*. In adopting that term, Freud was merely dealing with the topic in a manner that was extremely common among twentieth-century Jews and is fully consistent with Marx's dismissive attitude, which has succeeded in summoning a vast reservoir of human apathy towards the notion of divinity.

Here's how I would summarize that attitude, which I saw quite clearly as the child of a Marxist mother: religion offers us a path to happiness, but it is the happiness of a fool. Those who "believe" are as superstitious as the silly old lady who avoids black cats or is scared of the number 13. Their worldview is based on the worship of a God who is no more real than the Easter Bunny. Yes, that worship can make them happy, but it is the happiness of the brainwashed and the ignorant. We, who wish to look forward, not backwards, have the power to brush this nonsense aside for ourselves, and ultimately, for others too. And here's how: the next time you hear someone mention God, just shake your head and laugh.

Nietzsche never would have laughed. But my beloved mother would giggle for years whenever she set foot in a church or synagogue.

⊹

An argument can be made that everyone "believes in God;" the only difference among us is precisely which God we believe in. To buy into that conclusion, we need only adopt Paul Tillich's notion that a person's God is "that which concerns man ultimately."[6] Presumably, we all have an Ultimate Concern, whether it's God the Planner, God the Interconnected Web, world peace, or good old greenbacks. In at least one sense of the word, therein lies our God. But that's not how I think of the term. To me, for something to count as "God," it needs to have more than just a scant resemblance to what the term traditionally connotes. In other words, a person's subjective concerns do not alone confer divinity status on some object or conception. To be worthy of the term, what we're talking about

5. Marx, *Contribution*, 250.

6. Tillich, *Systematic Theology*, 220.

must seem grand enough to assume the status of ultimacy in relationship to Being itself, and not merely our little planet. In that sense, I would grant that for many people, there is no God. And when they use the term disparagingly as a strawman—when they build up a particular conception of the Divine, only to tear it down—they may, unlike Nietzsche, be speaking about the only "God" they truly think about.

As a God-slayer, Marx's genius was in marrying an antipathy toward religious supernaturalism with an appeal that would make much of humankind apathetic toward the notion of spiritual transcendence. But like Nietzsche, this does not mean that Marx himself was completely non-religious in the broad sense of that word. He simply substituted for the God of Abraham an alternative system of faith, which includes the belief in: (a) matter as the substance of all reality; (b) the intelligibility of human history; (c) the centrality of economics to human evolution; and (d) the perfectibility of the human condition, given sufficient development in our economic infrastructure. I would agree with Marx that such a faith is indeed "Godless," but that doesn't make it any less of a religion—like other grand systems of faith, it is an impressively coherent framework from which to resolve ultimate ethical and metaphysical issues.

Following in Marx's footsteps, at least with respect to their thorough rejection of traditional religions, are the so-called "New Atheists." Spearheaded by the British biologist Richard Dawkins, the New Atheists have written many a best-seller in recent years and have managed to insert themselves with some prominence into the public discourse on God. Dawkins' *The God Delusion*, like the other New Atheist screeds, continues incessantly for page after page with a single set of related goals: to prove the stupidity and the dangers of believing in God. Generally speaking, Dawkins' book has the subtlety of a sledgehammer. But I wouldn't say that applies to the initial chapter. In essence, Dawkins says there that before he whips out his metaphorical Uzi and starts firing away at the concept of divinity, he is going to exempt from his cloak of disrespect the pantheism of Spinoza and his disciple Einstein. Why? Because, Dawkins' said, "pantheism is sexed up atheism."[7]

From Jacoby, that would have been viewed as an insult. From Dawkins, it's a compliment. In support of his contention that the pantheists are really okay, he quotes Einstein in saying that "I believe in Spinoza's God who reveals himself in the orderly harmony of what exists, not in

---

7. Dawkins, *God Delusion*, 18.

a God who concerns himself with fates and actions of human beings."[8] You would think that Dawkins would recognize in that philosophy an opportunity to foster social unity and healing. This is a conception that might attract some theists, who have come to question whether the Old God isn't just a tad too anthropomorphic, whereas at the same time it could also attract a fair number of atheists, whose antipathy to the supernaturalism of the Old God has blinded them to such notions as cosmic unity or transcendence. But Dawkins doesn't go there. Instead, he notes that while not intending any disrespect to "the God of Einstein and other enlightened scientists," they really should stop using the word "God" in a non-traditional sense because it gets confused with the supernatural God and "[d]eliberately to confuse the two is, in my opinion, an act of intellectual high treason."[9]

That bit of hyperbolic intolerance illustrates why, in *Saving God*, Mark Johnston aptly referred to Dawkins and his fellow travelers as "undergraduate atheists."[10] Displaying infinitely more intelligence than they do wisdom, these polemicists remind me of some of the sharpest, and yet most angst-ridden, minds I knew in college. In whatever domain most captivated their interest, these undergraduates sought the comforts of a simple, consistent platform on which they could place their faith, unencumbered by the stresses of ambiguity or shades of gray. From this platform, they would rain down argument after argument, and heaven help any interlocutor who displayed even a shred of humility or open-mindedness. I remember encountering such individuals waxing eloquently about religion—either from a traditionalist or atheist perspective. Rarely did they ever seem conflicted or puzzled about what to believe, whether the subject involved God, politics, or just about any other topic of significance. For example, I frequently found such personalities attracted either to Marxism or laissez-faire libertarianism, both of which center largely on the fear or hatred of specific institutions (in one case, private; in the other case, public). Such is always fertile ground for orthodoxy.

Just as the Nurturing God may appropriately be seen as a concept worthy of small children in need of affection, the Strawman God of the New Atheists may be seen as a worthy outlet for adolescents who are coping with angst and could use a whipping boy. It is easy enough to dismiss

8. Ibid.

9. Ibid., 19.

10. Johnston, *Saving God*, 39.

both of these perspectives as "immature" and not suitable for adult consideration, but as we have seen, this would be a mistake. The Nurturing God revealed many deep emotional needs that we are well advised to satisfy if that can be done with integrity. Similarly, the tremendous popularity of the New Atheists' screeds is just as revealing, particularly to those of us, like Johnston, who are interested in "saving God."

The millions who read the works of Dawkins, Sam Harris, and Christopher Hitchens may or may not giggle when they show up at church, but at least they're not bored. And that separates them, I suspect, from those "unbelievers" who regard religion less as an evil than as a mere nuisance—more like the droppings in a litter box than anything worthy of a 300-page diatribe. Just as some unabashed atheists are writing books, an increasing number of others are organizing in networks and forming societies. These organizations include "humanist" groups as well as groups that unabashedly refer to themselves as "atheist." Clearly, there is a significant demand for communities that are able to provide an overarching purpose in life without being grounded in supernatural myths. Those who join these communities are looking for a religion; they just don't want to call it that.

For the majority in Western Europe and certain developed nations of Asia, and for an increasingly large minority of America, the supernatural God is indeed dead as a doornail. But what the atheist movement shows is that the widespread demise of the Old God does not necessarily portend the demise of religion. Many atheists thirst for a sense of meaning that is difficult to derive from secular life. Even Dawkins, the would-be deicide, left open the prospect that, for him, pantheism might well be an attractive alternative to an uncompromising secularism. He simply doesn't want to call the object of pantheistic love "God," as that would defang his rhetoric against the Lord of Scripture.

Can we have religion without the Old God? We can certainly get many of its traditional benefits. Just go to a humanistic church, synagogue, or fellowship and you'll find all sorts of coming-of-age ceremonies, instruction in moral values, and celebrations of community. The better question is, can we have God without having to buy into all aspects of the Old Time Religion? And an even more interesting issue is whether we can re-conceptualize what we mean by God, without sacrificing "his" ultimacy and in a way that fosters an appreciation for divinity among non-believers.

For some, these issues may be of secondary interest, but not to me. Given my own journey to date, I can relate as much to those who oppose traditional religion as to those whose lives revolve around it. That is why I view the highest expressions of religion to be as heretical as they are pious. Now, allow me to explain how my own love for heresy arose.

CHAPTER 5

Autobiographical Interlude

"If you believe in God, you are an idiot."

—Evelyn Spiro

"Judaism has a layer of bullshit. Christianity added another."

—Julius Spiro

WE ARE ALL ALLOTTED as children both a set of crosses to bear and a set of wings with which to soar. How we evolve as adults is a function of which of these implements come to dominate our psyches.

Personally, one of the greatest gifts I have received in life is to grow up in a house where thinking for oneself about matters of religion was a supreme value. I was exposed to alternative approaches for resolving religious issues and permitted complete freedom to select my own path. Plus, I was mentored by people whose lives were profoundly impacted by the way they confronted religious questions and institutions. So I had no choice but to conclude that religion mattered fundamentally, and yet was afforded the liberty to choose for myself what to do with such knowledge. For that, I am eternally grateful to my parents, Evelyn and Julius Spiro.

In some respects, my religious upbringing was very conventional. My parents ensured that I received a standard Jewish education. They also went out of their way to give me an appreciation for the majestic cultural heritage of the Jewish people, one that spans thousands of years and continues today. But what was perhaps most notable about the importance they assigned to raising me "Jewish" was that it was juxtaposed against their own absolute disdain for some of the core myths of the Jewish religion. The two quotations at the top of this chapter come from my mom and dad, and were expressed to me when I was a child. To this day, when I try to summarize for myself their views on religion, those quotations come first to mind.

If you don't come from a Jewish background, you might view people like my parents as rather odd, but in the Jewish community, they are quite common. Judaism, you see, is as much a *folk* as a *faith*, and there are many who see themselves as deeply "Jewish" because of their connection to the Jewish culture, even though they find little that is appealing about the religion. That would certainly characterize my mother. My father's situation was a bit more complex. He kept kosher for his entire life and truly enjoyed attending synagogue. Yet if you asked him why he did so, he would say that it connected him to his roots, and especially to his devout father (who died before I was born). My dad would *never* say anything affirming about the belief in God.

Unlike my mom, who is always willing to poke fun at religion if given the opportunity, my dad didn't like to say much about it. When he did break his silence, his words took on even greater significance. As is apparent from the above quotation, he had no tolerance whatsoever for talk about biblical miracles or a supernatural deity. He had an even greater distaste for the hypocritical way in which politicians and clerics utilized religion. I cannot count the number of times my dad used the term "*big macher*"—a mocking English-Yiddish term for a big shot—to refer to some of the most prominent religious leaders in our society.

Clearly, my father retained a sense of the sacred from his own childhood, and especially from his father, a pious lower-middle class insurance salesman who had immigrated from Russia, settled in Brooklyn, and somehow supported six children. Yet just as clearly, my dad failed to find this sense of the sacred in the verbiage of most rabbis, ministers, or others who claimed to be experts on matters of faith. Perhaps this is why he always had more appreciation for the *chazzans* (cantors), whose music led the congregation in prayer, than for the rabbis, whose words led the congregation down a path of "bullshit"—at least in his view and that of my mother.

I mentioned earlier that two books played the greatest role in shaping my spirituality as a child. The first of the two, *Bible Stories for Jewish Children*, gave me a sense of enchantment for the stories of the Bible that will stay with me forever. But it was the second book that came to dominate my thoughts about God from midway through my elementary school years until I began to study philosophy in college. It was not, ostensibly, a book about religion, and yet it convinced me for many years that my mom was indeed correct. God, I decided, was a figment of our imagination, and those who believe in him may not literally be "idiots," but they are at least willfully blind.

The book I am referring to is now one of my most cherished possessions. I inherited it from my mother's mother after she died. I first saw it inside a glass bookcase in my grandparents' apartment. They lived in the poverty-stricken region of the South Bronx known as Hunts Point. That had been their home from early in the twentieth century until roughly 1970, when a local thug pushed my grandfather down a flight of stairs and broke eight of his ribs. As a child, I could only read the book when I left my upper-middle-class home in Bethesda, Maryland and visited my grandparents. It was impossible to make that trip without obsessing about poverty, injustice, and racism. The South Bronx was that bleak. But my grandmother's book was even bleaker.

Its cover is brown and bears but a single symbol: a swastika. Only on the spine and the inside of the book can you read its name, *The Brown Book of the Hitler Terror*. When I opened the book, it bore an inscription: "Feb. 13 1934—To a buddy of social science from a Veteran." As my mother explained, the "buddy of social science" was my grandmother, who was a serious student of both history and philosophy, including Spinoza. The book was actually published in 1933, the year Hitler first came to power as the Chancellor of Germany, and my grandmother's copy was part of the book's fourth printing, which came out in November of that year. Apparently, I wasn't the only one interested in what this book had to say.

Before I started reading its text, I was transfixed by its photographs. One shows a picture of a man with a mustache and his mouth open, beneath which were the words "Hitler speaks!"[1] There are also pictures of two other orators, Dr. Josef Goebbels and Hermann Goering, the latter of whom is quoted as saying "I would rather shoot a few times too short

1. World Committee, *Brown Book*, 36.

and too wide, but at any rate I would shoot."[2] And there are pictures of men from rival political parties who were said to have been "silenced" or "arrested."[3]

As the book progresses, the photographs and inscriptions beneath them become increasingly chilling. One photo depicts a store owned by a Jew, on which a large swastika had been painted on the front window. The inscription says "Boycott of a store: 'Let the hands of the Jewish pig rot away!'"[4] Another photo shows a swastika cut into the hair of a Jew; it was said to be made into an official post card.[5] Later photos show the Nazis forcing men, women, and children to stand for hours holding their hands behind their heads.[6] Then came the final chapter, entitled "Murder." I'll never forget staring at the photos in that chapter. One depicts a woman who was said to have been "shot down in the street by a storm trooper, and bled to death."[7] Another shows a man with multiple bullet wounds in his face, who was "shot while trying to escape."[8] The book's final photo is that of a woman's backside after she had been "beaten for two hours with rubber truncheons, steel rods, and whips."[9]

As enchanted as I was by *Bible Stories for Jewish Children*, I was even more transfixed by *Hitler Terror*. It fascinated me not merely for what it could teach us about the human condition, but also for what it had to say about divinity. I first saw this book after I had been exposed to biblical stories and the idea that our world belongs to God. He is the one who spoke to Abraham at Moriah and Moses at Sinai. He is the one who once showered us with manna from heaven, and who continues to bless us with fertile fields and ample water. Yet, for some reason, he allowed the Nazis to commit acts of unspeakable brutality and inhumanity, which Americans were beginning to learn about as far back as 1933,

---

2. Ibid., 132.

3. Ibid., 148–49.

4. Ibid., 260.

5. Ibid., 261.

6. Ibid., 309.

7. Ibid., 324.

8. Ibid.

9. Ibid., 325. As an adult, I have come to learn that certain allegations that this book makes against the Nazis have been refuted. Yet I had no knowledge of that as a child. More importantly, the atrocities that I have come over the years to associate with the Nazis, especially during the Holocaust itself, dwarf anything that a propagandist could possibly have dreamed up in 1933.

when *Hitler Terror* was published. Nearly a full decade elapsed before my country joined the effort to stop these beasts—by which time it was too late to prevent them from torturing and slaughtering six million Jews and countless millions of others. If God is responsible for palm trees and blue skies, I wondered, why isn't he also responsible for the Holocaust?

Most parents wouldn't want their seven-year-olds reading about the Nazis, and mine didn't exactly hand me the book. But once I discovered it, they didn't stop me from looking at it either. They valued truth too heavily to keep me in ignorance. As a result, when I was young, I spent no dearth of time contemplating just exactly what it says about an omnipotent Lord that he gave us Hitler, the Russian pogroms, African-American slavery, and countless other atrocities.

I must have gone through an emotional process similar to that which New Jersey Senator Bill Bradley was attempting to evoke when, in 1992, he gave a speech illustrating the horrors of the way the Los Angeles Police Department brutalized Rodney King, a black man who was arrested after driving while intoxicated. Bradley told his fellow Senators that what King had done was "clearly wrong," but this hardly justified the brutality he encountered from the men in blue. The policemen beat him no fewer than fifty-six times in eighty-one seconds.[10]

In order to demonstrate the extent of such brutality, Bradley exclaimed the word "pow" fifty-six times.[11] Pow! Pow! Pow! Pow! Pow! Pow! . . . After literally fifty more instances, if you heard the speech, you felt Bradley's point shake you to the bone: those policemen had completely lost any semblance of humanity.

As a child, after I contemplated what it meant to allow millions upon millions of men, women, and children to be enslaved, gassed, buried alive . . . you name it . . . I got the point too. In essence, I had heard the word "Pow" in my head one too many times. This "omnipotent God" we had been reading about in Jewish school would have had to be as inhumane as the Nazis. Either that or he had never existed in the first place. If I were going to continue to believe that human life is sacred and torture is beneath contempt, I had no choice to but to view God as non-existent . . . or worse.

10. Bradley, "Speech," para. 1.

11. Ibid., para. 3.

⟿

Unbeknownst to me as a child, an entire branch of theology has been created to address the so-called "problem of evil." It is called theodicy. Perhaps, if my Jewish school teachers had been steeped in theodicy and rhetoric and knew exactly which of my buttons to push, they could have saved me from a decade of atheism. Frankly, though, I'm happy not to have known such people, because that period of my life has allowed me to appreciate what is most lacking in organized religion today.

In my experience, clerics from each of the Abrahamic faiths conventionally suggest that with enough exposure to the rhythm of prayer, the stories of Scripture, and the figure of God, anyone who is born to a particular faith tradition should inevitably come to embrace it. I have even found this attitude in the branches of Judaism that pride themselves on being liberal and modern. Judaism is premised on the idea that the great philosophical questions (like the ones addressed by theodicy) are truly secondary and what matters most is living an ethical life and observing the ceremonial rituals. I have personally seen otherwise progressive rabbis scoff at the notion that most people are by nature philosophical or otherwise troubled by the paradoxes embedded in the Lord of Abraham. When I once complained to a rabbi that he had been portraying God like a cosmic Santa Claus, the rabbi replied: "The only ones who would care are you and Maimonides." The rabbi was speaking in hyperbole, but I understood his point and appreciated the candor. As long as a congregation has a shul full of people who are willing to sing God's praises on Friday night and study his alleged miracles on Saturday morning, it really doesn't much matter to rabbis how these people conceive of God when they go to bed on Sunday night. Judaism, as I constantly hear from members of the clergy, is about *action*, not *beliefs*.

Thanks to a decade of atheism, I can safely say that such a mindset tragically ignores the millions, if not billions, of people throughout the world for whom *The Name* has become either moribund or dead. Christians and Muslims stand out in how much they profess concern that the people of the world find salvation through a belief in God. And yet their clerics are committing the same gaffe as the rabbis: underestimating the power of the reasons *not* to believe, especially for those who grew up with less of an appreciation for *The Name* than for the dignity of humankind. If you wish to persuade Secular Humanists to embrace a belief in the Divine, you have to treat where they are coming from with respect. There is, after all, a reason why clerics have needed to create an entire theological discipline simply to address the problem of evil. Perhaps that problem is not an indictment of God, but it must be a pretty powerful indictment of the way God is typically discussed. Otherwise, it could have been dispensed with in a few books, and not require more than a few libraries.

So how, you ask, did I emerge from the comfort of my secularism and go on to become what my mother once described as an "idiot"? Studying Kant in college, I came to appreciate the concept of transcendence, and especially the idea that human beings are unable to sense, let alone comprehend, entire dimensions of existence. That led me to the blissful, academic state known as agnosticism.

For many, agnosticism is a terminal point. It is a place that beckons searchers to get off the path and devote themselves to consumerism, workaholism, or some other lifestyle that would have bored Socrates. Once they stop searching, they can always take comfort in the fact that the great questions about God are truly unanswerable, so why in the name of Sisyphus should they bother asking?

For me, however, agnosticism was but a relatively brief sojourn. It ended shortly after I graduated from college and decided to visit Israel for the first time. It was the spring of 1981. I was twenty years old and knew nobody in the Holy Land. I came simply with a backpack, a bevy of Nietzsche books, and a desire to spend several weeks in Jerusalem learning about the Jewish religion. I thought that reading the "atheist" Nietzsche in Israel would create a pretty cool dialectic—atheism one moment, theism the next. What I didn't appreciate was how subtly spiritual Nietzsche was. Nor did I appreciate how the very vitriol that Nietzsche heaped upon the God of Abraham would ironically cause me to take that God *more* seriously. If he were worthy of obsessing Nietzsche, I reasoned, he was worthy of obsessing me. These factors, combined with the way my agnosticism had opened my heart as well as my mind, made me easy prey for the rabbis of the Jerusalem yeshiva who put me up without charge for weeks. The yeshiva rabbis were the rhetorically sophisticated theologians I had never been exposed to as a child. They specialized in "converting" confused young-adult Jews who were interested in their ancestors' faith but hadn't been able to summon a heartfelt love for God.

The next part of my story is something I've written about, in supposedly fictional form, in my first novel, *The Creed Room*. According to the yeshiva rabbis, we students had a simple choice. One option was to believe that life is inherently meaningless and consists of nothing more than random interactions of subatomic particles that evolved into living forms culminating in human beings at the top of the evolutionary chain. The other option was to accept the teachings of traditional Judaism, which holds that life is ultimately overseen by a perfect, yet inscrutable God who rewards and punishes in all sorts of ways that are beyond our capacity to understand.

I refused to believe that the Holocaust was some sort of divine punishment for human transgressions. Nor, however, did I believe that life was meaningless and that humans were the pinnacle of the hierarchy of being. The more that I heard about the God who loves us and yet demands virtue in return, the more I warmed to that idea and allowed my concerns with the "problem of evil" to fade into black. These concerns were replaced by the voices of the yeshiva rabbis and the coherence of their philosophy. Gradually, I was gaining a new purpose in life: to love the biblical God and do my part in honoring his Covenant. As for Nietzsche's nemesis (the Old God), I began experiencing him less in my mind and more in my heart.

With the help of the yeshiva rabbis, I rekindled the appreciation for the Divine that was snuffed out by *Hitler Terror*. Yet the God I came to embrace wasn't quite the same as my former beloved, the Nurturing God. He was more like Darryl Green's deity, minus the part about Jesus. You see, by the time I had returned to the States and incorporated everything that was taught at the yeshiva; I had definitely fallen head over heels in love—and not just with God generally, but with God the Planner in particular.

Everything that happens, I had come to believe, is attributable to God's will. He even had a plan for human society, albeit one that depended heavily on humankind's willingness to rise to the occasion. In truth, I thought, God gives us the power to turn this world into an Eden or a living hell. He made us in his image precisely so that each of us can exercise our own will freely. Whether we choose right or wrong, the power comes from God, but the responsibility falls on us.

Here's how I might expect Darryl Green to put it: All God does is set out the playing field and establish the basic rules. We have to execute the plays, and often under difficult conditions. We will frequently encounter temptations to blow off the rules and play our own game, but ultimately that is a losing proposition.

That was my philosophy during much of the summer before I matriculated in law school in 1981. Then, one day, I had what Christians would call an epiphany, though it might be more apt to call it an epiphany-in-reverse. While walking down the street in Cambridge, Massachusetts trying to make a bus, I was a bit late, and the next bus wasn't scheduled to arrive for another half hour. Just as I turned the corner, the bus left. Had I reached the corner seconds earlier, I would have made it.

For a short period of time, I was strangely fascinated with *why* I missed that bus. "God must have willed it," I thought, "but what was he thinking? Was he punishing me for something?" While I can't recall exactly how much time elapsed before reality hit me, it sure hit like a ton of bricks. I couldn't believe that a Harvard Law School-bound son of heretical parents attributed the fact that he had missed a city bus to God's will. "Dan," I said to myself. "Do you know what that makes you? An F-ing imbecile."

Yes, my life had grown in meaning. Yes, I had tapped into the power of *The Name*, a power that can carry an incredible rush of joy when you contemplate it. Still, I couldn't escape the fact that I had lost touch with the voice of reason and adopted a worldview that was grounded more in Scripture than in common sense. That's a no-no. I owed a duty to the muse of philosophy, the very muse that had opened my mind from a decade of atheism, to worship not just a God that made me happy, but the God that really *is*. In other words, it was time to get back on the path of confusion, or God-wrestling, and seek a conception of the Divine that married both my thirst for a compelling purpose in life and my commitment to truth.

↢

From that point on, the epiphanies have been less dramatic because my basic adult religious framework had been established. I was not about to give up my love for God. Nor was I willing to stop speaking to God or finding inspiration in *The Name*. Yet never again could I allow myself to feel the familiarity with God that stems from viewing the Divine in largely human terms. My God was not to be a Superman known in terms of qualities like empathy, mercy, love, justice . . . or even *will*. In other words, the issue for me would not be what God "wills" us to do, but what we choose to do based on our own deliberations. It is plausible, I thought, that there exists a cosmic consciousness who literally sees everything that occurs and opines about how each of us should live our lives. But those ideas would no longer be among my beliefs. When it comes to the phrase "God willing," I'm with Richard Dawkins and my dear mother: unless we change the meaning of the word "willing" beyond recognition, it makes no sense to worship a God who "wills." That's not a God who created us in his image, that's a Superman we've created in our own.

When I became enamored with the philosophy of Spinoza in the summer of 1982, it was as much because Spinoza kicked open the door to heresy as because of the specific type of heresy Spinoza taught. All of a sudden, a whole realm of options was available to me, and not merely the two presented by the yeshiva rabbis (meaningless secularism and fundamentalist Judaism). Spinoza's particular brand of heresy allowed me to feel God's presence in my life without having to fictionalize him as a superhero. The pantheistic deity that came to replace the Planning God as my object of worship sat well with my voice of reason and gave me great comfort. When I went to synagogue, as I continued to do in order to honor God, it hardly bothered me to hear about God's "will" or "mercy." The masses had their opiate, I figured. I had my rationality.

Yet one of the key principles of rationality is that when it comes to God, the truth must forever evade us. We are, after all, mere mortals. So whenever I came to gain an insight, it was just a matter of time before a counter-insight would come along, thereby reminding me that it is the love of the *search* for truth, and not its possession, that marks the life of philosophy.

In this regard, one quotation came to take on greater significance for me than any other. "When beginning to philosophize," said Hegel, "one must first be a Spinozist. The soul must bathe itself in the ether of this single substance, in which everything one has held dear is submerged."[12] On the surface, it is a tribute by Hegel to Spinoza's pantheism, including Spinoza's intellectual and emotional commitment to the notion of the absolute unity that transcends any physical thing or object of thought. Yet if you think twice about this quotation, you'll realize that Hegel was pointing out the limitations of Spinoza's philosophy every bit as much as its value.

Notably, Hegel said nothing about where we must *end* our search for truth; he was merely telling us where that search must begin. We start with the belief (or should I say "faith") in absolute unity—with the idea that the substance of the world and the substance of God are one and the

12. Beiser, *Cambridge Companion*, 5.

same. But we can take that insight in many different directions, and Hegel would be the first one to argue that some of the best directions were those that Spinoza had never enunciated.

This, then, became my challenge—to go beyond Spinoza, Kant, or for that matter Hegel, in seeking God. It is a challenge born not of hubris but of humility, for if those men could speak from the grave, they would surely urge every human being, whether a beginning student or a master philosopher, to assume that mantle. It matters not if we are considering a single book of philosophy or the collected works of human Scripture. They are all so terribly finite, so incredibly limited, when compared to the entirety and the essence of the Divine.

CHAPTER 6

God the Source of All That Is

"The closest we can come to thinking about God is as a process rather than a being. We can think of it as "be-ing," as verb rather than noun. Perhaps we would understand this concept better if we renamed God. We might call It God-ing, a process, rather than God, which suggests a noun."

—Rabbi David A. Cooper, *God Is a Verb*[1]

"We want Wholeness, a holistic understanding, now. I believe that people are moving from theism to pantheism. . . . What was the objection that people had to pantheism, God is everything? 'Are you going to tell me that the excrement of a dog is also God?' And the answer to this would be—'Yes.' What is wrong with that? It is only from the human perspective that we see a difference between that and challah. On the submolecular level, on the atomic level, they all look the same. And if you look from a galactic perspective, what difference is there between one and the other? So if 'God is everything,' why are you and I here? Because we are the appearance of God in this particular form. . . . So it's not that God created the world but that God became the world."

—Rabbi Zalman Schachter-Shalomi, *Wrapped in a Holy Flame*[2]

---

1. Cooper, *God Is a Verb*, 69.
2. Schacter-Shalomi, *Wrapped in a Holy Flame*, 20.

PERHAPS WHEN YOU SEE a piece of dog excrement on the carpet, you think that therein lies God. But I don't. And I don't really think Rabbi Zalman does either.

The beauty of pantheism is in its core insights, that there exists ultimate unity and that this unity alone is the most suitable object of reverence. The problems begin when pantheists lose their discipline and attach *The Name* to every thing or idea they encounter—or to whatever subset of things or ideas they choose to extol. One minute, a pantheist might toast *l'chaim*, "To Life!" and her thoughts would turn to God as the unity of all life. I'm fine with that. But what if she were to step on a chunk of dog dung and say "Damn, I've got God smeared on my shoe"? How are we supposed to react to that? Maybe by thinking that *this* God (yours truly) thinks *that* God (the smelly pantheist) is a goofball.

A philosophical pantheist would surely respond to my objection that I'm playing with semantics. If it is true that the All is One, and dog feces and challah bread are merely interconnected portions of a single web of being, it makes perfect sense to say that God is the All and God is every part. After all, if someone pointed to my face and said "There is Dan," they wouldn't be misspeaking; a "person" obviously consists of much more than his face, or for that matter, his entire body, but it is fully consistent with the way we speak to identify a face by the name of the person whose face it is. When Rabbi Zalman was using the name God to refer to the dog feces, he was merely pointing out that the feces *is* God in the same way that my face *is* Dan.

Sorry, but if pantheism is going to put itself on the map as a prominent foundation for faith, it had better concern itself with semantics. I'm reminded of a beautiful statement made by a pantheist writer, Jay Michaelson. According to Michaelson, "God is a name that lovers give to Being."[3] What Michaelson is telling us is not only that a pantheist might equate the word "God" with Being itself—with pure existence—but that as soon as we attach the name "God" to Being, it takes on so much more emotional power and brings into play our greatest emotional tool, the ability to love. Suffice it to say that something as grand as Being, existence, or even life, is worthy not only of love but of the supreme reverential love that is extended only to that which we deem *ultimate*. By contrast, if Michaelson had said "God is a name that lovers give to dog feces (and

---

3. Michaelson, *Everything is God*, 115.

every other thing)," I'd assume that the lovers he's talking about are flies, not people.

While some pantheists like to equate God with each earthly object, Michaelson wouldn't make that mistake. But that doesn't stop him from exhibiting what for pantheists is an even more common occupational hazard: reasoning that because everything is part of God, it must therefore be *holy*. At the beginning of his book *Everything is God*, Michaelson quotes Allen Ginsberg as follows: "The world is holy! The soul is holy! The skin is holy! The nose is holy! . . . Everything is holy! everybody's holy! everywhere is holy!"[4] Does that make Hitler and Goebbels holy? Apparently so. For near the end of his book, Michaelson discusses Anne Frank's comment that "all people are good at heart," and concluded that "Anne Frank was not naive. Imagine her knowing, even as she was victimized and brutalized beyond our capacity to conceive, that what was happening was not the evil essence of humanity, but a mistake."[5]

A *mistake*? Many words can aptly be used for our species' most extreme act of genocide, but a "mistake" wouldn't be one of them. When pantheists lose their discipline, they reason as follows: "God is Good, and each of us is God (or holy), so we each must be Good."

Michaelson correctly understands that good people make mistakes. What they don't do is marshal hatred and fear to such a degree as to wreak destruction of biblical proportions, which is precisely what Hitler and his friends managed to accomplish.

As far as I'm concerned, a better use of the word "mistake" is to describe any effort on the part of pantheists to deify tiny portions of reality. Once they resist that temptation and turn their worshipful attention to the divine unity itself, they can find a true launching pad from which to attain great heights. This is what Hegel was talking about when he said that when beginning to philosophize, one must first be a Spinozist (i.e., a pantheist). Pantheists stand for the profound proposition that, when speaking about God, we must take omnipresence seriously. We must constantly remind ourselves of the Qur'anic statement that God is closer to us than our jugular veins. We must recognize that there is no rational ground for positing an ontological chasm between, on the one hand, a leaf, a water molecule, a loaf of challah bread, and, yes, a piece of dog feces, and on the other hand, all the thoughts in the universe.

4. Ibid., frontmatter.
5. Ibid., 215.

The more we learn, the more we see interconnections and a common ground for all of reality, and the less sense it makes to worship a God who sits in a heaven that is not composed of the same basic ingredients as our own world. Such a God may exist, but neither our five senses nor our voice of reason encourages us to accept that hypothesis.

In philosophical literature, you often see the term "philosophies of immanence" used to refer to the pantheistic views of thinkers like Spinoza, Hegel, Giordano Bruno, and Gilles Deleuze. They are grouped together for having taught that one vital force or set of forces pervades (is "immanent in") all that exists. Traditionally, that phrase is contrasted with "philosophies of transcendence," such as those grounded in the monotheistic biblical faiths, which traditionally posit a perfect God that in his underlying makeup is separate and apart from this world.

More recently, however, it has become trendy for those who would once have been known as pantheists to avoid that term and to embrace instead the word *panentheism*, which literally means that the all is *in* God, rather than that the all equals God. Why the trend? Because it is one thing to adopt the rationalistic, pantheistic view that there is no ontological chasm between this world and any other dimension of reality, such as a "heaven." But it is something different, and much less defensible, to deny that there exist dimensions of reality that transcend what human beings are ever capable of perceiving or imagining. Spinoza's Parable of the Worm is, on the surface, an argument for immanence, but it is just as profoundly an argument for transcendence. That parable illustrates not merely that everything in existence is interconnected, but that there is so much to our interconnected web that no single living being could begin to fathom, and this applies to the finite creatures known as human beings as much as to the worms in our bloodstream.

For me, panentheism at its best is pantheism in its most sophisticated form. The "en" that is inserted in the middle of the word is meant as a reminder that pantheists must not forget the importance of transcendence in speaking about God or the divine unity. Yes, that unity contains processes that transcend the simple-minded way in which we perceive the world, even if it were to be the case that, at a submolecular level, the transcendent is composed of the same basic stuff as earthly objects. But more to the point, those divine processes that transcend excrement or challah bread also transcend you and me. We can fathom the notion of cosmic unity. What we can't begin to do is describe more than a tiny part of it—or as the Muslims might say, the part we can understand in relation to the whole of the unity is tinier than that of a single grain of sand in relation to the largest desert on earth. That's how small a portion of God panentheists should claim to know. It's a humbling religious philosophy if taken seriously.

I have mentioned before that for Spinoza, the Parable of the Worm and the affirmation of cosmic unity were his points of departure. It is time now to turn to how he launched his thoughts outward from that foundation—and you'll please forgive him if his particular form of panentheism is as complex as other forms of pantheism are simple. As with so many other great thinkers over the centuries, Spinoza's thoughts are susceptible to multiple interpretations. His mind was far too capacious to be constrained by the hobgoblin of foolish consistency. Consequently, I must also ask that he be forgiven for playing with alternative wordings to characterize God, each of which could give rise to altogether different religious philosophies.

Spinoza scholars argue to this day about whether he is best viewed as: (a) a traditional pantheist, who meant by "God" nothing more than what the rest of us mean by nature, except that he chose to deify nature (which is, for many people, just another way of calling him an atheist); (b) a panentheist who instead saw God as a transcendent, active source and ground of all the objects and ideas in our world; (c) a philosopher who was willing to write about God in different, and somewhat inconsistent, ways because he had no interest in being completely transparent about his innermost thoughts; or (d) some fourth alternative. I will leave for professional philosophers the joy of continuing that debate from now until the end of time—or until Spinoza rises from the grave, whichever comes first. For me, though, what is most interesting is not what Spinoza really meant, but how his writings can inspire us. In that regard, what I find especially interesting is how he has given rise to a form of panentheism that pays homage to the power of *The Name*, while respecting both the sense of immanence and transcendence that his philosophy is capable of conveying.

✧

Admittedly, Spinoza did use the term "Nature" as a substitute for "God." And I think it is also safe to say that his God is the Philosophical Absolute—there exists nothing that is truly outside of this God. But it is indeed imperative to keep in mind that for Spinoza, "Nature" can be used in two very different senses. I am referring to a distinction in medieval philosophy that is now primarily associated with Spinoza's work: the difference between *Natura naturans* (literally, "Nature naturing") and *Natura naturata* (literally, "Nature natured"). When Spinoza used the name "God" as a synonym for Nature, he generally evoked the idea of Nature as an active principle—as a *verb*, to use David Cooper's terminology. In other words, he typically equated God not just with Nature generally, but with *Natura naturans* in particular.

If you hate jargon as much as I do, you're probably shaking your head in frustration about now. Couldn't I, or Spinoza, have just said "God is a verb"? That sounds so much simpler. But for me, it is less precise. Spinoza's God isn't just *a* verb; his God is the *ultimate* verb. It most closely corresponds to what it means to exist. All things in nature that are in motion—or for that matter, every finite form insofar as it is thought to be at rest—demonstrate various properties, but none is more fundamental than the fact that they exist. In speaking of *Natura naturans* (Nature as an active principle), we are speaking of an indivisible force or power that, according to Spinoza, resides within all of existence. We can explain how some particular things have grown or evolved at specific points in time, but we can't explain why anything at all exists or why existence as a whole has taken one form and not another. To that mystery (the mystery of existence as such), and to that hidden wellspring or ground that underlies all cosmic processes and beings, Spinoza applies the word "God." In doing so, he is referring to *Natura naturans*.

Grasshoppers jump, birds fly, dogs bite, and people think. To Spinoza, all of this activity is simply the process of cosmic unity unfolding through an infinite number of things and ideas that are truly just finite manifestations of a single divine, and largely unknowable, nature. The essence of this unity, Spinoza taught, is to engage in self-expression through manifold forms. In fact, the essence of *Natura naturans* is to engage in self-expression through precisely those forms that are manifested in reality. In other words, everything that is real exists just as it is determined to exist by being a product of *Natura naturans*. Einstein's statement that God doesn't play dice with the universe simply reflects his own Spinozist determinism and denial of the existence of cosmic caprice. (That Spinoza didn't believe in free will in the classic sense of that term is one reason Nietzsche loved him so, yet it may also have been one of the reasons why the Amsterdam rabbinate excommunicated him from their community.)

Just as Spinoza used "Nature" as a one-word summary for God, he also used another one-word summary that is significantly more panentheistic: God is "Substance" (meaning, that which underlies). Just as a submarine cannot be seen from above the water's surface, so too is Spinoza's power-generating "Substance" imperceptible from the perspective of the world as we know it. The title of this chapter is taken from the subtitle of a book written by my friend Frank Dixon, entitled *Spinoza's God: The Source of All That Is*. Frank was speaking specifically about Spinoza's God as Substance—as that which underlies every thought, feeling, or physical thing. Again, this underlying ground is nothing more than our friend, *Natura naturans*. And speaking of jargon, the one time in the *Ethics* when Spinoza saw fit to define the word "God," he specifically chose to do so not by mentioning "Nature," but rather by mentioning Substance: "By God, I mean an absolutely infinite being, that is, substance consisting of infinite attributes, each of which expresses eternal and infinite essence."[6] No, it's not exactly easy reading, is it!

To Spinoza, each finite thing or form is part of a plethora of interrelated cause-and-effect chains. We all have definite antecedents (our parents and other ancestors, in the case of human beings), and there are a variety of spheres that we ourselves can influence. That is what it means to exist as one being among others in the world. Spinoza's *Natura naturans*, or Substance, is different. This formulation of God emphasizes the divine essence as being a first cause that exists eternally. In fact, Spinoza derived much of his understanding of God from his understanding of what it means to be "eternal." According to Spinoza, "the eternal does not admit of 'when' or 'before' or 'after,' [hence] it follows merely from God's perfection that God can never decree otherwise nor ever could have decreed otherwise."[7] Spinoza's Substance is also Absolutely Infinite—limitless in every way. Wherever and whenever you find beings in motion or at rest, you can be sure Substance lies within, shaping them into precisely the same limited forms that scientists strive to measure, poets to rhapsodize, and theologians to deify or demonize.

By contrast, every time we deify any one discrete form or being—whether it is "God the Son" on the cross or Adonai talking to Moses in the form of a burning bush—we are referring to God as *Natura naturata*. Any specific form that we can reference, be it through spoken words,

6. Spinoza, "Ethics," Part I, Def. VI, 217.

7 Spinoza, "Ethics", Part I, Prop. 33, Scholium 2, 237.

sounds, or historical actions, is necessarily viewed from the standpoint of nature *natured*. Note the use of the past tense, for the active principle is gone. This form is now viewed passively, as the result of what has happened, like an infinite array of photographic snapshots.

Look outside and reflect on the trees, the grass, the cars, the sky . . . and then consider being able to perceive or imagine all other forms in the universe. You are still dealing in the realm of *Naturata*, even if you perceive that you are dealing with an object in motion. You are still attempting in your mind to describe or characterize what existed at the time of your observation and presumably no longer exists in precisely that form. As Heraclitus realized thousands of years ago, we can never step into the same river twice.

The difference when we contemplate the Divine as *Naturans* is that we are no longer dealing in the realm of discrete, differentiated forms. We are now speaking *sub specie aeternitatis* (from the standpoint of eternity), a phrase that Spinoza popularized and is now part of common philosophical parlance. From that perspective, we find at bottom simple unity—not a complex manifold, but a single substance or source of all that is. And we also find that this unity is pregnant with the power to manifest itself in an infinite number of finite, concrete forms. Whenever that power is exercised, we have an example of what David Cooper was referring to as God-ing. This is not a word I personally use very often, but it does get the point across. Spinoza's *Natura naturans*, or Substance, is pure activity and encompasses the power to create, to destroy, and above all else, to exist.

Spinoza identified as the force that pervades all individual things, including what we know as "inanimate matter," one's endeavor to persist in one's own being. This is the lifeblood of Nature considered as a set of discrete beings or forms (*Naturata*). Yet the impetus of this power—its timeless cause or ground—is God or Substance (*Naturans*).

⊷

Thanks to the teachings of Spinoza, I became much less concerned about the so-called "problem of evil." In reference to that issue, Spinoza said the following: "[T]o those who ask why God did not create men in such a way that they should be governed solely by reason, I make only this reply, that he lacked not material for creating all things from the highest to the lowest degree of perfection; or, to speak more accurately, the laws of his nature were so comprehensive as to suffice for the production of everything that can be conceived by an infinite intellect."[8] Here, Spinoza is talking about God not merely as a process but as a being, or more precisely, as Being itself. Yet what I have always found striking is that this Being comes across more like a Cosmic Power Generator than like a Cosmic Santa Claus. And indeed, Spinoza's God has given us fictionalized stories about heaven and true stories about Hitler.

In short, Spinoza attacked God's "omnibenevolence" centuries before Nietzsche proclaimed the coup de grace. Specifically, Spinoza challenged the traditional notion of God's transcendent consciousness right along with that of his benevolence. In Spinoza's words, "The intellect in act, whether it be finite or infinite, as also will, desire, love, etc., must be related to Natura naturata, not to Natura naturans."[9] So Nature considered as *Naturata* contains plenty of feelings and thoughts. But Nature at its most transcendent (as *Naturans*) is not to be considered in terms of finite feelings and thoughts, but refers instead to the active and mysterious unifying principle that underlies all of our thoughts and feelings. Thus, if you wish to believe that there is an overarching cosmic intelligence that is aware of the specific number of grains of sand on every beach at every nanosecond of every day, an assertion I once heard an imam make about his beloved Allah, you're not going to find support for that view in Spinoza.

It has become chic to say that the transcendent God is indescribable—that anything we can possibly say about God is bound to be false, for who are we to understand the inner nature of the Divine? Accordingly, while modern Muslims are stuck with the traditional doctrine that Allah has ninety-nine names—the Holy, the Sovereign Lord, the Merciful, the Beneficent, the Forgiver, the Mighty, etc.—these attributes are said to be mere tools for people to use to look up to him, rather than keys to revealing the divine mystery, which shall forever remain locked.

Spinoza's panentheism shares this same respect for the inscrutability of God, but it does so without sacrificing the power of viewing God through the additional lens of *immanence*. In addressing the divine attributes, Spinoza said repeatedly that God has "infinite" attributes of which we know but two: extension and thought. In other words, our

8. Spinoza, "Ethics," Part I, Appendix, 243.
9. Spinoza, "Ethics," Part I, Prop. 31, 234.

bodies and ideas convey direct knowledge about the nature of divinity, for they manifest internal expressions of God, rather than a "creation" manufactured by an altogether separate "Creator" who presumably had grown bored with the heavens. But there may well be countless other dimensions of reality of which we cannot now conceive and will never be able to conceive, as long as we exist in human form. God is the source, indwelling, and lifeblood of those dimensions of reality as well.

As much as a fish depends on water, Spinoza's philosophy relies on his faith in absolute, ontological unity. However, as one who reads Spinoza to be a panentheist, I would argue that he went beyond a simple recognition of that unity and revered the dimension of transcendence that pervades the unity. For me, while it is fair to say that Spinoza's philosophy was one of immanence, his *theology* was one of transcendence. his God is ultimate, eternal, infinite, inscrutable, unique. The power of that God underlies everything that has occurred, does occur, or will occur. What's more, each thought or action can ultimately be attributed to this God.

Note that one difference between Spinoza's God and that of Abraham is that Abraham's Lord is separate from, and interacts with, the world. By contrast, Spinoza's *Natura naturans*, or Substance, truly encompasses all there is. In Spinozist language, the ideas I am conveying on this page are merely temporal manifestations or "modes" of God's infinite thought. Similarly, the fingers typing those ideas are mere modes of God's infinitely extended body. When we discuss the "modes," we are speaking in the realm of *Naturata*. When we discuss the Substance underlying the modes, we are speaking in the realm of *Naturans*.

To Spinoza, everything happens inside of God/Nature/Substance; all the activity we've been discussing resides within the cosmic unity that Spinoza has chosen to deify. Yet Spinoza has taken care not to deify every individual thought or thing. Given all the gnats, excrement, and conflict about, where's the majesty in that? Rather, he has emphasized the transcendent power that underlies and ties together the infinite number of forms (modes) comprising our world.

To a Spinozist, the God of Spinoza has even more claim to ultimacy than Abraham's God. In fact, by recognizing the divine power discussed in Spinoza's works, we can hope to put biblical mythology in perspective. That mythology has an incredible amount to teach us as ethical and emotional beings. And historically, it has played a monumental role in opening our eyes to divinity. But as a foundation for a contemporary philosophy of God, it has amply been discredited by Occam's Razor, the gas chambers of the Nazis, countless storms and earthquakes, and the existence of a medical field known as pediatric oncology. At least that's how I feel.

⊕

One of Hegel's favorite phrases was the Spinozist teaching that "determination is negation."[10] That phrase suggests to me that in order to determine the uniqueness of a rock, a tree, or a person, you need to locate that thing in a larger universe—its particular place, its particular time, and its unique powers. Yet in order to do that, you need to ascertain its limits—where it is not, when it is not, and what it is not. In other words, you must negate it and bound it in order to grasp its individual form.

For many years, Spinoza's Substance served as the one referent of which I was aware that is not, in that sense, determinable. His Substance is the pure absence of negation—absolute, limitless affirmation. Moreover, his Substance is infinite and eternal not merely in one respect but in all ontological domains. In contemplating Spinoza's God as Substance, I concluded that unlike all other conceptions of the Divine, this God is truly able to claim the mantle of the One and Only.

With the passage of time, however, I have come to learn that Spinoza's Substance has, if not a twin, then at least a mirror image, one that is expressed in Hebrew rather than Latin. This twin comes from the realm of mysticism, a realm that many believe to be inherently tilted toward panentheism. (I happen to agree with that perspective, because I view the essence of mysticism in all of its forms as the visceral recognition of a connection between the self, the other forms of nature as we know it, and that which transcends our visible world. Panentheism emphasizes this same connection.)

The conception of the Divine that I have in mind is known simply as the *Ein Sof*. It represents what one of my Kabbalah teachers referred to as the "God above God." Normally, I associate that phrase with Christian theologian Paul Tillich, who sought a God transcendent of the anthropomorphisms in conventional Christian doctrine. Yet it applies equally well to the *Ein Sof* and Its relationship to the Kabbalistic Sefirot.

10. Spinoza, "Letters," Letter 50, to Jellis, 892.

In ancient Kabbalistic texts, much respect was paid to the *Ein Sof* but little ink was spilled in explaining that term. Literally meaning "without end," the *Ein Sof* refers to the cosmic infinity that so transcends the world as we know it that virtually no words can be used to describe It. According to the authors of the Kabbalah, however, while we cannot come to know the mysteries of the *Ein Sof*, we can come to know God through the ten Sefirot (literally, "enumerations") that emanate from the *Ein Sof* and interact with our universe. The Sephirot are organized hierarchically, and each is supposed to reveal qualities of God. They are, in descending order, Keter (God's crown), Chokhmah (wisdom), Binah (intuition or understanding), Chesed/Gedulah (mercy or greatness), Gevurah (strength), Tiferet (glory), Netzach (victory), Hod (majesty), Yesod (foundation), and Malkut (sovereignty). The God that was said to be revealed in the Torah is quite clearly the God of the Sefirot. We can see in the Sefirot many of the very qualities that we have associated with Adonai from the time of our childhood. These qualities of the biblical God emanate from the transcendence of the *Ein Sof*. Given that the term "emanation" is classically analogized to the Sun's rays in relationship to the Sun, you realize just how much honor the authors of the Kabbalah were assigning to the *Ein Sof*. It is as if not only our world, but even the God of our Scriptures—with all his omnipotence and omnibenevolence—are mere rays of light emerging from the beacon of the One who is "without end."

Whether you wish to think of the panentheistic conception of God as a verb, as I've been discussing *Natura naturans*, or as a noun, as I've just introduced the *Ein Sof*, both evoke the notion of that which is infinite in *all* respects. This is what is meant by being without form, limitation, or boundaries. So why, you might ask, did I refer to these conceptions as mirror images rather than twins? Because when they are considered in the context of the respective theological schemes in which they were developed, they take on significantly different roles.

For Spinoza, *Natura naturans*, or Substance, represents a reminder of transcendence within a generally panentheistic philosophy of immanence. For the Kabbalists, by contrast, the *Ein Sof* represents a reminder of immanence within a traditionally theistic philosophy of transcendence. In panentheism, the focus is always placed in two directions: on what Franz Rosenzweig once referred to as the "bubbling plenitude"[11] of the world (in other words, the infinite interplay of discrete forms), and

11. Rosenzweig, *Star of Redemption*, 47.

on the cosmic unity that underlies the world's multiplicity. Considered as multiplicity, as the sum of the discrete beings and ideas we encounter on a daily basis, we have *Natura naturata*. Considered as the underlying cosmic unity, we have *Natura naturans*. But as I read Spinoza, these are just two different perspectives on the same thing; there is no intermediary posited between *Natura naturans* and the bubbling plenitude, and you never find one without the other. By highlighting *Natura naturans*, Spinoza is reminding us that just as we must view the world from the standpoint of temporality and finitude (the world as we know it), we must also remember that our world is grounded in eternity and infinity. Thus, the God that emerges from these teachings is necessarily associated with the bubbling plenitude, just as the world that emerges from these teachings is necessarily associated with the cosmic unity. When we speak about Substance, or *Natura naturans*, we are simply evoking the perspective on the All that allows us to recognize and revere the transcendent unity that resides within it.

As for the *Ein Sof*, it is but a hint of panentheism within an overarching, hierarchical, monotheistic system that ranks various levels of reality. The sub-human realm—that of Spinoza's worm in the bloodstream—is at the bottom. The realm of human beings, who are said to be created in the image of God, is on a higher plane of existence. Above that is the domain of the Sefirot, which are commonly referred to as the divine attributes and which allow us to recognize divinity to the extent we are able. The Sefirot keep alive the notion that while there may be a more profound truth about God than what is conveyed in Scripture, that Scriptural message represents virtually all of what we feeble human beings can possibly understand. With the fourth and top level of this hierarchy, that of the *Ein Sof*, we are generally left in the position to which Wittgenstein was alluding when he said that whereof one cannot speak, thereof one must be silent.

Jews are proud of their strict adherence to monotheism and would never admit that their God has intermediaries. But an argument can be made that, unlike Spinoza's *Naturans*, the *Ein Sof* comes with plenty of intermediaries—the Sefirot. They may be conceived as intimately connected to the *Ein Sof*, but they are viewed as inferior to its mysterious unity. They remind us constantly that to be human is to live entirely within the realm of the bubbling plenitude, and an often cruel plenitude it is. We can gain glimpses of holiness through such spiritual notions as strength, glory, mercy, and majesty, but the unity of the *Ein Sof* remains as unspeakable as it is unreachable. Consequently, when it comes time for us to forge associations with the *Ein Sof*, it is seen less as the All than as the Naught. Therein lies the mirror image to Spinoza's God. Spinoza's *Naturans* or Substance, the Source of All That Is, is viewed as all-encompassing and complete. By contrast, the *Ein Sof* is conceptualized as the No-Thing—in other words, it is seen less in terms of Being than in terms of the abyss or nothingness. For once we start talking about "things" or even "the sum of all things," we are speaking about a level of reality that is qualitatively beneath that of the *Ein Sof*.

The more that I reflect on the central significance of monotheism to the Jewish faith, the more puzzled I become by the Kabbalistic idea of a hierarchy in which the scriptural God is an object of worship and yet is *not* found at the top of the hierarchy. No Muslim I know would ever say that about Allah, just as no Spinozist would ever say that about her deity. From a Jewish standpoint, though, theoretical, intellectual statements about God take a back seat in importance to the biblical God's relationship with humankind; after all, as we have said, Judaism prides itself on being a religion of action, not of belief. Consequently, though the *Ein Sof* might be ontologically superior to the Sefirot, the latter have the advantage of being infinitely more relevant and instructive to our lives. They imbue the objects in our world with meaning, whereas the *Ein Sof* remains forever enveloped in mystery.

The different roles played by Spinoza's *Naturans* and the Kabbalah's *Ein Sof* in the overall philosophies with which they are associated prevents me from looking at these concepts as identical twins. But nobody can deny their profound similarities. And perhaps their most striking similarity is that when it comes to modern Jewish theological literature so little tends to be said about them. That could easily enough be explained in the case of the *Ein Sof*, which is arguably the ultimate conversation stopper. For what can be said about the cosmic Naught? But how do we explain why even progressive Jewish theologians frequently fail to acknowledge their debt to Spinoza for his insights as a panentheist pioneer? Is it because he was excommunicated from his own synagogue? Or because, as a commentator on the Torah, he squarely challenged so many of the "truths" expressed in that book, rather than simply searching it for hidden meanings? Clearly, Spinoza had the chutzpah to speak far more from the tradition of philosophy (Athens) than theology (Jerusalem), and the official Jewish world may be responding to such chutzpah like any group of entrenched bureaucrats responds to the threat of outsiders—by minimizing the importance of their contributions. To the extent officialdom is confronted with ideas, it is always better that they come from inside the fold. In this context, Spinoza, though born Jewish and steeped in Judaism, is the ultimate outsider.

Personally, I am impressed by that fact. And I say that not simply as a student of philosophy but also as a Jew. It reveals a courageous and committed intellectual who never let the value of fitting in with a group prevent him from speaking his mind about the Word of Words. From my perspective, this seventeenth-century heretic may have captured a more modern theory of God than any of his more traditional contemporaries, or for that matter, any others who followed him in the next century or two.

And yet, as I have been exposed to twentieth-century theologians, I have realized that there is indeed something profoundly lacking in Spinoza's teachings, something a person like me who was raised in a secular home might not detect, however obvious it may be to others. While this hasn't caused me to lose my respect for Spinoza, let alone my appreciation for all he has taught me, it has reminded me that Spinoza merely embarked down a path, and we have the opportunity to continue further in any number of directions. What follows is my attempt to build on the foundation that Spinoza has provided while remaining cognizant of his limitations.

CHAPTER 7

God the Summoner

"As absolute ... or sub specie eternitatis ... the world repels our sympathy because it has no history. As such, the absolute neither acts nor suffers, nor loves nor hates; it has no needs, desires, or aspirations, no failures or success, friends or enemies, victories or defeats. All such things pertain to the world qua relative, in which our finite experiences lie, and whose vicissitudes alone have power to arouse our interest."

—William James, *A Pluralistic Universe*[1]

"When a man loves a woman so that her life is present in his own, the You of her eyes allows him to gaze into a ray of the eternal You. But if a man lusts after the 'ever repeated triumph'—you want to dangle before his lust a phantom of the eternal? ... What does the voluptuous delight of rapacity and hoarding have in common with the joy over the presence of that which is present? ... God, the eternal presence, cannot be had. Woe unto the possessed who fancy that they possess God."

—Martin Buber, *I and Thou*[2]

1. James, *Pluralistic Universe*, 47–48.
2. Buber, *I and Thou*, 154–55.

*"This gaze that supplicates and demands, that can supplicate only be-
cause it demands, deprived of everything because entitled to everything,
and which one recognizes in giving . . . this gaze is precisely the epiphany
of the face as a face. The nakedness of the face is destituteness. To recognize the Other is to recognize a hunger. To recognize the Other is to give.
But it is to give to the master, to the lord, to him whom one approaches
as 'You' [the 'Vous' of majesty] in a dimension of height."*

—Emmanuel Levinas, *Totality and Infinity*[3]

UPON FIRST HEARING ABOUT Spinoza's idea of *sub specie aeternitatis* (the
standpoint of eternity), I felt entranced. There at once was the notion
that all the troubles of the world are of little moment compared to the
cosmic Substance that resides within and unifies all of Being. From the
standpoint of eternity, all of us are brothers and sisters—cut from the
same divine cloth, expressed by the same sublime author, sung by the
same enchanting singer. From the standpoint of eternity, every earthly
form is simply a part of an infinite, non-humanlike God whose nature
is grand enough to generate all ideas and creatures, great and small, loving and hateful. This might not be the pinnacle of our dreams, but it is
nevertheless an uplifting vision. For it revels in the majesty of an infinite
plenitude, and in the love we feel for a God that transcends that plenitude
by both giving rise to it and sustaining it. Upon initially grasping this
perspective, I found it nurturing, liberating, and enlightening. What I
hadn't yet realized was that I was about to stumble upon what would
become another God the Strawman—only this time, unlike with the "Old
God," it would be mainstream theologians and philosophers who would
do the honor of serving as deicide.

The series of William James' lectures from which the above quota-
tion was lifted was given at Oxford in 1908 and 1909, not long after Marx,
Darwin, and Nietzsche had changed the world's religious landscape.
From a perusal of James' lectures, it was clear that pantheism in one form
or another had grown tremendously in popularity and that, at least in
his high-brow circles, the "God of the philosophers" (of which Spinoza's
God is a prime example) was gaining ground on the Lord of Abraham.
James' background was in philosophy, not theology, but that didn't stop

3. Levinas, *Totality and Infinity*, 75.

him from making a statement that would soon become de rigueur for twentieth-century theologians. Spinoza's God, James essentially argued, like any abstract notion of the "Absolute," is a bloodless academic construct, one that might be attractive to eggheads but could never serve as a living, breathing deity for poets, paupers, pirates, pawns, or kings. As Heidegger once said in reference to the so-called "god of philosophy," "man can neither fall to his knees in awe nor can he play music and dance before this God."[4]

As a man who once joined the Nazi party, Heidegger can't exactly speak for mainstream Jewish theologians on every issue. But they surely would adopt his statement about the god of philosophy and apply it to Spinoza's God. Consider, for example, the theology of Abraham Joshua Heschel. Only weeks before his death, Heschel gave an interview to NBC. The interview showed this grey eminence at his most impressive. It is difficult to imagine a man whose very visage, not to mention his egalitarian spirituality, more conveyed the impression of a modern-day prophet. And just as the prophets could be ever so critical, so could Heschel. He clearly was irritated by the Spinoza-inspired teaching of Paul Tillich that God is the "Ground of Being." In Heschel's mocking words, "ground of being causes me no harm. Let there be a ground of being. . . . It's meaningless. Isn't there a God who is above the ground? Maybe God is the source of qualms and of disturbing my conscience. Maybe God is a God of demands. Yes, this is God, not the ground of being."[5] Heschel's close friend, Dr. Martin Luther King, Jr., was similarly dismissive when he wrote that Tillich's "Being-itself"—another concept with profound significance to Spinozists—is "little more than a sub-personal reservoir of power, somewhat akin to the impersonalism of Oriental Vedantism. Being-itself is a pure absolute, devoid of consciousness of life."[6]

In using the term "sub-personal" for what many Spinozists take to be the holy of holies (Being-itself), King put his finger on the pulse of the pantheism-theism debate. His thought was expressed even more explicitly by Martin Buber. While nobody would take Buber to be an orthodox theist, he was nevertheless critical of Spinoza's decision to deify Being. According to Buber, "The fundamental error of Spinoza was that he imagined that in the teaching of Israel only the teaching that God is

4. Heidegger, *Identity and Difference*, 72.
5. Heschel, "Carl Stern's Interview," 408.
6. King, *Papers*, 546–47.

a person was to be found, and he opposed it as a diminution of divinity. But the truth of the teaching is that God is *also* a person, and this is, in contrast to all impersonal, unaddressable 'purity' of God, an augmentation of divinity."[7]

So now, the shoe is on the other foot. Buber is famous for seeing in God the "Eternal Thou" who we don't conceptualize as an "It" but rather *meet* through our worldly encounters. Surely, Buber would recognize that when we approach God via mutual, meaningful encounters, we may indeed subconsciously convey upon him (or her) facets of a human-like personality. But, Buber might ask, isn't that preferable to refusing to approach the Divine at all—save as a lifeless, abstract concept that, as we have seen, can just as easily be equated with "Nothing at All" as to the All? In other words, in their desire for intellectual integrity and purity, haven't the Spinozists sacrificed the one indispensible ingredient for a functional deity: relevance to the concrete, emotional lives of the deity's followers?

Spinoza had a point. But so did Buber.

⊕

Before examining the teachings of Martin Buber and that other "philosopher of the encounter," Emmanuel Levinas, let us consider briefly the thoughts of a man who is associated primarily with the realm of fiction. This writer has helped me not only to better appreciate Spinoza's teachings, but also to recognize how Buber and Levinas can build upon those teachings. I am referring to someone whose greatness was such that Napoleon, upon first laying eyes on him, exclaimed "Voila un homme!" (Now here is a *Man*!).[8] More impressive still is the fact that Nietzsche, who always seemed to have something insulting to say about everyone, could only compliment this man. Apparently, I am not the only reader who has been smitten.

If Spinoza was the epitome of calm, or at least tried to be, Johann Wolfgang von Goethe was his opposite: he personified passion with a

7. Buber, "Spinoza," 92.

8. Nietzsche applies his characteristic flair when describing this historical meeting: "One should at last have a sufficiently profound comprehension of Napoleon's astonishment when he caught sight of Goethe: it betrays what had for centuries been thought was meant by the 'German spirit'. [sic] 'Voila un homme!'—which is to say: 'but that is a *man*! And I had expected only a German!'" Nietzsche, *Beyond Good and Evil*, 121.

pen, which is why perhaps more than any other writer, he is identified with eighteenth-century Germany's *Sturm und Drang* (Storm and Stress) period. Nevertheless, as a panentheist from the time he was a young adult, Goethe adored Spinoza. In words that would have left Heschel, Martin Luther King, Jr., and William James scratching their heads, Goethe wrote that Spinoza "does not prove the existence of God; existence *is* God. And though others miscall him atheist, I name and praise him as Theissimum [the most religious] even Christianissimum [the most Christian]."[9] Indeed, perhaps it is due to his own admiration for Goethe, and Goethe's devotion to Spinoza, that Nietzsche came to say of Spinoza "I have a *precursor*, and what a precursor! . . . [My] solitude, which, as on very high mountains, often made it hard for me to breathe and made my blood rush out, is at least a dualitude."[10]

While Spinoza was clearly Goethe's favorite philosopher, Goethe did not fully share Spinoza's view of blessedness as the intellectual love of God. Goethe, a celebrated romantic, sought a much more holistic existence than what can be attained strictly through the life of the mind. It was, in fact, his willingness to move beyond Spinoza's thoroughgoing intellectualism that allowed him to inspire generations of pantheists who are anything but bloodless. Thanks to the influence of Goethe, when I read James' lampooning of pantheism, I recognize it for the strawman that it is.

Then again, Goethe was not merely a muse; he was himself a disciple. Whenever I think of the Goethe-Spinoza relationship, I see Goethe as if he were a worldly and insightful young man who recognizes true genius in an older and underappreciated scholar. Not lacking courage himself, the young man takes it upon himself to push his elder out of the library and into the society at large. In this case, sad to say, my beloved Spinoza plays the role of the underappreciated scholar.

In Goethe's philosophical novel, *Wilhelm Meister's Apprenticeship*, the title character, who was neither a scholar nor a genius, was no match for an androgynous woman named Natalie, to whom the awestruck Meister would refer as "the Amazon." Near the end of the book, Natalie guided Meister into a place known as the "Hall of the Past." She was obviously very much in control of herself and her environment, which is exactly the key to freedom in the philosophy of Spinoza. As worldly as

9. Gullan-Whur, *Within Reason*, 308.
10. Yovel, *Spinoza and Other Heretics*, 105.

Natalie was, she was largely created in the spirit of Spinoza's teachings. Indeed, in many ways, she is to Spinozism what Muhammad is to Islam: a human exemplar of righteousness.

Natalie could completely put aside her appetites. She also knew not to pine for mere information or facts. She arose less from the masculine world, which is ruled by knowledge, than from the feminine world, in which wisdom is supreme. She was especially endowed with the capacity to intuit and to use that intuition for the betterment of the human condition.

Saint Natalie had but one overarching drive. "I remember that the strongest impression of my youth was that of human need everywhere; and I had an irresistible urge to do something about this. . . . My greatest delight was, and still is, to be presented with some deficiency, some need in others, and be able to think of some way of repairing or alleviating it."[11] She personified a line in Spinoza's philosophy that Goethe once called a "wonderful sentiment . . . [that] filled my whole mind":[12] "He who loves God cannot endeavor that God should love him in return."[13] In Natalie's case, however, she felt that way about seemingly everyone she encountered.

"You have never been in love?" Meister asked her.[14]

"Never—or always!" Natalie replied. The answer depends on whether we define love strictly as eros, as thirsting to possess what one desires, or in more spiritual senses of the word. One particular object of Natalie's affection was the Hall of the Past, the final resting place of her dear deceased uncle. There, she accompanied Meister with flowers, the very same that her uncle most enjoyed.

Meister was expecting to find a gloomy tribute to the dead, but what he saw instead was a world of light—of architectural triumphs, of brilliant and various colors; in short, of art at its finest. But there was more. In Goethe's words: "Across from the entrance, on a magnificent sarcophagus, stood the marble effigy of a distinguished man, his head resting against a pillow. He was holding a scroll in front of him which he

11. Goethe, *Wilhelm Meister's*, 322.

12. Goethe, *Auto-Biography*, 26.

13. Spinoza, "Ethics," Part V, Prop. 19, 372.

14. Goethe, *Wilhelm Meister's*, 330.

appeared to be reading attentively. The scroll was so placed that one could read the words written upon it. These were: '*Remember to live.*'"[15]

One of Judaism's leading sages, Rabbi Hillel, was asked to summarize the whole Torah while standing on one foot. He famously replied, "what is hateful to you, don't do to your fellow man—that's the whole Torah and the rest is just commentary. Go then and learn it." I suspect that if Hillel were alive today and asked to summarize Goethe's philosophy while standing on one foot, he would raise a glass and be even more succinct: "Remember to live! For life itself is worthy of reverence. L'Chaim!"

This is the same summary one might give to convey the philosophy of Nietzsche, Goethe's disciple. And it probably represents the parting words Buber or Levinas would have provided had they encountered the "madman" Nietzsche wrote about—the one who was looking for God. But first, they would have explained *how* to live in the way that most swiftly unlocks the key to divinity: namely, by opening not merely our mind but our whole spirit, and especially our heart, to *the other*.

✦

Traditional theism begins with the belief in a fundamental principle: we are all subjects of an omni-excellent Lord, whose inscrutability does not detract from his justice and love. Modern secularism responds with its own key principle: the supreme reality of the realm of science, a realm of matter and energy that is largely measurable. Pantheism, too, has its essential principle: cosmic unity, or the idea that the deeper our perspective, the more we find everything to be interrelated. What we are about to discuss involves yet another religious framework, one that is founded on an altogether different principle, only this one is less about metaphysics (the ultimate nature of the real) than about epistemology (how we can come to know what is real).

According to the philosophy of thinkers like Buber and Levinas, enlightenment can be attained primarily through our encounters with *the other*. Any philosophy that neglects to emphasize these meetings or to place profound demands on all who enter them will have relinquished the best possible opportunity to know and experience the Divine. Just as Goethe's Natalie saw a human face and invariably received a plea or

15. Ibid., 331.

summons, Buber and Levinas would experience the same thing, but they would also recognize this event as an encounter with God.

The Buber quotation at the beginning of this chapter invokes a metaphor that we've seen earlier in a different context: the metaphor of a ray of light. To Buber, every time we encounter another earthly being as a "Thou," instead of an "It," it is as if a ray of light shines directly from our eyes into the face of *the other* and then towards God, the Eternal Thou. But this isn't merely a one-way street, Buber said. For just as one "ray" is sent in the direction of God, another heads back in our direction— from God, through the earthly object of our encounter, and back to us. In the process, we come to understand and appreciate one another and to recognize our relationship to the One who Buber called the "Absolute Person."[16]

By speaking of God as the Absolute Person, Buber walked a fine line in the extent to which he anthropomorphizes the Divine. His eminent interpreter, Maurice Friedman, made this point in terms that are antithetical to the philosophy of Spinoza and Goethe, when he referred to Buber's Absolute Person as "Being which becomes Person in order to know and be known, to love and be loved by man."[17] Yet Buber also saw fit to point out that "The personal manifestation of the Divine is not decisive for the genuineness of religion. What is decisive is that I relate myself to the Divine as to Being which is over against me [i.e., encountered in relationship to me as the *other*]."[18]

To Buber, God's essence cannot productively be analyzed and expressed in words. What we can do is enter into a mutual relationship with the Divine by either addressing God directly as a Thou (in whatever way the address would be most authentic, given our present state of spirituality) or by engaging in an I-Thou meeting with some worldly being or thing. Those who are able to reach out to an earthly Thou, Buber suggested, even if they claim not to believe in God, are encountering the Divine. In the case of Goethe's Natalie, Buber would need no more information than what I have already provided to conclude that she had forged a closer bond with God than have most men and women of the cloth.

16. Friedman, *Martin Buber*, 267.

17. Ibid.

18. Ibid.

The key to approaching God according to Buber's philosophy is to open our heart to *the other* as a Thou. We will find that we are meeting not merely another earthly form but the Eternal Thou who gives unity to all that exists. In these kinds of encounters, the one we meet is regarded as a fellow subject and not as an object of our own desires. We throw our whole being into the meeting and encounter *the other's* whole being. Moreover, we engage in this meeting fully in the present and bring to the encounter such qualities as respect, honesty, concern, warmth, responsibility, and love. Even a quick glance at that list should indicate why so many people prefer the canine species to our own; the I-Thou bond seems to be easier to forge with dogs than with our own kind.

Buber would be the first to recognize that an I-Thou encounter isn't always possible or even appropriate. I-It, the alternative mode of human interaction, serves us well in numerous situations. Still, in Buber's philosophy, if we hope to deepen our relationship with an otherwise hidden God, all the academic reading in the world is no substitute for encountering one another with an I-Thou mindset. Ironically, it is precisely by living in the present with other finite, concrete forms, Buber taught us, that we can best attain whatever wisdom is available to us about the Eternal.

✦

Particularly for those who grow up without the benefits of unconditional love, Buber's I-Thou encounter must seem daunting to the point of utopian. Yet when compared to Emmanuel Levinas' face-to-face encounter with *the other*, the I-Thou is like a stroll in the park. You could say that Levinas' philosophy of the encounter is Buber's on steroids.

Having spent much of World War II as a French Jew in a Nazi prisoner of war camp, Levinas wrote as one who understood the profundity of pathos. Levinas reminds us that it is not enough to view *the other* as a Thou. We must see her, at least in part, as if she is in a POW camp and we are her guards. This applies to every authentic human encounter, even if the one we meet seems to be more fortunate in life than we are. After all, as Natalie would surely acknowledge, everyone we meet has unmet needs. Part of what it means to be human is to suffer, and suffer profoundly, on multiple levels.

To enter the world of Levinas, imagine being hypnotized to respond dramatically to a particular stimulus. In this case, the stimulus is a human gaze. The initial request that *the other* makes by gazing at us is just what you would expect Levinas to suggest as a former POW: "Do not kill me." There at least is a request most of us can and do grant whenever we meet another gaze. But then what do we do? Do we, as Natalie would, continue to take the face of *the other* as the source of a gentle plea for help? Or do we assume that once we have decided not to kill or actively harm *the other*, we can go about our business and ignore our responsibilities to the face that has summoned us so intensely? Levinas would argue that our ethical obligation upon noticing another's gaze is not only to give of ourselves, but to do so in the spirit that the biblical patriarchs brought to an encounter with Adonai.

"Here I am," Abraham said to Adonai, just before he was directed to sacrifice Isaac (Gen 22:1). "Here I am," responded Moses, when Adonai appeared in the form of a burning bush (Exod 3:4). "Here I am, send me," answered Isaiah, when Adonai asked who should go to the people to serve as a prophet (Isa 6:8). Levinas's God expects nothing less from us. We must take the opportunity to encounter another human face, Levinas said,

> [As a] marvelous accusative: here I am under your gaze, obliged to you, your servant. In the name of God. . . . The sentence in which God comes to be involved in words is not "I believe in God." The religious discourse prior to all religious discourse is not dialogue. It is the "here I am" said to the neighbor to whom I am given over, and in which I announce peace, that is, my responsibility for the Other.[19]

To Levinas, the face of *the other* cannot help but beckon us with the look of one who is both naked and ashamed of her nakedness. In response, there is much we must do to show the hospitality that we, as empathic human beings, are required to show. And it is precisely when we show this hospitality that we are honoring not merely the suffering soul we meet but the holy God, who Levinas also refers to as the "Infinite" and the "Absolute Other." This God is hardly identical to the Lord who is described in Scripture. He is said to be "beyond being" and fully unknowable, or at least inexpressible by our language. Yet, as we saw in the quotation on the first page of this chapter, Levinas' God is one whom we can approach through a relationship between the self and *the other*, a relationship characterized by *asymmetry*, much like our relationship to

19. Levinas, *Of God*, 75.

the suffering human face that beckons around every corner. When we get used to honoring our demands to one another in the same spirit that Abraham, Moses, and Isaiah stood up when Adonai called, we still will not be able to describe God in words, but at least we will know what it means to serve God in deeds.

✧

Buber and Levinas are both original thinkers with unique messages. Yet what I find especially gratifying is to consider the harmonies in their teachings. To begin with, both believe that there are few verbal statements we confidently can make about God. We may use words that suggest the unwillingness to limit God's grandeur—words like absolute, eternal, or infinite—but anything we say about God's personality or essence will tell us more about who *we* are than about what God is. Nevertheless, just because we are limited in what we can learn *about* God does not mean we are limited in what we can learn *from* God. To these thinkers, God is constantly summoning us whenever we open our heart, and it is our misfortune that we usually ignore or refuse to recognize the summons.

Just as Levinas' God calls on us to stand up and live the words "Here I am, Ready to Serve" whenever we see a human face, Buber's God also is one to issue challenges. According to Buber, whether we are encountering a person, a dog, or a tree, whenever we approach them as a "subject" or a Thou, we should carry with us such deep affection and concern that inevitably we don't merely ask the question "Who are you?" but "How, my friend, can I help you?"

After reading Buber and Levinas and taking their teachings to heart, God can no longer be seen primarily as the Nurturer. Rather, he becomes the Summoner—one who captivates, inspires, and, above all else, *demands*.

In a very deep sense, these thinkers are anti-philosophers because, far from valuing wisdom above all else, what they preach is *action*. Their focus is not on universal principles but rather on the here-and-now encounter. They are less interested in what *the other's* gaze can tell us about the Eternal than in how the Eternal can inspire us to stay fixated on that gaze so as to best figure out how to lend a hand as if our own virtue depends on it.

In the fictional character of Natalie, we find the rare bird who would actually exemplify both Buber's and Levinas' teachings. She gives of herself, habitually, viscerally, and happily. Imagine what it would be like to be "always" in love. I can't, but Goethe is asking us to try. Buber and Levinas are asking us to imagine something almost as difficult: to live in a constant state of heightened empathy and to turn that state into action. Somehow, they're telling us, therein lies the path to God. It must have something to do with how we listen and how we look.

Those most attentive to the Eternal Thou will find that God is talking to us, both orally and visually. Perhaps we cannot see God in the form of a burning bush, but what about bushes that don't burn? Or seas that are not being parted? And are we not especially able to view and hear God in the faces and voices of the people we encounter? Indeed, I must ask those of you who are happily married, as Buber reminds us in the sentence that opened this chapter, are we not able to find God most clearly of all in the face of our own cherished spouse?

Once we learn to open our eyes, ears, and hearts to our family . . . then our friends . . . then our species . . . then our world . . . we will surely have achieved a high level of spirituality. Still, something important could be missing. Buber, no less than Spinoza, would recommend that we invoke *The Name* and all the power and meaning that comes with it to recognize the unity that pervades all of life. After all, Buber was a devout, if untraditional, Jew, and he recognized that "Judaism's fundamental significance for mankind . . . [is] that it . . . proclaims a world in which dualism will be abolished, a world of God which needs to be realized in both the life of individual man and the life of the community: the world of unity."[20] For Buber, our blessedness requires both the appreciation for the glory of the divine unity and the willingness to embrace other concrete, earthly forms in I-Thou relationships. His is a philosophy of balance, something that he felt was missing in that of Spinoza.

If the subtext of this chapter is to take *the other* seriously and bestow it, him, or her with honor, we have not yet finished our work. We have been discussing *the other* primarily in terms of the individuals we meet face to

20. Buber, *On Judaism*, 33.

face. But what about groups of people? Or institutions we create? Or the world's ecosystems? And yes, what about God?

Everything that has been said with respect to an individual applies to those others as well. What is critical is that we encounter them as one lover encounters another, and not as a pedestrian scientist encounters a microbe. We must meet them with our whole self—all the receptors must be open, and particularly the receptor for empathy. But let's assume for the sake of discussion that we could open the floodgates of love and empathy. It still doesn't tell us the whole truth about God, now does it? It so happens that empathy and other expressions of love are the most useful signs of life in the human world. But does that really tell us that our God is an exemplar of love and empathy? Or have we come right back to Spinoza's point that a triangle contemplating the Divine would assume that God is triangular, whereas a circle would view God as circular?

Perhaps Buber, for one, would feel that there's nothing wrong with that. I suspect he would say that as long as you bring authenticity to your encounter, whenever you address God as the Absolute Person, it stands to reason that he would address you back with a human-like personality and you would come to see him in terms of qualities like love and mercy. To Buber, as with Martin Luther King, Jr., that attitude would sure beat the alternative of worshipping a sterile, abstract Sub-person.

Fine. Maybe it does. But I would question why that strawman is the only alternative. It is one thing for students of religious philosophy to seek help from Buber in order to supplement the depth of our insights, yet that hardly means we should ignore altogether the lessons that Spinoza and other voices of reason have taught us. That is why it behooves us to continue to look for a conception of God that makes as much sense as possible, rather than settling for something that feels good to the heart but enfeebles the mind. By losing interest in the importance of what precise words we use to characterize the "Absolute Person," Buber has violated one of his own critical teachings. Remember what was said about the characteristics of the I-Thou? One of the critical features is that we bring honesty to the encounter. In Buber's words, "I and You do not only stand in a relationship but also in firm honesty."[21]

If that is true, it leaves someone like me in a real dilemma if I wish to take Buber seriously. On the one hand, when I consult the teachings of my *mind*, I agree with Spinoza and Goethe that there is no rational

21. Buber, *I and Thou*, 151.

ground for attributing to God any human personality characteristic, even love (unless we are willing to attribute to God such emotions as hatred). On the other hand, when I open my *heart* to God and address this Absolute Person in prayer, the glow and the wisdom that I might gain from this experience cannot help but make me feel loved in return. So which is it? The mind or the heart?

"Let passion be your sail, reason your keel, and empathy your rudder." Those were the words I used in *The Creed Room* to sum up my protagonists' philosophy. There's an old saw that first novels are autobiographical, and indeed, I subscribed to that philosophy when I wrote those words and continue to do so today. Passion is surely needed if we hope to make things happen and not simply to watch things happen. And if asked to identify the single best indicator of whether individuals are helping to steer us all in a positive or a negative direction, I would point to their ability to empathize. But when it comes to laying the foundation of a boat, you should start first and foremost with the keel. Just as we need a sturdy keel to keep a ship above water, we need total honesty to keep ourselves grounded when it comes to God. In other words, in selecting a religious framework, never go against what your intuition tells you makes the most rational sense.

Fortunately, there are many ways to enliven and enrich one's worship of a non-humanlike God that do not involve lying to ourselves. Meditation, relaxed contemplation, certain forms of prayer, and love of our fellow human beings come immediately to mind. In fact, one of the subtle benefits of basing our religion on our religious philosophy, and not the other way around, is that it creates the most stimulating and satisfying of challenges. Instead of worshiping a deity who could fulfill us emotionally, but requires us to brainwash ourselves to accept his existence, we could seek the truth about God to the best of our ability and not worry about the joy we are missing by refusing to believe in the Cosmic Santa Claus. And while we are engaging in this search for truth, we can nevertheless enlist our heart, as well as our mind, in taking the wisdom we've acquired to date and making the most out of life. Lord knows, that approach worked for that remarkable novelist, poet, playwright, scientist, statesman, and panentheist named Goethe.

CHAPTER 8

The God Who Needs Man

"Oh ye men! It is ye that have need of Allah. But Allah is the One Free of all wants. . . . Allah stands not in need of any of His creatures."

—The Qur'an (35:15; 3:97)

"There is a partnership of God and man. God needs our help. I would define man as a divine need. God is in need of man."

—Abraham Joshua Heschel, from his December 10, 1972 Interview with Carl Stern[1]

IN THE LAST CHAPTER, we considered the religious significance of our various daily encounters with *the other* and why our inter-personal relationships have the potential to deepen our bond with the Eternal God. In that regard, we spoke about how God may be seen as summoning us through these encounters with challenges, even demands, for those who are willing to listen.

Yet the question remains: what does the feeling of being beckoned by God teach us about the true significance of humankind? Are we to conclude that human beings represent a divine need—in other words,

---

1. Heschel, "Carl Stern's Interview," 397.

that there exists some sort of inadequacy within God for which we are required to provide assistance? Or is the Qur'an correct in stating that God "stands not in need of any of His creatures"? These are the questions to which we will now turn. Once they have been resolved, I will finally be ready to assimilate all that has been said and reveal where my journey in search of a sensible, fulfilling conception of God has led . . . to date.

"Does God need us?" For the longest time, this question would have made me laugh, or perhaps even annoy me. I would have viewed it to be an insult to God's ultimacy.

That is certainly the perspective of Islam. The passage from the Qur'an included at the top of this chapter explicitly states that Allah has no need for any of "His creatures." According to all the commentary I have seen or heard, this passage refers as much to the praying man as to the praying mantis. Moreover, a similar statement could be made by anyone who conceives of God merely as the Ground of Being, the Infinite Source of All That is, or *Natura naturans*. Such a deity needs nothing. In fact, one of the things Spinoza pointed to in criticizing the doctrine that God acts in accordance with a will was that it "negates God's perfection; for if God acts with an end in view, he must necessarily be seeking something that he lacks."[2]

On this issue, my thinking has changed drastically. The change began when I rephrased the relevant question. For me, the inquiry can no longer be simplified as, does God need us? Now, we must ask, does God need us *to live righteous lives*? And when we fail to do so, are we somehow injuring the Divine?

In addressing these questions, I have followed the admonition of Buber and Levinas to take the *encounter* seriously. So I put aside my Spinozist dogma and opened my heart to anyone or thing who could provide clues—including the works of thinkers who have anthropomorphized God a lot more than I have been comfortable doing ever since I missed that fateful bus in Cambridge.

As has been discussed, taking the encounter seriously involves coming to grips with the abundance of suffering that seems to be experienced universally and on many levels. Clearly, I can imagine a God who does not suffer, and Aristotle's Unmoved Mover immediately comes to mind. But that is a lifeless deity. By contrast, when we encounter the Eternal Thou through our interactions with *the other*, the last thing we

---

2. Spinoza, "Ethics," Part 1, Appendix, 240.

experience is lifelessness. Instead, we experience a summons to act—to alleviate the suffering that corrodes the soul of the beloved *other* and, accordingly, our own.

When we contemplate the summons to alleviate suffering, new questions abound. What does this tell us about the nature of the summoner? Is God suffering as well? Is that why there seems to be so much at stake? Or is the summoner really nothing more than our own psyche playing theological tricks on us? The Spanish philosopher, Miguel de Unamuno, found the answer in his native Christianity. For him, the significance of Christ on the Cross is, at bottom, the revelation of the Divine in suffering, for in the words of Unamuno, "only that which suffers is divine."[3] Unamuno went on to call suffering "the substance of life and the root of personality[;] . . . suffering is that which unites all us living beings together; it is the universal or divine blood that flows through us all. That which we call will, what is it but suffering?"[4]

Clearly, Unamuno is thinking of suffering's universality in the sense that anyone who experiences desire will necessarily suffer, since much of what we desire is what we do not have. A great religion, Buddhism, is largely based on the need to reduce desires so as to alleviate suffering. But unlike the followers of Buddha, Unamuno came not to bury suffering but to praise it. And this is why the image of God's Son on the cross is so powerful to him—the suffering it reveals, not just in Jesus but in God the Father, "is the revelation of the very heart of the Universe and of its mystery."[5] As Unamuno went on to explain, "There is no true love save in suffering."[6]

Spinoza's *Natura naturans* or Substance might transcend "will" or "suffering," but that is not Unamuno's deity. He referred to God as the "Consciousness of the Universe," one that is "limited by the brute matter in which He lives, by the unconscious, from which He seeks to liberate Himself and to liberate us. And we in turn must seek to liberate Him."[7] To a person who is struck by the suffering in the world and then approaches God as a cosmic mind in which all this suffering is played out, it can only be expected that God himself would be viewed as the focal

3. De Unamuno, *Tragic Sense of Life*, 204.

4. Ibid., 205.

5. Ibid., 204.

6. Ibid.

7. Ibid., 207.

point of all suffering. As a result, when we hear that voice summoning us to announce ourselves and help, we are not only being asked to assist whatever finite, earthly being is suffering, but God himself. In the words of Unamuno, "Charity, then, is the impulse to liberate myself and all my fellows from suffering, and to liberate God, who embraces us all."[8]

The idea of the divine pathos may seem to lend itself more to Christianity than to the other Abrahamic faiths, yet it can also be found in Judaism and especially in the work of Heschel. Here is Heschel's attempt to drive a clear distinction between his beloved God of Jerusalem and the deities of Rome and Athens:

> "The gods attend to great matters; they neglect small ones," Cicero maintains. According to Aristotle, the gods are not concerned at all with the dispensation of good and bad fortune or external things. To the [biblical] prophet, however, no subject is as worthy of consideration as the plight of man. Indeed, God Himself is described as reflecting over the plight of man rather than as contemplating eternal ideas. His mind is preoccupied with man, with the concrete actualities of history rather than with the timeless issues of thought.[9]

Heschel goes on to say that God does not merely "reflect" over our plight but is emotionally involved. Interpreting one biblical passage, Heschel attributes to God the statement that "I have *sympathy* for, I am *affected* by" human suffering. In another instance, he interprets the text to mean that God "*had pity*."[10] Thus, when Heschel concludes that the prophets disclose a "divine pathos, not just a divine judgment," or claims that "[t]his divine pathos is the key to inspired prophecy," he is describing a God whose concern about our welfare is far from casual.[11] Empathically, as they say in poker, Heschel's God is "all in."

Heschel threw down the gauntlet to anyone who would dare neglect the lessons of the biblical prophets. He clearly saw the spirit of the prophets alive in himself, and few students of the African-American Civil Rights Movement would argue to the contrary. This was a man who personified empathy and the acceptance of responsibility. In the nationally televised interview that he gave shortly before his death, the sixty-five

8. Ibid., 211.
9. Heschel, *Prophets*, 5.
10. Ibid., 57.
11. Ibid., 24.

year old Heschel—who didn't look a day over ninety-five—said that "the greatness of man is that he faces problems. I would judge a person by how many deep problems he's concerned with."[12] You could tell it from his face, his philosophy, and his biography: this man truly internalized the suffering of other people, no matter who they were or where they lived; for him, "loving thy neighbor as thyself" was a commandment, not a cliché.

Accordingly, when Heschel talks about the divine pathos, it brings greater power than when the concept is discussed in the typical academic conference. Heschel's God does not merely request but *demands* that we repair his world, and these demands are made for *God's* sake as well as our own. When Heschel tells us that "to us, injustice is injurious to the welfare of the people; to the prophets it is a deathblow to existence: to us, an episode; to them, a catastrophe, a threat to the world,"[13] it is clear that he is speaking not just about the prophets, but even more so about God. According to Heschel, how we treat God's creation generally, and one another in particular, is second in importance to nothing. God feels that way. God's prophets felt that way. And we, too, had better feel that way if we wish to alleviate the suffering of the One who suffers most from human anguish.

⊸

Unamuno's and Heschel's words are directed squarely to the heart. Examining them intellectually does them injustice. But I did promise to return to the keel and thereby determine whether the words of those thinkers sacrificed some precious rationality in order to make their poetic, heart-felt appeal.

I am fortunate when it comes to encountering Heschel in particular that my left-wing upbringing prepared me to appreciate his work. Heschel's "Prophetic Judaism" is largely mother's milk to those who come from progressive, secular backgrounds. It locates the fundamental spirit of the faith in terms of working for justice and peace, rather than in punctiliously obeying the ceremonial rituals. In this tradition, the great saints and sages were those who were willing to bend the rules as long as a

---

12. Heschel, "Carl Stern's Interview," 402.

13. Heschel, *Prophets*, 4.

higher purpose, like alleviating human suffering, was at stake. To the extent Heschel stood for that philosophy, I am right there with him.

Emotionally, I'd love to find a way to support Heschel's decision to enlist God in the social action movement. I'd love to fight this "War against Suffering" with all hands on deck. Given the ability of *The Name* to inspire and even command us, why wouldn't I want to believe that God himself is suffering whenever a bully grabs a smaller boy's lunch money, or whenever a bureaucrat soullessly looks into the eyes of a needy applicant for government benefits and says "What is it about the word 'No' that you don't understand?"

For that reason, I could wholeheartedly embrace the idea of incorporating God as a participant in this holiest of struggles, if only this could be done with integrity. But there's the rub. I cannot compromise my religious philosophy in the process. As a result, I have not been able to go as far as Heschel's or Unamuno's words would take us—at least not if they are to be taken literally.

Ultimately, Heschel's theology is consistent with Unamuno's: both posit a Cosmic Consciousness capable of experiencing joys and sorrows, much like our own mind yet on a qualitatively grander scale. For me, though, the belief in such a Cosmic Superman is a leap of faith I see no reason to take. It seems to bring us back to the absurd idea of some omniscient force that is able to count the number of grains of sand on every beach, or the number of water molecules in every ocean, on every planet, at every moment. And even if we ignore that notion and focus instead on a less trivially-minded but equally cosmic mega-heart that suffers every time any organism experiences an unfulfilled desire, what *reason* do we have to posit such an entity—other than wishful thinking? Are we also saying that this Cosmic Superman is empowered to use its heart or mind in order to create the "best of all possible worlds," or have we conceived merely of a brain/heart in a vat that is able to watch over the world but is powerless to do anything about it? Either way, we seem to be making assumptions based neither on observations nor reasonable inferences. At a minimum, we would be violating Occam's Razor (the principle of parsimony) even to entertain that such a Cosmic Superman exists. For me, as a rationalist, that would go too far.

But that is not to say that our lives as human beings are inherently meaningless. Or that acts that alleviate earthly suffering do not matter. Or that we should relish the idea of waging the great War against Suffering without all hands on deck, including *The Name*.

So, can we say that God, in some *rational* sense of that word, truly needs us? Thanks to my encounters with Unamuno, Heschel, Buber, and Levinas, I think we can. It is now time to explain why that is and how this realization has transformed my view of divinity.

CHAPTER 9

God the Ultimate Synthesis

"Say: He is Allah. The One and Only. Allah, the Eternal, Absolute. He begetteth not, nor is He begotten. And there is none like unto Him."

—The Qur'an, Surah 112

"Trinitarian monotheism is not a matter of the number three. It is a qualitative and not a quantitative characterization of God. It is an attempt to speak of the living God, the God in whom the ultimate and the concrete are united. The number three has no specific significance in itself, although it comes nearest to an adequate description of life-processes. Even in the history of the Christian doctrine of the trinity there have been vacillations between trinitarian and binitarian emphasis. . . . The trinitarian problem has nothing to do with the trick question of how one can be three and three be one. . . . The trinitarian problem is the problem of the unity between ultimacy and concreteness in the living God. Trinitarian monotheism is concrete monotheism, the affirmation of the living God."

—Paul Tillich, *Systematic Theology*[1]

1. Tillich, *Systematic Theology*, 228.

BEFORE MOVING FORWARD, ALLOW me to attempt to encapsulate the journey described above. There has been a definite method to this madness, and it centers on a search for meaning that strives to be intellectually honest. In other words, the fundamental goal has been to arrive at a conception of God that satisfies the heart, but not at the expense of the mind. This conception must inevitably be supported by that inner voice of reason—or more specifically, intuition grounded in reason—that tells every person when s/he has stumbled on an approach that makes at least as much sense as any known alternative.

As much as we might wish to deny it, our voices of reason do not work alone. For each of us, the rational faculty shares the same mind as a very biased set of emotions. Scientists might want to pretend that their hopes, fears, pleasures, and pains are irrelevant to their search for truth, but students of philosophy should know better, at least when it comes to any attempt to conceptualize God. We have so few objective facts to draw from relative to what is not known that the task necessarily includes speculating about inscrutable metaphysical questions. And when you are aware that your answers are mere speculation, why not pick one that satisfies us emotionally? After all, we may not know what we should think, but we might at least know how we feel.

What's more, even after engaging in such speculation, students of philosophy must figure out how to express their conclusions in words. Once again, their decisions on how to resolve the critical semantic issues may ultimately be based less on their logical thoughts than on their feelings. Consider, for example, that two people could make similar assumptions about the underlying nature of reality, and yet one might call herself an "atheist" whereas the other would term herself a "believer." Why the difference? Because, for purely emotional reasons, the first person is more gratified by fighting the concept of God and the second by worshipping God.

In searching for truth and meaning about God, those who deny that their emotions are largely guiding their journeys are kidding themselves. Rather than hiding from that fact, I have embraced it. It has been my conscious goal to find a conception of God that is as emotionally fulfilling as possible. Still, that goal is subject to one overarching proviso: my beliefs must never conflict with the dictates of that small, subtle voice of reason. At the end of the day, that voice should remain the final guide.

Staying for a bit longer on the issue of "method," I have identified certain principles to adopt as tools of rationality. One is Occam's Razor, which is also known as the principle of parsimony, or simply KISS ("keep it simple, stupid"). In other words, when selecting between alternatives of otherwise equal merit, choose the one that avoids unnecessary assumptions or complications.

Another principle is to avoid basing one's metaphysical conclusions primarily on mythology, no matter how beloved it might be. Mythology can dramatically enhance our passion for living by presenting ideas in ways that speak directly to the heart. But that is precisely why people need to be careful to ensure that mythology complements logic, and does not substitute for it. Our mythology is centered upon human-like figures, and idealized figures at that. And yet, who are we to think that our personalities are a microcosm of the lifeblood of Being, or that our ideals are replicated in some heaven above? In fact, isn't it presumptuous to the point of conceit for us to posit at the center of all reality a being that resembles a human saint, with the same love for mercy, justice, and peace that characterizes homo sapiens at their best? The voice of reason, from what I can tell, urges us to be skeptical about any effort to conceive of God in our own image.

Armed with those principles for finding a meaningful, intellectually honest path, I have described a number of sights that were encountered along the way, each of which has left its mark on my spirituality. The first such sight—or, to be less metaphorical, the first conception of God we discussed—emerged from reading children's stories taken from the Hebrew Bible. These stories collectively depict a "Nurturing God" who deeply loves humankind and takes care of all who obey him. While acknowledging that there comes a time in our lives when the Nurturing God no longer seems realistic, I have contended that the ideal religious philosophy would provide some of the same benefits of believing in such a comforting conception of the Divine. Moreover, the biblical stories we read as children can be praised for teaching profound truths about the nature of reality. Namely, we learn that there are indeed greater forces at play in the universe than the ones that are commonly accessible to human beings, and that recognition of the transcendent may provide us with the fulfillment, security, and sense of purpose we so desperately seek. The question becomes, is there a way to incorporate those lessons into a framework that does not require adults to think with the naïveté of children?

I did not find a completely satisfactory answer in the so-called "Planning God," the idea that is commonly held among adults from

Abrahamic faiths who subscribe to the most traditional interpretations of Scripture. These "true believers" tend to view God's capacity to punish just as centrally as his capacity to nurture. He is seen as a partially inscrutable and partially human-like figure (the Big Guy Upstairs) who deliberately establishes plans for people that we disregard at our own peril. Adults who adhere to this view are frequently mocked for seeing God in such human-like terms, and indeed, it would appear that the Planning God is merely a nuanced version of the Nurturing God, one that enables adults to take into account the tragedies in life that children are encouraged to ignore. Still, those who worship the Planning God should find themselves with incredible motivation to walk the straight and narrow path, free of some of the vices that have destroyed many a human life. In addition, if they are sincere in their religious faiths, they could well become paragons of loyalty and humility. Finally, as was illustrated in the case of a Hall of Fame football player, this path can also launch people to accomplish impressive feats and do so in a way that shows respect and love for others. In short, when we observe people who truly devote their lives to the "plan" of the biblical God, we can see just how sweeping the emotional benefits of religious belief can be. But the question remains, does this Planning God truly exist outside of people's dreams and fears?

After discussing conceptions of divinity inspired primarily by Scripture, I introduced a simple alternative: the pantheist idea that reality is pervaded by a cosmic unity that can itself be viewed as God. Under this approach, the beings and ideas that people encounter in life should be regarded simply as internal expressions or manifestations of the Divine. In other words, each of us can be seen as *parts* of God, rather than as God's external creations. The principle of parsimony lends support to pantheism, for the dictates of reason hardly require us to posit an invisible chasm between the natural world and some separate, immaterial deity.

After introducing the idea of simple pantheism, I described my own voyage, which led me to adopt a more complex form of pantheism known as panentheism. For example, I described how I gained and then lost faith in the Planning God, and yet didn't want to give up the joy of "belief." *The Name* offered too much satisfaction to the psyche. More importantly, I continued to believe in a domain of existence that both transcends and unifies the world as we know it. I wanted to deify that transcendent domain but remained plagued by my associations of "God" with all the anthropomorphic personality traits that people have assigned to him. As a result, I lived for about a year in a state of thoroughgoing spiritual confusion until I examined the *Ethics* of Spinoza and interpreted it to be imbued with a panentheist spirit.

Spinozist panentheism seemed to me the one place where mysticism, monotheism, and atheism could shake hands. It appealed to my sense of eclecticism, combining the best of those three traditions: that there exists fundamental ontological unity (mysticism); that at the heart of such unity is a transcendent, all-embracing power who alone is worthy of our worship (monotheism); and that to the extent organized religions have championed a God that is replete with human-like personality traits (loving, merciful, jealous, etc.), they have been breeding ignorance (atheism). The connection to mysticism opened for me the gates of meditation and relaxed contemplation, and even a feeling of universal brotherhood and sisterhood. The connection to monotheism opened up a channel to appreciate, once again, the great Abrahamic texts and the comforting, even blissful, idea of a single overarching beloved. And the connection to atheism opened up the liberation of iconoclasm and heresy, which can be more devilishly rewarding than any trip to the liquor store.

What I found especially appealing in my grappling with Spinozism was how it built a sense of the transcendent into pantheism. For example, Spinoza viewed Being or Nature both as *Natura naturata* and *Natura naturans*—in other words, in terms of the discrete beings and ideas that populate the realm of the senses, and in terms of the mysterious, all-pervasive, and indivisible power that underlies everything that exists. One could refer to *Natura naturans* as Substance or the Source of All That Is. Spinoza simply used the term God . . . and for a long time, that worked for me.

At some point, though, I came to question the limitations of worshipping *Natura naturans* alone as God. These limitations became the focus of the previous two chapters of this book. As I explained, modern theologians and philosophers have taught me that any conception of God that is so abstract as to be equated simply with the Ground of Being is clearly missing something—a connection to the world as we know it. Nowhere, for us, is the connection between the world and the divine unity more apparent than in our own personal encounters with *the other*. So it felt right to bring the search for divinity into the realm of these day-to-day interactions, and especially those involving other human beings. This led me to wonder whether the clarion call to action that emerges from these interactions—the "commandment" to stand up, announce oneself, and pledge one's assistance—doesn't ultimately come from God.

Though that issue wasn't definitively answered, it was clear that I was intrigued by the idea of associating God with *the other* in all its concrete forms. Intuitively, it would appear that whenever *the other* deeply penetrates the human heart, as in the case of a plaintive gaze, God is present in the encounter. If the Qur'an is correct that God is closer to man than his jugular vein, it only stands to reason that the Divine is fully alive in these face-to-face interactions.

Finally, I addressed the issue of whether it is preferable to think of human beings as needs of God. From the standpoint of Spinozism, the idea that God (as Substance or the Ground of Being) needs *anything*, let alone anything from planet earth, borders on the absurd. But in considering the blessed human capacity to alleviate suffering—or, what is largely the same thing, to unleash freedom—perhaps we the people have cosmic significance after all. Indeed, perhaps there is no greater formula for turning oneself into a vehicle of holiness than by viewing oneself as a divine need. So the question had to be asked: is there a path to God that would embrace such a formula without sacrificing intellectual integrity?

For me, as a Jew, the answer came from two curious sources: the emphasis on *greatness* in the Muslim concept of Allah and *balance* in the Christian concept of the Trinity.

⟜

After writing my second novel, a book primarily about Judaism but secondarily about Islam, I had the privilege of asking Jewish audiences if they could identify one positive Muslim contribution that is truly unique. The silence in response was deafening.

As a student of Islam, I could come up with a number of responses to that question. But as I have already suggested, easily the most important involves the extent to which Islam emphasizes Allah's *greatness* above Allah's *likeness*. Yes, I have noted that a number of Allah's ninety-nine attributes resemble human-like personality traits. Yet the Muslim never loses sight of the notion that those so-called attributes are mere teaching tools for the creatures known to us as human beings, whose capacity to understand cosmic truths is tiny indeed. The much deeper teaching, one taken directly from the Qur'an, is that "Allah is the One and Only. . . . There is none like unto Him" (112: 1, 4).

That idea is hardly foreign to Judaism. Rabbis have said similar words for millennia. But rabbis also have a different agenda: to encourage people to appreciate the fundamental importance of the human condition. You can find elements of that agenda in Islam as well, but in Judaism (not to mention Christianity) it is so important that rabbis allow it to affect our view of God. The result is that man becomes elevated in importance, and as that occurs, God is brought down a bit closer to the human level. I have sometimes seen the Jewish God referred to as our "partner," but perhaps it is more accurate to say that Adonai is experienced like a parent or an employer. Anybody familiar with the character of Tevya in *Fiddler on the Roof* will recall the role the Divine played for him. Whenever difficulties ensued, Tevya would look up to the sky and challenge God. It was as if God had just walked into Tevya's office, and Tevya was sitting at his desk, looking up to his boss in puzzlement and frustration. "Am I not a nice Jewish boy?" Tevya is essentially asking. "Do I not deserve better? Why are you letting this happen to me?"

You would never hear such a dialogue between a devout Muslim and his God. In that faith, Allah is the Great One and man is but a creature. To be sure, people are said to be the most supreme of earthly creatures, but *a* creature and *the* God to whom we must all submit are two fundamentally different concepts. Consequently, when bad things happen, it is much easier in Islam for a God-worshipper to shrug them off. Muslims do not demand so much apparent rationality and beneficence from their God. They accept more readily that a God for whom it can be said that there is "none like unto Him" cannot be expected to act like a human ideal.

In short, the Jewish God is fundamentally good. But the Muslim God is fundamentally great and powerful. To a Muslim, that is something that can be said about Allah and Allah alone.

What I have found so incredibly inspiring in my association with Muslims is how deeply they have incorporated that belief. Combine the sense of awe for the divine greatness with the extent of the Muslim's love for her beloved Allah, and you have an amazing recipe for spirituality. This is why one of my rabbi friends says that it "just feels right" to pray with Muslims. When it comes to giving the Divine not just the affection but also the respect that God deserves, they *get* it.

To be candid, there are elements of Islam that frustrate me, and I am not even referring to the extremist, violent elements that we hear about constantly in the media. Most Muslims are peace loving and respectful of diversity, yet they remain largely orthodox in their theology. At this time, there is no established counterpart to Reform or Reconstructionist Judaism within the Muslim community, which I think is unfortunate. But to seek truth requires looking for inspiration from anywhere and everywhere, including orthodox theology. After studying Islam and forming an interfaith community with Muslim people, I was determined to honor the fundamental lesson that their faith had taught me. It was not a completely new lesson; in fact, it was something I accepted some time ago. But that is the point: this was a teaching that had rung true for years, and yet having witnessed a community of people who adopted it made me redouble my efforts to take it seriously. The lesson can be stated in three parts: (a) if a God is to be treated as a *God*, and not merely a utensil for the service of humankind, people must stop creating God in their likeness; (b) if a God is to be treated as *the* God—the One and Only—people must start granting God the ontological greatness that goes with the moniker; and (c) just because you grant God the greatness that God deserves doesn't require you to sacrifice the extent of God's relevance to the meaning of your life, for if anything, that relevance should grow the greater you view God to be.

My task became clear: to appreciate that God can be supremely relevant and infinitely great. To accomplish that task, I needed to contemplate what exactly it meant to be great ontologically. New words found themselves higher and higher in my list of interests: power, scope, majesty. Those were a few examples. But no word felt more meaningful than *ultimacy*. Without ultimacy, how can we possibly find divinity?

Stated differently, given two possible religious philosophies, both of which rest on the same basic approach to metaphysics, I wanted to choose the one whose God comported most with the criterion of ultimacy. My search wasn't for the God with the ultimate ratio of "goodness" to "evil," because those qualities, while critical to the realm of human ethics, are not supreme in the realm of ontology. When I used the term "ultimate," I did so with regards to the scope and depth of existence.

Since nobody had dissuaded me from viewing reality through a panentheist lens, the issue then became what approach to panentheism allots to God the greatest possible ontological ultimacy, while retaining from traditional monotheism God's supreme relevance to our emotional lives. I found that answer in Christianity.

⊕

In light of my embrace of panentheism, it only stands to reason that for many years, I have been a fan of the works of Paul Tillich. As has been noted, Tillich was mocked by Heschel for positing that God is the "Ground of Being." He also offered such other pantheistic definitions of God as the "infinite power of being" and "being-itself."[2] Superficially, those expressions would appear to be synonyms for Spinoza's Substance or *Natura naturans*.

In fact, however, when I re-read Tillich more recently, it became clear that he was using the above expressions not merely symbolically, but within a Trinitarian framework. In other words, he was speaking the way Christians frequently speak about the Divine—in terms of one realm or "person" of a multi-faceted, and yet unified, deity. Tillich's "Ground of Being" is to be viewed as a supplement to the so-called "ground of revelation," which he defined as the "'Ground of Being' manifest in existence."[3] This is just another way of differentiating between *Natura naturans* and *Natura naturata*. The latter is the realm of concreteness, of finitude, of form; it is the only realm "manifest" or intelligible to human beings.

For a Jew, it is hardly foreign to take two perspectives on the same basic unity and place one hierarchically above the other. As I have discussed, you'll find this kind of hierarchical ordering in the Kabbalistic discussions of the Divine, which assigns separate ranks to the ten Sefirot and places them all beneath the Ein Sof. Similarly, Spinoza appears to rank *Natura naturans* over *Natura naturata*, with one being seen as the ultimate cause or ground of the other. In both cases, the hierarchy is linear—one dimension is placed above the other, but the two can and should be connected. Yet for a Christian, or at least one with the sensibilities of Tillich, whenever we see two pairs of complementary poles connected together, this is an invitation to synthesize the two into a higher unity. The line, in other words, becomes a triangle. Dare I say the word? It becomes a type of *trinity*.

I find that dialectical approach much more amenable to panentheism than the old Aristotelian logic. Instead of taking two related, yet distinguishable, concepts X and Y and focusing on their non-identity, why not locate a Z that transcends X and Y and yet incorporates the essential character of both?

2. Ibid., 235–36.
3. Ibid., 155.

The casual reader of Tillich must be careful not to misunderstand him whenever he invokes *The Name*. It is not immediately clear whether he is speaking about the symbolic analogue of God the Father, God the Son, or some sort of unity between the two. What is clear, however, is his desire to elucidate the nature of divinity by dialectically opposing two complementary concepts.

At one point, for example, he draws a distinction between "God as being and God as living" and defines life as "the process in which potential being becomes actual being."[4] With that one simple distinction, Tillich has brought the entire realm of concrete forms into the Divine.

Similarly, in another instance, he remarks that,

> The divine life is the dynamic unity of depth and form. In mystical language[,] the depth of the divine life, its inexhaustible and ineffable character, is called "Abyss." In philosophical language[,] the form, the meaning and structure element of the divine life, is called "Logos." In religious language[,] the dynamic unity of both elements is called "Spirit."[5]

What is implicit here is made explicit elsewhere in Tillich: the Divine is not merely a synthesis of contrasting facets of Being but one that places complementary elements of unified Being in balance with one another. That dynamic balance represents the highest unity of all.

Semantically, I find his Trinitarian approach cumbersome. The idea of making one equal three is both bad math and confusing English. Still, while I may not care much for *speaking* like a Trinitarian, what Tillich has done is to help me appreciate *thinking* like one.

⊷

If I am correct, a person's conception of God will be a function of whatever that individual deems to be the *Ultimate*. In searching for that conception, I came to embrace the device of Trinitarianism, but not Trinitarian *Christianity* as it is commonly known. My continuing reluctance to go that far begins with my refusal to view Jesus as truly ultimate because I see him merely as human. To be sure, he appears to be an ideal man from a moral standpoint, but that is still a long way from the *Ultimate*, as I understand that term. Stated simply, *ultimacy* and *humanity* don't

4. Ibid., 241.
5. Ibid., 156.

go together in my mind. Similarly, I can't view God the Father, or more broadly, the God of the Abrahamic Scriptures, as the *Ultimate*. For all the reasons discussed above, I still see that God as largely fictionalized and, much like Jesus, anthropomorphized. The Christian Trinity thus doesn't work for me as a description of God. But that is only because the elements constituting that Trinity appear to lack the necessary claim to ultimacy. The idea of Trinitarian thinking—of taking a complementary, co-equal pair, combining them into a synthesis that contains them both, and looking at them separately and synthetically as God—has come to dominate my religious thought.

Everything changed once I took the liberty of substituting for "Jesus" the "sum of all concrete forms" and substituting for "God the Father" the "Ground of Being." Now, I found myself confronting realms that for me are truly ultimate. In the "sum of all concrete forms," I envision the entire world as we know it, plus all of the other distinct forms in existence (past, present, and future) that we cannot even begin to fathom because of our limited human capacities. As for the "Ground of Being," I envision what Tillich called the "abyss" and Spinoza calls "*Natura naturans*"—the ineffable force that propels and sustains all the forms that comprise our world. For me, they comprise the two central components of the Divine.

As Tillich explained in the quotation at the top of this chapter, Trinitarian monotheism (or panentheism) is not necessarily about the number three. It is about bringing into the Divine multiple components, each of which by itself is worthy of association with *The Name*, and all of which together form an ultimate unity. The notion of properly balancing these different components is critical to any form of Trinitarianism that professes to be based on a compelling religious philosophy. When one of the components is exaggerated or otherwise distorted, it can throw the entire philosophy out of whack. Yet when the components are balanced—when we are taught to give each component of the Trinity its due as a co-equal partner that plays its own unique role in the totality—then we have the potential for something that is both profound and beautiful.

There seems to be a bias within the family of Abraham to rank God's ineffable, thoroughly transcendent dimensions above that of "nature" as that term is commonly understood. I have mentioned that we saw this hierarchy in Spinoza and the Kabbalah, but it is notable that Tillich himself may have suffered a bit from the same bias. After all, that same passage in which Tillich disavows the importance of the number three in the Trinity and that appears to emphasize two components of divinity contrasts the notion of "concreteness" with that of "ultimacy."

I would freely concede that the realm of the concrete is less transcendent and more familiar than the abysmal ground of all that exists. But that does not make it any the less *ultimate*. Indeed, I am here to say that it is time to stop placing the world of things and thoughts beneath the realm of the abyss. In other words, it is time to reclaim the balance in our views of God by confronting the prejudices within our religious traditions. To me, the sum total of what exists in limited form is every bit as exalted as that invisible and indivisible mystery that has heretofore been viewed as "superior" and "heavenly" by our ancestors. To quote my friend, Dr. Dennis Skocz, a philosophy of God that does not do justice to the realm of the concrete is lacking in "thickness"—i.e., that same layered depth that is present in all great art and that is essential to making any philosophy satisfy the human heart.

In my philosophy, the world—the bubbling plenitude—is no less divine than that which powers and unifies it under the surface. Whenever we look up and see the sky, we are glimpsing a fragment of God, not merely some outgrowth of God. The world of discrete forms is where and how God comes fully alive. Similarly, to the extent we wish to extol love, will, intelligence, and all the other mental faculties that we have come to know and love, we are referring to the realm of the concrete and *not* the Ground of Being (at least not directly). And while I believe that there are infinite dimensions of reality that transcend our perceptive abilities, including within the realm of the concrete, that doesn't make those imperceptible dimensions any more divine than the world we experience. To worship God is to respect divinity in what is *not* mysterious every bit as much as to respect the mystery. Whether we're talking about order or abyss, field or ground, we don't need to rank them. We can simply deify them—both separately and in their unity.

⤙

It is only recently that I have been able to conceptualize in words what I have been able to understand for some time in my heart. Despite my commitment to strict monotheism, I have been conceiving of the Divine in three specific ways: as the "world" as a whole (including all the past, present, and future forms that shall forever remain unintelligible to us), as the Ground of Being, and as the synthesis of these two majestic, complementary, and unified domains. Each of these facets of Being, in my opinion, is worthy of *The Name*. This is because, taken separately or together, they appear to satisfy a robust standard of what it means to be truly *ultimate*.

The two realms that form the base of this conception of God are both infinite, eternal, and broad enough to encompass the known universe and beyond. Further, these realms fully complement one another rather than restricting each other. Moreover, taken tog9ether, they appear to comprise the totality of Being. And finally, in affirming each of these realms, I don't feel like I am merely conceptualizing a fiction, such as a theological myth. Rather, my voice of reason tells me to infer not only a realm of the concrete, but a realm that grounds and unifies all concrete forms. So, for example, even though I cannot *see* beyond the concrete realm, I can rely on inference and intuition to justify believing in the unified power or ground that resides within it. To borrow a phrase from a legal dictionary, I take each of these realms, "jointly and severally," to constitute God.

Is this an arbitrary way of conceiving of divinity? Not if you take seriously the Muslim phrase "Allahu Akbar." For if the Muslims are correct that "God is (the) greatest," what can be greater than *The Synthesis of Ultimates*—or, if you prefer a more streamlined formulation, *The Ultimate Synthesis*? I view these two designations as saying largely the same thing; after all, what synthesis can be more *ultimate* than the "synthesis of ultimates?" In both cases, God is seen as the dialectical unity of complementary domains of reality, each of which is infinite, eternal, unencumbered, and which collectively encompass the whole of reality. Personally, though, I prefer conceiving of God as *The Ultimate Synthesis* because the word "Ultimates" in the other formulation places an emphasis on the plurality that is within God, whereas I would prefer to place the emphasis on God's unity.

Am I saying that there is but one possible complementary pair of "ultimates" that can be synthesized to comprise a conception of God? No, I am merely acknowledging my awareness of only one candidate for this job. Just as Spinoza has said that God has infinite attributes of which we know only two, extension (matter) and thought (ideas), I am happy to posit that at least in theory, there are infinite pairs (or, more precisely, triads) of *Ultimates* that can satisfy the above standard. And yet, in each case, we will have simply identified different perspectives on the same God. That God remains *The Ultimate Synthesis*—whether what is being synthesized is one pair of ultimate, complementary realms or other groupings of ultimate, complementary realms doesn't change this simple fact. At most, it affects the way we may use *The Name* in referring to certain overarching facets of *The Ultimate Synthesis*.

↭

Now, I can rest, at least temporarily, with the satisfaction of having identified a conception of God that appears to meet the central goals established for this portion of the journey. This conception is emotionally fertile—for it allows people to deify the *world* and not just the heavens, and to see in every human action and emotion a direct effect on (the concrete) God. This conception is respectful—for it allows people to deify a God that meets the Islamic test of being greater than any other possible God. This conception reflects humility—for it does not require people to deify our own kind in spite of all the evidence that we don't deserve such an honor. This conception is honest—for it does not require people to take myths and other fictions and mistake them for literal truth. And most importantly, this conception is just—and by that, I mean it does justice to the term "God," which denotes the *Ultimate*, for it is precisely the concept of ultimacy that has served as the brightest star that has guided this search.

The worship of *The Ultimate Synthesis* is fully consistent with the panentheistic worldview, which is itself consistent with the principle of parsimony. Panentheists need not posit some kind of ontological chasm between this world and some kind of "heaven" above; the assumptions, in other words, are kept to a minimum. Moreover, the idea of *The Ultimate Synthesis* comports with the notion that, as an abstract matter, of all the concepts that have ontological reality, *The Name* is the greatest that can be conceived. Considered as *The Ultimate Synthesis*, it is appropriate to say that *God is in everything*, when God is considered as the mysterious infinite power that is presumed to reside within and unify all that exists. And yet, it is also appropriate to say that *everything is in God*, either when God is considered as that same indwelling power (in which case finite beings may be viewed as expressions of that power) or when God is conceived as the sum of all concrete forms in the past, present, and future.

Similarly, as has been discussed, the concept of *The Ultimate Synthesis* provides a sense of balance that does not exist when one particular perspective on reality is deified to the exclusion of others. Spinozism has always rung a bit hollow insofar as it treats human beings as mere "modes" or expressions of God. Indeed, in Spinozism, all the individual beings that exist, have existed, or will exist, considered in their aggregate, are viewed as but a single, collective "mode" of God—albeit, one would have to say, an "infinite mode." The realm of beings deserves more respect than that. As Tillich recognized, they may not be the Ground of Being, but they are God's *becoming*. They reflect the fullness of God's *life*. And just as it seemed arbitrary for Heschel to single out for ridicule the idea that God is the Ground of Being, it would seem equally arbitrary to assume that all the world's beings, taken together, are somehow less divine than the unifying power that underlies their existence. Indeed, when we begin to see the realm of beings from the framework of *The Ultimate Synthesis*, wanton acts of murder and other types of destruction are revealed in their fullest possible depravity because they attack not only something God has made or expressed—something derivative of God—but the very life of the Divine.

By the same token, while it is important to insert life into the notion of divinity, it is also important not to render the deity so overwhelmingly concrete as to become fictionalized. While clerics commonly acknowledge these days that the true God possesses personality traits only symbolically and did not literally do or say what has been attributed to the Divine in the Abrahamic Scriptures, the fact is that many continue to describe God in all-too-human terms. Why? Perhaps that is because these clerics fear the alternative. Presumably, they have convinced themselves that creating a truly balanced conception that respects both God's existence as the indivisible Ground of Being and God's primarily *non*-anthropomorphic reflection in the world of beings would make their Lord a yawner for too many people.

As a post-Enlightenment searcher, this philosophy of God is about as concrete and emotionally evocative as I dare adopt. Unfortunately, because it is not grounded in concrete mythological narratives of the type commonly associated with Scriptures, I can easily imagine traditionalists responding that the idea of God as *The Ultimate Synthesis* sounds like an abstract concept so void of concreteness and meaning as to attain the dubious distinction of being *sub*-personal. Surely, some would argue that what Heidegger said about Spinoza's God would apply to this one as well: "man can neither fall to his knees in awe nor can he play music and dance before this God." Other than to present this conception of God at academic conferences, the critics will say, it has no function.

Therein lies the most obvious objection. And yet it doesn't trouble me. Given that people are used to hearing descriptions of God with a human-like personality, any other conception of the deity will appear inadequate at first. People do, after all, deify human beings as the lords of the earth. So it only stands to reason that the Lord of reality would be human-like, and any attempt to sap God of that quality will be met with emotional resistance.

The task, though, isn't to find a conception of God that has the most superficial appeal; it is to find one that will be appealing *upon reflection*. It is in that regard, I submit, that *The Ultimate Synthesis* holds up so well to scrutiny—not only in terms of honoring God's greatness, but also in elevating the relevance of *The Name* to our emotional lives.

⟜⟞

If *The Ultimate Synthesis* is going to work as a conception of God, it will have to give us satisfactory answers to a number of key questions, including the basic inquiries of religious philosophy. When perceiving the Divine as *The Ultimate Synthesis*, answers to philosophical questions about God will commonly be framed in the form of "from one perspective, the answer is yes; from another perspective, the answer is no." To the Western mind, that sounds like a cop-out. To the Eastern mind, it just sounds like realism.

For example, consider the question: if God is *The Ultimate Synthesis*, do people have free choice or are they determined by God's very nature to act as they do? From the perspective of God as the Ground of Being, it would appear that all things exist as they do because they are fated to so exist by the nature of the God that encompasses them. Stated differently, the eternal God has an essence, which is to exist just as it does, and from the standpoint of that God, everything is happening in the present. Individual manifestations of God, including human beings, cannot truly be "free" to change their lives from one moment to the next, since dimensions like time and space do not even exist from the standpoint of the eternal, infinite ground of all Being, and it is precisely that active, eternal power that underlies every human action. By contrast, from the standpoint of God as the sum of finite, ephemeral beings, human beings are indeed free. From one moment to the next, we make choice after choice, and these choices are determined by forces that reside within each of us to consider options and evaluate those that are preferred. A less powerful individual could not have the same range of "freedom," which is why we don't say that dogs are free to learn calculus, even though nobody is stopping them from doing so.

Similarly, consider the question that was raised before: if God is *The Ultimate Synthesis*, is it true that God needs people? From the perspective of God as the Ground of Being, what could God possibly need? Such a God is complete in every way. Moreover, it would be odd to think that the Ground of Being experiences "desires" or "pains." The most I would be willing to say about God from this perspective is that God exists, infinitely and eternally, as an active power (which perhaps can best be thought of as "is-ness"). However, from the perspective of God as the sum of finite, ephemeral beings, God has all sorts of needs. Anyone who reads the newspaper can tell how flawed this realm is. Those flaws are very much *in* God—all the suffering, all the injustice, all the unfulfilled potential. Anyone who would dare stand up and come to the rescue of the world around her would serve the needs not only of her world but also of the concrete God who lives and breathes through such worlds.

Still, that is not to say that the answer to every question about God as *The Ultimate Synthesis* would be "yes and no." What if the question is: Is God omnibenevolent? If, by "omnibenevolence," we are referring to God's loving or merciful nature, that word would clearly *not* apply to *The Ultimate Synthesis*. There is plenty of hatred in the world, and therefore in God, when expressed from the standpoint of the sum of all concrete beings. Moreover, if God is considered from the standpoint of the Ground of Being, there is no reason to posit any emotions at all. That is what led Spinoza to say that "He, who loves God, cannot endeavor that God should love him in return. . . . [For if] a man were to so endeavor, he would therefore desire . . . that God whom he loves should not be God."[6] In other words, the Ground of Being—the Source of All That Is—is so far from human comprehension that it is absurd to attribute any human emotions to that God, including even love.

And yet, we would get a very different answer if we asked whether there is love in *The Ultimate Synthesis*. Yes, there is love in this God, just as there is hatred. In fact, every human emotion and every human

6. Spinoza, "Ethics," Part V, Prop. 19, 372.

thought is in God. God both encompasses and transcends all the mental and physical components of reality. Anything less just wouldn't be worthy of *The Name*.

So, getting back to the earlier challenge, is *The Ultimate Synthesis* a name for God that would make anyone want to sing or dance? Perhaps not. But that's not its purpose. *The Ultimate Synthesis* is not a name I would use when addressing my deity. In those moments, I harken back to my own religious tradition and use words like Elohim, Hashem, or simply, "God." *The Ultimate Synthesis* is merely a short description of who it is I am addressing. When I need names for God, and not merely conceptions of the Divine, I prefer something that is more emotionally charged. What I don't need is a name that is emotionally charged with human-like qualities. Having a human-like God makes us look like some primitive species in a science fiction movie—like the creatures on *Planet of the Apes* who worship the ape-God, Semos. I guess that's what separates us as human beings from those apes; we can conceive of God as *The Ultimate Synthesis* and feel satisfied, without having to erect statues and build myths that deify our own kind. Our God can be greater than that.

↬

But what about the *really* basic questions? This God of Synthesis, this yin/yang God, is it truly one God or multiple Gods semantically draped in the cloak of unity? Is it a God to whom people can meaningfully pray? Is it a God that inspires loyalty and righteous conduct and that makes commands? And how can people come to know this God better?

To the first question, the answer is simple: *The Ultimate Synthesis* is very much One. In fact, as the Qur'an states about Allah, it is the One and Only. There is nothing outside of this God. However, inside of God there is awe-inspiring variety composed of seemingly infinite fragments or forms of Being, the bulk of which must presumably remain beyond our grasp. In using the word "God" in a Trinitarian sense, I am willing to apply the term to less than *The Ultimate Synthesis*, but as discussed above, I am only willing to apply it to those "*ultimates*" that entered into that synthesis. In no respect will you find me applying *The Name* simply to Rabbi Zalman's dog feces or, for that matter, our own individual bodies and egos. We all may be divine beings, but we alone are not "God."

Can people meaningfully pray to *The Ultimate Synthesis*? Absolutely. With a reach that extends infinitely beyond the furthest star, *The
Ultimate Synthesis* is even closer to people than our jugular veins, for
this God includes all of our veins and whatever underlies them. Praying
to *The Ultimate Synthesis* should provide many of the same benefits as
praying to Abraham's Lord. To cite just one example, anyone who truly
loves his God will feel compelled to express that love and appreciation,
and that indeed is a form of prayer. Hoping that prayer would result in
supernatural intervention was always beside the point; just ask those who
have watched their loved ones die prematurely and painfully.

Is *The Ultimate Synthesis* a God who inspires and commands? Like
the previous question, this one will be addressed in greater detail in the
following part of this book. But the short answer is "yes and yes." There is
immense power in praying to a God whom we view not only as great, but
as Absolute. Even if we don't regard *The Ultimate Synthesis* as the owner
of an omnibenevolent "will," it remains the case that this deity has provided us with the gift of life, and what gift is greater than that? How can
we not be inspired by the opportunity to repay our greatest benefactor by
honoring that benefactor through our conduct? And what better way is
there to honor our benefactor than to devote our lives to nurturing this
world, which not only belongs to God but is part of God?

As for the idea of commanding human action, there is no reason to
suspect that *The Ultimate Synthesis* provided concrete, mandatory, and
eternal laws to Moses at Sinai or to Muhammad in Medina. Yet that hardly renders this God impotent as a commander. The love of God compels
the service of God. For how can anyone claim to serve this God without
a firm, undying commitment to alleviate suffering, unleash freedom, and
produce harmony in our world?

Finally, if God is conceived as *The Ultimate Synthesis*, how is it possible for us to grow in our knowledge of God? Quite simply, *all* knowledge
of any kind is of God, for *The Ultimate Synthesis* encompasses all things.
Thus, even if we are merely learning about the mundane things in life, we
are increasing our knowledge of God. It remains the case, however, that
the deeper the significance of our knowledge or wisdom, the more of the
Divine it captures, and for human beings, the depth of our knowledge
is tiny compared to the depth of our ignorance. This is especially true
when it comes to what we know about the abysmal Ground of Being,
which is pretty much nothing. Accordingly, even though "God" under
this philosophy is a name that lovers give to the unity that transcends all

multiplicity, God is *known* virtually entirely through the divine multiplicity, in all its forms and all its depth.

Most importantly, this God is best approached in the same way that Abraham approached his God—through a heart that is effusive with love. Yes, this philosophy compels us to look at every divine form realistically, and when we do, we will find some of these forms to be unworthy of our love. Just ask a genocide survivor; she'll tell you all about them. But honestly, they're the exceptions, not the norm. It remains the job of all who extol *The Name* to open our hearts and extend the net of compassion as widely as our sanity and integrity will allow. The greatest challenge of this philosophy is to allow *The Name* constantly to inspire our love—for God, for ourselves, for other people, for animals, for life—without envisioning an ever-merciful cosmic parent who consciously repays this love with interest. This is easier said than done. But to quote the final line in Spinoza's *Ethics*, "all things excellent are as difficult as they are rare."[7]

---

7. Spinoza, "Ethics," Part V, Prop. 42, Scholium, 382.

PART II

GOD IN THE SECOND PERSON

So, do you view God primarily as some*thing* to be studied and conceptualized or some*one* to be encountered and addressed? The chic answer, in theological circles, is the latter. To say that "God is beyond conceptualization" has become the theological equivalent of "2+2=4." According to conventional wisdom, those of us who can adroitly discuss the meaning of the word "God" are nothing more than *homo intellecticus* and are missing the whole point of the Divine. Conceptualizers are said to be brains without souls, pedants with tunnel vision, and novices in the realm of the spirit. By contrast, those who can pray with all their hearts, deeply meditate on the mantra "One," or approach every earthly meeting as a divine encounter are extolled not only for their spirituality but also for their wisdom.

I can't tell you how many times I've seen that theme in print. And I still don't fully buy into it. Obviously, we can never completely capture God in conceptual form. But does that mean we need not try? When even many of our brightest theologians and clergy don't attempt to conceptualize God in a logically coherent way, we as individuals tend to be left to our own devices . . . or to the preaching of charlatans. And if that means that large segments of society become apathetic or dismissive about the whole domain of religion, whereas other segments look to God's supernatural intervention to solve our greatest problems, we all must live with the consequences.

If we are to communicate with one another about divinity, it is invaluable that you understand who or what I mean by the word "God." That is why we began this book by considering God in the third person. But it was never my plan to limit ourselves to that third person framework. In fact, we couldn't pull that off even if we wanted to. In the Spinozistic words of Jay Michaelson, "the heart loves what the mind knows."[1] In other words, the more we learn about the Divine—the more coherent, subtle, and reasonable our conception of God becomes—the more we come to love God. And it is impossible truly to love something, or someone, and not desire a meaningful encounter with this beloved. I feel that way about the birds that nest on my back porch just as I do about *The Ultimate Synthesis*.

In this part of the book, I will attempt such an encounter with the Divine. Every statement will be made directly to God and God alone.

In connection with these statements, at least three fundamental questions arise. First, by speaking to God, am I expecting to receive a response? Second, if indeed the answer to that first question is yes, from whom do I expect that response? From God? Or only from myself? And third, whenever I use mere words to address the boundless mystery that is the Divine, am I inevitably resorting to anthropomorphizing God—the very activity that I have vociferously argued against in Part I?

Hopefully, Part I has enabled you to glean how I would answer the first two questions, but I'll leave it for you to answer them for yourselves. As for the third question, I must address it here and now, lest you think that I refuse to see in myself what I have been pointing out in others.

Do I anthropomorphize God whenever I use words to address the Divine? To some degree, yes. The words we use, just like the feelings we experience, are grounded in our all-too-human realm. They reflect an entire array of perceptions—our words for sights, for sounds, for tastes, even for abstract concepts. If only at a subconscious level, we will interpret these words and feelings in human terms—and that applies to a beloved book, a treacherous blizzard, or a philosopher's idea of God. That's the way we're hard-wired. But it doesn't mean we must be completely trapped by our anthropomorphizing.

1. Michaelson, *Everything Is God*, 38.

Once we start conceiving of the fundamental nature of the *Ultimate* in essentially human terms (e.g., in terms of loving, hating, desiring, etc.), that's when I feel we've gone too far. It is this type of false characterization—the willingness fundamentally to mischaracterize the Divine so that we can more easily relate to "him"—that I strive to avoid like the plague, regardless of whether I'm addressing God in synagogue or in solitude. And that is why, when I speak to God, I don't assume that there is some overarching cosmic intelligence processing my words and deciding how to respond with love, justice, and wisdom.

Why then do I speak to God at all? Keep reading, and hopefully that question will be answered easily enough.

We'll speak again in Part III and attempt there to figure out why all this God-talk can be meaningful not only to us as individuals, but also to our society and our planet. For now, though, you must excuse me. I have a different audience to address—an audience of one.

CHAPTER 10

My Ultimate Benefactor

IT IS NICE TO be alone with You. Without distractions. Without temptations.

And when we are alone, I always approach You with candor. That's part of our deal, isn't it? I give you my innermost thoughts and feelings, and in return, You give me as much of this world as I dare envision. For me, it's a great deal.

If I must be candid, then, the truth is that I am disappointed with myself, or more specifically, with my worship. Decades ago, when invoking Your name for the first time, I was more excited. Sometimes, I'd feel an almost physical rush of pleasure, like I was taking an intense, chemical stimulant, when all I was doing was contemplating You.

Where has that rush gone? Why has it abandoned me?

Maybe what I felt for You was puppy love, but I miss it just the same—that childlike sense of belonging to You and feeling cared for by the Omnipotent One. I keep thinking that if I work at it, I can get some of that intense, worshipful feeling back. Only next time, it will be a more mature feeling of worship. That's my goal.

When it comes to rejoicing in Your name, I'm not nearly what I once was. But I'm not willing to blame that loss on my rationalistic philosophy. If I were accused of abandoning You for the worship of reason, I'd plead not guilty. I don't worship reason. I'm just trying to worship You with my eyes wide open. Is that a sin?

Years ago, when for the first time as an adult I fell in love with You, You were a *personal* God in every sense of the word. Purposeful. Caring. Just. Fair.

And then, I found sobriety. I refused to believe that whatever happens is because of Your will. I got back in touch with my philosophical side. I stopped attributing anything to Your "will" and began attributing everything to Your *nature*.

You became less a person than a concept. Gentler on the mind. Colder in the heart.

I could try right now to go back to a time when I'd frequently feel Your loving presence touch me as if You were my parent and I was Your precious child. I'd like to feel those jolts of pleasure again. But not if it involves turning You into something You're not. I can't do that to You, God. I can't strip You of Your reality just because I could use an imaginary friend in heaven.

So, You see, this is why I can't fault my commitment to philosophy— it is no more at fault than You should be criticized for not resembling a human being. I am what I am—a man who tries to value truth even when it hurts. And You are what You are—infinitely more mystery than man.

But fortunately, You have given us more than just the mystery. You have also bestowed what we call "knowledge." And this has given rise to our cherished beliefs. One of mine is that You are the ultimate benefactor.

You have breathed life into our lungs and handed us an entire world to utilize and care for. A world to use as a laboratory, a conservatory, an amusement park, a tunnel of love.

How can I not feel the need to give praise in return? And when giving praise, do I not owe the respect of worshipping You as I find You, not as I would design You in my own image?

No, I won't blame the discipline of philosophy for hardening my heart. In fact, I credit philosophy for allowing me to approach You in the sunlight, where the truth often hurts, but at least it is the truth.

Then again, the human mind's "truths" can only take us so far. We are capable of going so much further. The real challenge You pose is not to know You, but to *feel* You—all the while knowing that You are so much greater than we are. So familiar, yet so alien.

It is a challenge. But we owe You nothing less. And when I finally meet that challenge—when I can finally feel You *as You are*, and not as we have created You in our own image—worship will be doubly intense and doubly sweet. Or so I tell myself.

-⊙-

This morning, before I sat down to write, I opened the cupboard and picked out a mug for tea. It was the one that said "Stanford."

Some of my friends here in the Washington, D.C. area may wonder—why do I love Stanford University so much? It is, after all, associated with California generally and Silicon Valley in particular, whereas I am an East Coast guy who, by nature, is a Luddite.

But the answer is simple. I love Stanford because I went to school there at a time in my adolescence when I was willing to open my mind, and that school and its terrific professors taught me many wondrous things. I love Stanford because, no matter what else can be said about it, that school was my benefactor. And if there is one thing I have learned from worshipping You it is to love our benefactors.

There's that word again, "benefactor." Four syllables. Anything but poetic. And yet, in that one word, we can find our surest pathway to You.

I love my parents. My wife. My daughters. My extended family. My true friends. They, too, are my benefactors. They give, I take. I may give back, but that's not the point. They bestow their gifts whether or not I give back, just like You do.

In the title of this chapter, I called You "My Ultimate Benefactor." I fully recognize that all gifts come from You, including the most precious—the gift of life.

Sometimes, though, we only see the gift-giving through the face of one of Your distinct *forms*. It could be a person, an institution, a dog, or a tree. Each one is a potential benefactor.

Let's take trees as an example. I'm still awed by the beautiful trees I saw on my walk this morning. When I looked up at them, I felt myself living in a Lilliputian society by contrast. The trees made me think about hills and mountains, the sky on a sunny day, and above that, the stars, or just deep space and whatever we cannot detect that lies beyond that. But it all begins with trees and our ability to look up and notice something beyond ourselves.

Scientists are lucky. They're able to identify benefactors that most of us cannot. The rest of us look outward, to see a face, or upward, to see a tree or the sky. But scientists also look inward. And then, they can contemplate an electron, see a microbe, and feel a sense of understanding, belonging, and awe.

Mystics are luckier still. They're always able to find a benefactor. Whenever they see a tree, they see *Your* tree. Whenever they see a face, they see *Your* face. Whenever they see a microbe, they see *Your* microbe. Benefactors one and all.

⤴

Sometimes I ask myself, do I want to look at the world the way the mystics do—and not just occasionally but every second of every day? Then I remember that most of my greatest heroes aren't mystics. They're fighters, or more precisely, they're activists—agents of social change.

They don't think about You 24/7. They get carried away with their fights. As a result, they don't see benefactors around every corner. They don't feel blessed every moment of their lives. Candidly, neither do I.

Like most of my heroes, I often get consumed by societal battles and try to join in—as a fighter either for justice or peace. Those are lofty and worthy ideals. But when the battle begins, I often lose focus and get consumed with things that are the opposite of lofty: the duplicity, the pettiness, the selfishness, the ignorance, the inevitable destruction. That stuff is as ubiquitous as empathy, love, and wisdom.

My greatest heroes live in the world of activism and strife. Some of them don't ever give You a thought, at least not by name. Yet they are still my heroes. They might not think of this world as Yours, but all their tireless activism goes into perfecting it just the same.

These activist heroes of mine, their effort is destined never to be complete. For Your world is imperfect. Eternally imperfect.

My God, I must admit that I see You largely through the prism of this world. For me, it is our greatest teacher about Your nature. You are the mystery that transcends the world. But You are also the world. And to me, the world is imperfect. So You . . . can I finish the sentence? So You are imperfect. At least that's how I feel.

I don't wish to criticize You or even to limit You. Please may I not be disrespectful. I wish to embrace Your infinity in every respect.

In you, I imagine infinite vectors heading in infinite lengths and depths. Outward, upward, inward . . . through the mind as well as the body . . . and through dimensions we human beings cannot ever begin to understand.

I can imagine Your power extending over the entire domain of morality: over the good, the bad, the indifferent. You share responsibility for all of it. Infinite responsibility.

No, I don't wish to limit You. But apparently, I do wish to deny Your so-called "perfection." I associate that word with purity—pure goodness—whereas I associate You with something far greater: reality in its entirety. And that begins with what we call "the world."

This world is many things. "Purely good" just doesn't happen to be one of them.

That's okay, though. I love our world just the same. And I love You for giving it to us.

Baruch ata, Hashem.

I can't sincerely thank You for every single thing in this world. I can't thank You for Auschwitz. But I can thank You for life itself, and for this world, taken as a whole.

Perhaps, someday, I will learn to thank You unconditionally, no matter how many more Auschwitzes should appear.

CHAPTER 11

My Source of Enchantment

SOMETIMES, I FEEL UNSUITED to call myself a panentheist, let alone a peacemaker. Those terms usually refer to people who are moved above all else by Your unity and the challenge of replicating that unity here on earth. That's not me. What I appreciate most about Your world is its *diversity*. I might philosophize about Your overarching unity. But I spend a lot less time contemplating that unity than I spend focusing on the differences that exist within Your world.

I enjoy examining what distinguishes us from one another. I love to analyze, or even to argue. Why do You think I practice law for a living? I've always enjoyed verbal sparring. So sue me.

Some might think that a panentheist would be just the opposite. Stereotypically, she is compelled above all else to seek the common root, the common energy that lies within. She looks more for Your all-encompassing hand than for the variety of Your handiwork. Her focus is on the Ground of Being beneath multiplicity, where time is transcended, and only You remain—ever present, ever active. In that Ground of Being, she locates Your home. Not in heaven above, but in an inner domicile of mystery, sublimity, and radiating light. And she envisions our world as if it is but the outer skin of an artichoke—far away from the heart of it all.

Personally, I find You inside, but outside too. I find You in the sky, the molecules, and in that which is beyond words. To me, You are no more present in one place or time than any other. Your essence is as much revealed in a lightning bug as in light itself. I find You in a destructive volcano no less than in the holiest house of worship.

Whether I speak of human love or hatred, I recognize that they are both among the infinite ways in which Your powers are expressed. I love to contemplate You as infinite variety.

I like communities of eccentrics, in which no two members are alike. I like collections of individuals who disagree with each other on fundamental issues. And that's why I love my Jewish-Islamic dialogue society—we're a community of *non* like-minded individuals.

What I don't like is witnessing people preach to the choir. That's what makes talk radio so insufferable. That's what makes me averse to Fox News, MSNBC—or, for that matter, political parties.

I read in the Qur'an that You made people into nations and tribes, so that they "may know each other, not that they may despise each other" (49:13). We all know that with diversity come the seeds of discord, even death. But to me, the benefits are well worth the cost.

Yes, God, this diverse world of Yours is so rich, so provocative. There are muses everywhere. Every face can be one, if we really take the time to admire them.

Sometimes, I like to think of Your world as a world of faces. Each one is different, whether it belongs to a person, dog, or cat. Every face can inspire empathy. And when I become empathic, that's when I feel most worthy of breathing Your air. That's when I become confident that I will do good and not bring the discord that we often associate with diversity.

Diversity—or should I say, variety—is, after all, a double-edged sword. The spice of life can easily turn into the insanity in life. But at least Your world isn't boring.

No, it's not the least bit boring. To anyone whose eyes and ears are open, it's enchanting.

‹›

Ironically, one of the reasons I am so in love with Your *name* is because even though it is supposed to symbolize cosmic unity, it actually adds incredible diversity to this world.

In my society, people are making less and less room for Your name. Many associate it with antiquated thinking, dogmatism, even oppression—in other words, the *threats* to diversity. For me, though, a world without Your name would be as absurd as a world without math, science, literature, or sport. It would be smaller, duller, less meaningful, and yes, more homogeneous.

Our sense of the holy would be gone. Our sense of unity, of wholeness, equally gutted. And we would struggle to imagine the transcendent, the mysterious.

If we stop remembering Your name, we may stop reminding ourselves that there is always more than what meets the eyes. And we may forget that even our greatest scientific truths pertain to just a tiny fragment of Your world.

My God, You don't simply ground being. You ground our appreciation for the value of diversity. Panentheistically, everything that exists can be fully known only in relation to Your name. All beings belong to You. They all occupy a part of You. Your name has the power to make each thing seem more connected and more beloved.

Panetheistically, everything is a window onto You. And what little we have already learned about You is a window onto everything else we are about to envision for the first time.

When we try to take away the majesty of Your name, erase the notion that each of us is but one of Your infinite number of forms, and remove the "eternal Thou" from each worldly "Thou," we would strip the world of much of its enchantment.

For me, Your name brings a sense of overarching enchantment. Instead of a world of "creatures" and "things," we are given a world of the sublime. All of a sudden, life becomes a miracle—a combination of mystery and logic, knowable in part, and yet mostly unimaginable.

Spinoza coined the phrase "God, or nature," as if those words are synonyms. To me, though, that was one of his biggest mistakes.

"Nature" may be loved, whereas Your name is *revered*.

When we experience "Nature" we feel fortunate, but when we contemplate Your name, we feel *blessed*.

"Nature" as a term is largely neutral. Your name is laden with emotional significance. Some call it "baggage." I call it liberation.

⊹

My country has a motto—*E Pluribus Unum* ("Out of the many, one"). Your name offers much the same creed on a cosmic scale—Diversity within Unity.

Real unity isn't so much sensed as celebrated. We can close our eyes, remove all thoughts of separation, and contemplate what it means to be unified in You.

Then, when we "come to," we're left with the enchanting thought that every object of our eyes and our heart is divine. That is what I call something to celebrate.

I don't mean to reduce You only to the sum total of Your "expressions," though. I realize that You are more than just the objects of nature.

But all the things in the world—the people, the animals, the ideas— play their parts in revealing who You are. Ultimately, these parts come together, and while it may not exactly be the world of our dreams, most of us never choose to escape from it. We also know that if we were to try to recreate a world of our own, it couldn't possibly measure up to the beauty You have expressed.

Whatever should happen in my future, I wouldn't trade my life for any alternative. I feel blessed to play my part, and it's not because that part is any better than anyone else's. It's because I have fallen in love with the whole. And because I recognize what an honor it is to participate in the drama unfolding inside of You.

I call it the Play of Plays—the only play worthy of the term *Ultimate*.

God, when I'm waging one of my battles against wars or injustice, I often find that I'm tilting at windmills. Working for justice is a slow, painstaking process, and you never know when you will succeed. As for peacemaking, it often feels downright impossible. That's why would-be peacemakers sometimes feel like Sisyphus—either tragic or comic figures, depending on the day.

But that's okay. In the scenes from Your Play of Plays—those incredibly-varied and often-conflicting scenes known as the workings of human society—there are no small parts. Just small-minded actors.

Simply by contemplating Your name, we can get less small-minded and more enchanted every day.

CHAPTER 12

My Magical Muse

PLEASE MAY I NOT be guilty of abusing Your name.

I'm not so worried about saying things like "God damn." Yes, that's crude, but it's hardly the worst kind of blasphemy.

I reserve that label for when people invoke Your name for selfish purposes. And especially when they credit You for someone's misfortune, or pray for others to suffer or die in Your name.

That's religion at its most depraved. But really, any time we bring You into the equation when we're trying to advance our own interests at the expense of others, it's blasphemy.

Why do I feel that way? It comes back to something Kant wrote:

> Act so that you use humanity, as much in your own person as
> in the person of every other, always at the same time as end and
> never merely as means.[1]

Kant gets no style points for those words. But they're beautiful just the same. They give us a foundational principle of ethics. A secular commandment.

I love how Buber took that commandment and moved it into the realm of religion. When he distinguished between the I-It and the I-Thou relationships, he brought Kant's commandment into the house of Abraham. He used words like "rapacity" and "hoarding" to refer to the I-It realm.[2] And when he wrote about the I-Thou encounter between one

1. Kant, *Groundwork*, 46–47.
2. Buber, *I and Thou*, 155.

person and another, he spoke in terms of experiencing "joy over the presence of that which is present." [3]

"As soon as we touch a You, we are touched by a breath of eternal life." [4] That's Buber's way of saying that when we stop using people merely as a means to an end, only then can we begin to encounter You, worship You, and honor You.

So how sick is it that people don't simply treat one another strictly as a means, but treat *You* that way? How is that not blasphemy?

I agree with Buber that the I-It pairing creates a sense of ultimate separation. I agree that when we're trapped in that mentality, we're alienated from truth—and from You.

If Buber was right that You are the "Eternal Thou"—the Thou that grounds every other I-Thou encounter—how can we possibly justify treating You simply as an instrument for achieving our own selfish goals? Your name evokes the *unity* grounding the multiplicity. That name is supposed to bring us together, not split us apart.

I don't want my life to be one big fencing tournament. I want it to be an exercise in exploring, nurturing, and loving. Sports aside, I want to fight because my world needs me to, not purely for the fun of it. I can't justify stepping on people just to get ahead.

Now, don't get me wrong. We don't always have the time for I-Thou encounters. And we sometimes encounter people who will make it impossible to experience "joy over the presence of that which is present." Take it from a lawyer who fights fraud for a living, there are moments in life when we shake another guy's hands, and we're not so much reminded of the Eternal Thou; we just want to take a shower. But there is never a reason to feel that way when we contemplate Your name.

I would argue that our ethical compass begins with the ability to recognize *any* unneeded I-It contact between people as a shame, if not a sin. But when the one we are treating as an "It" is You, now *that* is a sin.

For me, that's what it means to take Your name "in vain." Though it doesn't offend me as much as, say, the murder of a human being, it still frustrates me whenever I think about it.

3. Ibid.
4. Ibid., 113.

᪥

Yes, God, Your name is too precious to treat as a mere instrument to be *utilized*. Above all else, it must be honored. It must be praised.

Not just Your name but, more importantly, *You* must be thanked. For so many reasons, we owe You that.

I may not be the world's most spiritual person, but at least I know enough to begin all my prayers by thanking You for the gift of life. Then, when I have expressed that sentiment, I might even name some people and things for whom I am especially thankful.

And then, I generally ask what work I can do to help out the world. Peace work. Environmental work. Work for the poor. Prayers for inner strength so that I can stay focused and productive.

Prayers not followed by hard work ring hollow.

Please God, may my prayers advance the ends of others, not just my own. I feel blessed whenever I'm at prayer and I remember to ask to do my part to enrich the world. Even my atheist friends probably wouldn't begrudge me those kinds of prayers. They're not the kind that people subject to ridicule.

Ah, but I have engaged in those *other* kinds of prayers too. Like the ones I address to You on stressful Monday mornings. When I walk into a bathroom at an office building at 8:20 a.m., ten minutes before a deposition is about to start, and ask You for assistance. I pray for strength, insight, patience, courage—all the usual suspects.

These are many of the same requests that fundamentalist business-men make before a big meeting, or that fundamentalist football players make before a big game. When they kneel down on the playing field, with their hands on their foreheads, and create for themselves a peace-ful space. Little do many of these athletes know that they have suddenly become objects of condescension outside of the Bible belt.

Where I live, it's generally understood that only an idiot could think that You would care about the outcome of a football game, a business meeting, or a deposition. So, the argument goes, why should anyone pray to you in connection with these events?

Sometimes, I think about Einstein's statement about how he believes in Spinoza's God, who is revealed in the order and harmony of existence and doesn't care about the fates and actions of human beings. How can I quote that line, call myself a Spinozist, and then pray to you before every deposition, which I do? Some would call that a level of hypocrisy worse than that of the fundamentalists. At least they admit who they are. I'm living a lie, right?

Here's the thing, though: there is incredible power in invoking Your name. Maybe it is black magic. Maybe it is white magic. But there's no denying that it can be magical.

If, with integrity, I can justify using that magic, why wouldn't I do it? As long as it's ethical, wouldn't I be a fool to turn my back?

↦

Long before I called myself a "believer," I would talk to myself. For example, I would try to get the proper focus and just the right energy level before a test in school.

I would make an appeal to my own psyche because I've always sensed the value of a strong internal monologue.

But those monologues became qualitatively more valuable when I began directing them to You. Suddenly, the words grew in significance. These were no longer monologues; they were *moments*.

Just by beseeching You, we acknowledge our limitations and needs. What's more, by invoking Your name in support of our enterprise, we proclaim our cause laudable and pure. At least that's how I feel. Otherwise, I wouldn't be invoking Your name in connection with a particular cause.

Once the prayer begins, how can I not be invested? How can my self-respect not be on the line? But not only that, I've also brought Your *honor* into the equation. I might be willing to disrespect myself, but am I really willing to dishonor You as well?

This is why petitional prayers must not be taken lightly. This is why those who cannot sincerely put their hearts behind these prayers may be better off avoiding them altogether.

The problem with praying before a business meeting has nothing to do with insincerity. Professionals are plenty sincere that we want to do well at that meeting. We truly want strength, insight, patience, courage.

We badly want to succeed. The question is, why bring *You* into that enterprise?

Obviously, we do it in part because it's effective. For the reasons I've said, invoking Your name motivates us like nothing else can. More than just invested, we're inspired to obtain what we seek both for our own sakes and for Yours.

But that doesn't answer the question. Let's assume Einstein is correct. Certainly, I would agree with him that You in Your capacity as the Ground of Being are not concerned about whether we succeed or not. Why then should we stake Your honor on our success?

I have but one answer: because to me, You are more than just the Ground of Being. You are also the Grand Totality of the World—or as a Spinozist might say, *Natura naturata*, taken in the aggregate. In that capacity, whether or not You care about what transpires in this world, You have a stake, just like we do.

When I beseech You for things that directly affect my own self-interest, I don't need to know that You care. I just need to believe that if I receive what I seek, it will matter to Your world.

As one who makes a living fighting fraudsters, I need to believe that my proper conduct at a deposition matters, because fighting fraud matters and so does proper conduct by anyone who enters that arena. Because of that belief, I allow myself to invoke Your name during some of my internal, work-related monologues.

What of football players? Do they have a right to invoke Your name before a big game?

It depends what they're asking for, doesn't it? If they're asking for concentration, focus, power . . . that's all fine. In sport, no less than in art or business, it matters that we all do our best. It enriches the whole activity.

But sometimes football players ask for Your help to make them win. Or to make their opponents falter. "Please God, make them miss that field goal."

That's a horse of a different color.

Winning a competition is a zero-sum game. Your name has no business being invoked to help one competitor win a zero-sum game. That's just using You as a means to our own ends. It wouldn't cut the mustard with Kant or Buber, and it shouldn't with the rest of us either.

❧

Your name, God, is my Magical Muse. Whenever I summon it, I seek inspiration and virtue. Wholesome inspiration. Righteous inspiration. Profound inspiration.

The last thing I ever want to do is pervert the magic in Your name. Please don't let me do that. Help me feel my devotion to You more as a source of duties than as a source of power.

And please don't let me confuse You with Your name.

We come from You. Your name comes from us. Therein lies a big difference.

CHAPTER 13

My Well of the Purest Substance

MOSTLY, I LIKE TO find You by looking up and looking out. Then there are days like today, when I seek You by looking inside. I stop viewing You as the totality of forms and start contemplating You as the Ground, the Source. I stop locating myself in You, and start locating You in me and our world.

No longer do I seek You in Your infinite complexity. Now, I seek You in Your eternal simplicity.

When I drill down, I can give thanks to You. In fact, I must give thanks. Benefactors merit gratitude.

What I don't do while drilling down is make requests—*any* requests, even righteous ones. These occasions aren't times for me to think about myself or even my planet. They are all about Your unity and Your mystery.

While I drill down, I'm not even thinking about Your *name*. My focus is on You as the One who is beyond names or words of any kind.

Deeper and deeper I drill. Until I stop seeking and simply bask in Your glory.

It is then when You are no longer a challenge. You provide nothing to overcome. You offer no tasks. You simply let us be. And finally, I stop feeling You in me. We are One.

❧

This morning, when I drilled down, I was struck by having experienced the sense of total simplicity. Void of all form. One voice underlying all of life's songs. *Pure Being.*

Then, at some point, I started thinking about that word again— "pure." You could say I have a love-hate relationship with it.

Who doesn't love the idea of a pure heart, a pure marble statue, or a pure sound on a violin? But I also see sacrilegious elements in the idea of purity. I can't help but notice the way it is used to suggest that You are smaller than You truly are. And I can't help but notice how it is used to divide my planet.

In human society, Your unity is commonly ignored. In the dualities that are created in its stead, much is praised, but at least an equal amount is vilified. The latter often gets attributed to evil forces *outside* of You, even though, as far as I'm concerned, there are no such forces.

The contrast people draw between Your beauty and the ugliness of the "devil" can be attributed largely to the concept of purity. It may not be a sacrilegious word, but it sure is a dangerous one. It can turn part of Your world (the "purely good") into an icon, and the other part into the realms of the so-called "a-religious" or "irreligious."

I don't believe any of those separate realms exist. Everything that is, is in You.

This morning, no sooner did I focus on the idea of purity than my attention was turned away from my mystical interlude and towards organized religion. I'm talking about religion as it is commonly understood in our world. Through rituals modeled by clerics. Through symbols and myths ingrained in our cultures. Through a field of study that can be learned in school—and that has no more to do with You than any other discipline, be it biology, math, or history.

Some would say that religion has *less* to do with You than those other disciplines, but I'm not that cynical. I'm fascinated by the study of religion. I simply disagree with much of what is said in its name. And my disagreement starts with the traditional obsessions with *purity* and *holiness.*

Many clerics may not acknowledge those obsessions, but they exist. They're merely hidden by the typical nature of religious language.

In the field of religion, simple definitions are generally avoided. Instead, we get the sense of mystery—even when what we're dealing with is easily enough defined. The meaning of "purity" in the religious context is hardly mysterious. It refers to the perception that something is absolutely good and a superb exemplar of its kind.

I associate You with purity insofar as when I contemplate You as Substance—as Source or Ground—I sense You as pure, undifferentiated Being. But I also recognize that in the field of religion, You are traditionally associated with purity because that concept has such a close relationship with arguably the one word that has come to dominate religion even more than Your name. I'm referring to "holiness."

Traditionally, whenever clerics find things that they deem pure and worthy of awe, they will invoke the notion of holiness. And in each case, they attribute these "holy" things to You.

Sunsets are deemed holy. So, too, are other expressions of nature that people find beautiful and unthreatening.

We also use that word for memorials to soldiers who gave their lives in the field of battle. Actually, people admire as holy *any* sincere acts of charity. Charity seems like such a refreshing rebuke to our creaturely selfishness, which most of us aren't very proud of. In fact, all situations in which we sense Your "presence" are deemed holy.

Weddings are deemed holy, at least when the couple seem to be suited for each other. Some people would never acknowledge that single-sex couples could have a holy wedding, for that would violate their view about what makes marriage "holy." That's part of the tragedy of the word.

Scriptures are deemed holy, but only the Scripture for the religion we ourselves practice. Other religions' Scriptures are often criticized. (I still bristle when some of my Muslim friends refer to the Torah as a "corrupted text" that pales in comparison to their own "perfect" text. Of course, that insult is nothing compared to what a lot of my fellow Jews say about the Qur'an.)

Whether we're talking about a book, a memorial, or a situation, we associate Your holiness most often with whatever we perceive as "pure." And when someone threatens to introduce "impurities" into what we deem to be holy, we feel threatened and strike back. A lot of violence comes from that impulse.

People like to associate You with holiness and holiness alone. What's frustrating to someone with my philosophy is that those people tend to ignore that You are just as responsible for all the sickness in the world.

Your *unity* might be pure. But Your multiplicity? Just the opposite. And yet, when we talk about objects of holiness and purity, we are typically talking about elements of Your multiplicity.

I don't deny Your presence in what we deem to be most pure and holy. But aren't You equally present in *all* Your multiplicity—the living hells as well as the harmonies?

It is always such a special treat to drill down and seek You inside as the source of Unity. Inevitably, though, some irritating concept enters my head and snaps me back to the world of multiplicity. Whenever I find the opportunity to slice and dice concepts, I take it. I am like a fish, and over-analyzing is my water.

Why must my experiences of Your unity be so brief? Am I afraid of what would happen if I didn't snap out of my reverie? Am I so addicted to my own ego that I don't want to take the risk of losing it and becoming a "different person"? What if that "different person" could be holy and pure?

If I were to become a 24/7 mystic—a true portrait of holiness—I would need to change my personality, and I mean dramatically. But the fact is that I'm not willing to change it so much that I would feel like a different person. That would seem almost suicidal. And it wouldn't be nice to my family or friends. They're nearly as accustomed to my neuroses as I am.

Generally speaking, I am at peace with my neuroses. Despite all my worries and feelings of inadequacy, I accept that it is the human condition to be neurotic and to fail to live up to our potential. Even at my most self-satisfied, I still wouldn't care for the idea that someone like me—a mere human being—was ever "made in Your image." If I were forced to think of You as having an "image," it would be the whole world—both knowable and unknowable—not some neurotic Jewish guy from Maryland.

But I have to say this much: if I am right that You have traditionally been associated with purity and holiness, then how could human beings ever see ourselves as having been made in Your image? That wouldn't make sense if we were talking about the Old God, and it certainly doesn't make sense if we're talking about You.

CHAPTER 14

My Friend

I LOOKED UP THE noun "friend" in Webster's Dictionary, and here's what I found:

1. A person whom one knows well and is fond of; intimate associate; close acquaintance

2. A person on the same side in a struggle; one who is not an enemy or foe; ally

3. A supporter or sympathizer [a *friend* of labor]

4. Something thought of as like a friend in being helpful, reliable, etc.

5. [F-] Any member of the society of Friends; Quaker[1]

As long as I can identify You as a "something," I can then officially call You a friend. After all, You are certainly reliable and helpful. In fact, You are the *most* helpful and reliable.

Whenever I feel that I need You, I can find You. Every nanosecond of every day, You envelop me. All I have to do is say Your name and open my heart, and I immediately become aware of Your presence. That's what I call reliable.

I don't mind that our friendship lacks the mutuality of a friendship between two people. What it lacks in mutuality, it gains in being eternal. I don't worry about You moving to Denver and our losing touch. As long as I breathe, I will have You as a friend.

1. "Friend," *Webster's New World College Dictionary*, 567.

As for Your being helpful, You are always available as a confidant and a true antidote to loneliness. Plus, You are a muse who inspires us to be virtuous and productive. Who can possibly be more helpful than You?

I'm hardly the only one who calls you a friend. Many people feel the same way, and they would say as much if anyone cared to ask. Actually, it is because some of them did say as much to me that I was intrigued by Your name even when, as a teenager, I doubted Your existence.

Yet despite all the testimonials You receive, the same skeptical question is raised, and from what I can tell, it is raised more and more often these days: *Why do we need God?*

Well, for starters, it's because without You, there would exist nothing at all. So in the most basic sense of the word, we absolutely do need You, whether we choose to admit it or not.

But not everyone thinks about You panentheistically. So when I'm asked the question, "Why do we need God?" maybe I should answer in the style of Webster's:

1. We don't; we only need fluids; even intravenous fluids would be sufficient

2. God is a reality, not a need

3. We can live a meaningful, happy life without believing in God; we don't need God

4. Belief in God can be a wonderful luxury to have, but it's not a necessity item

5. Ask the Quakers

God, I don't mean to be glib, but the "Why do we need God?" question exasperates me. It makes me feel like I'm back in a law office, and someone is engaging in what we lawyers call "burden shifting."

One of the reasons I love philosophy so much is that philosophers are taught to approach the great questions with a completely open mind. There's no burden of persuasion placed on one side more than any other. Nobody puts a thumb on the scale.

The world of religion is different. Traditionally, the burden was shifted to anyone who would deny the truth of Scripture. And now, in secular circles, people have just replaced the old orthodoxy with a new one. Just as burden shifting was once used to affirm Your existence, now it is used to *deny* that You exist. We who would come to Your defense must now bear the burden of proving with almost mathematical certainty that You are a human need.

Honestly, I'm not sure I could provide that proof for anything but water. Certainly not truth. Many of us seem to thrive without that.

If I were to try to argue that You are a human need, and if I were to back that up by talking about all the ways that Your name has inspired me, I'd surely be told that You are nothing more than a fiction and that I was just using Your name as a crutch. Perhaps my secular interlocutors wouldn't begrudge me my "crutch." Perhaps they'd even acknowledge that we all need crutches. But then they might say that they prefer their own, because their crutches come with less baggage. I can just hear them saying "I'll take gardening over God any time!"

So, when people ask "Why do you *need* God?" maybe they are really asking a different question:

> Given that the name "God" is a fiction and at best nothing more
> than a crutch, and given all the divisiveness and oppression that
> crutch has caused, can't we please stop using it?

For some reason, I don't find that question nearly so exasperating as the shorter one. It doesn't seem so rhetorical. It invites a verbal answer, not a sigh.

My answer is this book.

⊷

Let me get back to Webster's definition of "friend." Perhaps I was too quick to gloss over a problem.

According to Webster's, a friend is "something thought of as like a friend in being helpful, reliable, etc." Your *name* is a "something." But I wouldn't say the same for *You.* A "something" is part of a class known as "things." You transcend that class. So, does that mean "Your name" can be my friend, but "You" cannot?

Some Jews take especially seriously the difference between speaking about You and speaking about Your name. Whenever they refer to their God in conversation, they use the Hebrew term *HaShem* ("The Name"). I like that term. It reminds me of Your transcendence and of the uses and limits of language.

You are, and shall always remain, a mystery. For every single thing we understand about You, there are infinitely more we cannot. No set of words, be it in Hebrew or English, could possibly do You justice. Even HaShem.

And yet, just as we feel compelled to praise You, we feel compelled to name You. As verbal creatures, if we can't name You, we can't fully encounter You, and that, for many of us, is not an option. So perhaps it is best to say that Your name is our eternal friend and You are our eternal mystery.

But between friends, sometimes we don't need to be so precise with our words. You are still the one I am attempting to address—not some human conception, some mere moniker, but You, in the flesh, in the spirit, in the dimensions beyond flesh and spirit.

You, God, are my friend—or at least I will continue to think of You that way. Maybe I am anthropomorphizing a bit. Then again, the only way to avoid doing that completely is to address You with no words at all. When it comes to any of my friends, I'm just not willing to do that. And I *certainly* wouldn't be willing to do that with You.

I remember what life was like when I was in grade school and college, and Your name wasn't in my life. Once it was, I never again lacked for a sense of purpose. Or a companion.

That's what I call a friend.

CHAPTER 15

The Commander
of My Conscience

MY LORD.

I do so love to refer to You by that name.

Whenever I'm alone and I say the words "My Lord," I am comforted. In other contexts "Lord" sounds so stultifying. But not in this context. Not to me.

It gives me comfort to think that this world is a unity—one You both propel and pervade. When I call You "Lord," I proclaim Your infinite power over all that exists, and I cast out the notion that we human creatures are lost souls in a sea of unconnected creatures.

By calling You "Lord," I feel more like part of a brotherhood. We are all brothers (and sisters) *in You.*

A lord demands. A lord commands. In other contexts, commands can be an imposition. Not with You. It is invigorating to tackle Your commands.

Any other lord may inspire more fear than love, but not You. I serve You out of love.

The more I think about You, the more my fears subside. And when I contemplate my errors and limitations, I accept them, for I accept my own humanity.

So, I appreciate the name "Lord" because it can both comfort and invigorate. Mostly, though, I appreciate it because You should be praised in a manner that is worthy of Your name, and I know of no title more honorable than "Lord."

THE COMMANDER OF MY CONSCIENCE 149

Believe me, I realize how often this term has been used to refer to men of "nobility." For some, it inevitably has both sexist and elitist connotations. Perhaps if I were from England, I might feel the same way. But I'm not, and I don't.

Here in America, those human lords don't exist. In fact, many if not most of us are put off by the whole royal enterprise. We're small-d democrats and small-r republicans, and we don't believe anyone has a right to confuse his own family with You. Who are they to usurp Your proper title?

Are these human lords omnificent (unlimited in creative power)? Are they ultimately responsible for all that exists? Spare me.

By calling You "Lord," I remind myself of how little I care for caste systems among human beings, and how I recognize only one true caste system. You are at the top, and the rest of us—and I mean every solitary finite form in your infinite realm—are lower down.

Together, we may comprise You, or at least one facet of You, but there is only one of You, my Lord, and we are so tiny and insignificant by comparison.

"Lord" is a beautiful word. You own it, not the aristocrats. Those posers are not going to stop me from using it any more than the fundamentalists are going to stop me from calling You "God."

⊖

Still, it is undeniable that most people who address You as "Lord" tend to be much more conservative than I am when it comes to religion. They associate Your Lordship with Your supposed power as a lawgiver. I have serious issues with that.

I don't deny *that* You command. What I'd put at issue is *how* You command.

Traditionally, clerics derive Your commands from Scripture—books written centuries or millennia in the past.

Many clerics attribute the statements in those books to You—and not in the way that I attribute *all* statements to You, but in a much more direct way. They view those books as the products of supernatural divine intervention. In that regard, I stand with the atheists.

To the ultra-Orthodox Jew, the laws of the Torah are Your laws. Supposedly, You have given the rabbis the power to interpret them, but they remain laws just the same.

So, for example, the Torah says, "If a man lies with a male as he lies with a woman, both of them have committed an abomination. They shall surely be put to death. Their blood shall be upon them" (Lev 20:13). Fortunately, rabbis don't interpret that passage at face value—they don't require us to put gay people to death. But ultra-Orthodox rabbis do take that, and other passages, as grounds for proclaiming that homosexual conduct is sinful. As a result, to this day, many Jews feel commanded by You to disparage such conduct.

As for me, I don't feel that You have proscribed homosexuality. That's because my views of Your commandments are more the product of my own conscience than the Torah. And yes, God, I realize how ridiculous and morally relativistic my words would sound to some people.

How can I say both that You command me and that my conscience is my ultimate guide? Isn't that a blatant inconsistency, not to mention an insult to Your Lordship?

I don't see it that way, because I don't view You as a cosmic law giver who descends from the heavens and verbally dictates right from wrong.

Ultimately, we human beings are making up the rules of the road as we go along. We ourselves decide what to include in our books. We decide which of those books are deemed to be Scripture. We decide how to interpret Scripture. We decide when to put aside Scriptural passages altogether.

In other words, in those situations when Scripture doesn't hit the spot, we decide whose teachings do. Sometimes—perhaps even most of the time—the teachings come from our own reflections.

But that doesn't mean You're out of the picture as a commander.

Whenever I have a big decision to make, I think of You. Whether it's a business decision or a personal one, if the stakes are high, I will invoke Your name.

Immediately, the stakes are raised even higher. And yet I feel more equipped to deal with them.

Why? Because whenever I call out to You in the context of, say, an ethical dilemma, I agree to serve as Your partner—to follow the path that *serves* Your world and *honors* Your name. And I'm hardly alone in this regard: whenever people truly feel that they're on that path, they can't help but gain in confidence and resolve. They are determined to do the right thing for the sake of Your name.

Sometimes this is a good thing, and sometimes it's a tragic thing.

If our moral compass is functioning, we will feel *commanded* to nurture, to conserve, and to assist those who need our help. If our moral compass is broken, we might feel commanded to engage in conduct that is hurtful and perhaps even violent. In either case, though, if we sincerely are moved by Your Lordship, we will feel commanded.

I fully subscribe to the notion that religion makes wise people do blessed things and foolish people do horrible things. And it all comes back to the power of feeling commanded to do what we feel is best. Once we acknowledge Your Lordship, as soon as we decide what is right and what is wrong, we no longer feel free to choose either path.

↭

Which brings me back to Scripture.

Do I feel compelled to follow its every word? No.

Do I feel compelled to buy into every traditional interpretation of the rabbis? Or for that matter the imams or priests? No, no, and no.

But do I feel free to treat the Torah as just another human-authored book? Again, absolutely not.

You inspire me—You command me—to show respect. Respect not only for those who are alive today but also for those who came before us, and especially those who have built traditions that have stood the test of time.

My ancestors are especially worthy of my respect. It's that gratitude thing again.

You can count me in with those who deny that the Torah is *Your* book about humankind. Yet as a Jew, I won't go so far as to deny it is *our* book about You. I joke that Spinoza's *Ethics* is my Bible, but really, I have but one Bible. The Torah. The book I started reading in its abridged form when I was just a small child. The one that is largely responsible for forging my moral compass. The one that, for its time, is an extraordinarily progressive piece of literature—anything but the reactionary tract that some people today make it out to be.

When it comes to the prohibitions in the Torah, I must admit that I *do* try to follow them, unless there is a really good reason not to. I won't let that book make me a homophobe or a sexist, but all else equal, I would like to honor my people's traditions.

Long before I became a vegan back in the early nineties, I stopped eating pork and shellfish. There was no ethical reason I could think of for continuing to eat chicken but not those foods, and yet that is exactly what I did. I felt compelled to honor the Torah—both for Your sake, but even more, for the sake of my ancestors who worked so hard to praise Your name.

Of course, the Torah's greatest value is in its ethical spirit, not its ritual injunctions. That's the case with any great scriptural text. That's what makes those texts so awe-inspiring and allows us to speak of them and You in the same sentence, without feeling completely insane.

I have no problem saying the words: *Your* Torah. Or, for that matter, *Your* Bible. *Your* Qur'an. *Your* Vedas. The love of Your name has so profoundly inspired each of those works. How can we not treat them with respect?

Whenever I encounter conduct that not only is contrary to my modern sensibilities but is also prohibited by Scripture, the commandment takes on double significance.

Thou shall not kill.

Thou shall not steal.

Thou shall not bear false witness against your neighbor.

Thou shall not commit adultery.

I hear it loudly and clearly: these are commandments, not mere guidelines.

It is my honor to respect them for the rest of my life.

CHAPTER 16

My Beloved

I REMEMBER A RECENT flight home from a business trip. I felt too antsy to read, so I gazed outside at the clouds in the sky and the earth below. It was a typical airplane scene on a daytime flight. Only I decided not to make it typical. I imagined myself as a man from the sixteenth century who had been whisked away from his own time and placed onto my seat.

Suddenly, my airplane window revealed a series of miracles. The cloud formations looked more magnificent than Michelangelo's David. And as I glanced further down to the farmland on the ground, I felt as if this was the view from heaven.

Those kinds of impressions are always available to people—all we'd have to do is use our imaginations. We need only walk down the street, picture ourselves as visitors from the sixteenth century, and suddenly, the cars on the road would become more spectacular than flying carpets.

If we wanted to, we could live most of our lives in awe of Your majestic world. Or, if we preferred, we could live out most of our lives basking in Your unity.

We could be meditating, contemplating, singing Your praises . . . all we have to do is decide to leave our beehives, and happiness awaits.

And yet, most of us don't leave our beehives, do we, God? In fact, we spend most of our time working—incessantly striving to produce goods or services that others will find useful. Sometimes we succeed, but many times we fail. And the fruits of failure can be as miserable as that plane ride was enchanting.

I am reminded of one of my own favorite ways of coping with failure. It's not a conscious thing I do; it's a purely visceral reaction to having had an awful day.

Upon waking up, I get out of bed and go to the bathroom. And there I am, sitting on the toilet of all places and saying out loud: *I hate myself.* I'm saying it to You, too. *I hate myself.* And though I don't verbalize anything else, I can tell You exactly what I'm thinking: *I hate myself. Take that, God!*

I call it a ritual because I've performed it many times during the course of my life. But I don't do it with a rote mindset. At those moments, I'm totally disgusted with what I've done or haven't done and feel like memorializing that emotion.

The problem is, no sooner do I come to grips with the self-loathing than I snap out of the whole exercise with laughter. I'm laughing *with* myself, not just *at* myself. Because even though I realize how crazy I'm being, I also realize it's the human condition to be crazy sometimes, just as it is to fail.

God, it's never dawned on me until today how much of a role You've played in that silly little toilet ritual. I've always thought I was talking to myself alone. Only now do I realize I was mostly talking to You.

I was saying, *Lord, I need some slack.*

I'm not so much saying *I hate myself* as *I've been hating myself and it needs to stop.* I can't justify hating myself for any length of time, because even when I fail in life, I am still just doing my part *in You.*

Strike that, I *can* justify hating Hitler and he's part of You. But when I contemplate that idea, I start to hate him less and find myself looking at him the way I'd look at a cancer cell.

I've lost some friends to cancer. But I don't hate the cells themselves. I just feel sad about my friends.

And besides, I'm no Hitler. If You'll pardon the redundancy, I'm just another flawed human being. To put it differently, I'm just another flawed and yet awe-inspiring collection of microscopic particles and macroscopic organs that collectively is capable of asking metaphysical questions, answering complex mathematical equations, manipulating a wide range of technological devices, and engaging in intricate and intimate forms of communication with others of my kind.

If a man born several thousand years ago were to meet me and see the way I live, he would be as amazed as I would be if I encountered a levitating pig.

So I guess that makes me a walking, talking miracle—surely someone worthy of a little slack.

What's fair is fair, right? I definitely cut You slack. And that's in spite of the fact that You are responsible for far more damage than any of us can ever do.

We could hate You for all Your deadly earthquakes and tsunamis. And for all Your genocides. Yes, those are Yours, too.

We could hate You for our mortality as individuals. Or for the deaths of our parents, or worse yet, our kids.

We could hate You for how different You are from the omnibenevolent God of our children's books. As a Spinozist, I could also hate You for the fact that when I pray, I don't expect any consciousness outside of my own to be lovingly processing the words. I could hate You, in other words, for not being a Cosmic Santa Claus.

Your world is no more ideal than I am. So, should I get up every morning, sit on the toilet, and say, *I hate You God*?

Never.

⦿

For some reason, *I hate myself* rolls off the tongue, even now when I'm not engaging in visceral self-loathing. But *I hate You God* sounds absurd. For starters, it is disrespectful. But more than that, it rings false. I don't hate You. I don't ever hate You. I can't even imagine it.

Even when I learned that my father died—when I keened like a wolf and one of my daughters had to cover her ears with her pillow despite being on a different floor of the house—even then I didn't hate You.

Why should I? Wasn't it You who was responsible for giving me such a wonderful father? Wasn't I blessed to have him around for decades of my life?

It's arguably crazy to hate ourselves, but it's *definitely* crazy to hate You. We owe You everything, and given the choice of everything or nothing, I'll take it all—the good, the bad, and the ugly.

I use that phrase a lot at the office. When I'm talking to a corporate defense lawyer, I tell them that when it comes time to interview their clients, I want to hear the good, the bad, and the ugly (which is also known as "the truth, the whole truth, and nothing but the truth"). But no sooner do I say that than I realize that I don't expect to hear them tell "nothing but the truth," even when they're under oath. I expect perjury like an Eskimo expects snow. Sometimes I'm pleasantly surprised, but all too commonly, when the going gets tough, the witnesses lie.

I hate that. But when it happens, I don't hate You.

I listen to political candidates bloviate about helping the disadvantaged. Then I watch as they take power, blow off the ideals they espoused as candidates, and spend the rest of their tenure raising money, pointing fingers, and failing to stick their necks out for the needy.

I hate that. But when it happens, I don't hate You.

Yes, I hold You fully responsible for those lying witnesses and those bloviating politicians. I hold You responsible for everything—for all the choices we make. And yes, we all screw up a lot, and You share in the responsibility. I just don't hate You when it happens.

The question is, why not? And the answer comes back to gratitude.

It says volumes that when we think about the problems with this world, we think first and foremost about the ubiquity of death. And yet, what is death but the termination of our ability to enjoy Your world? What is death but the mere absence of the life we love so much? Even those who kvetch incessantly tend to opt for life.

I can talk until I'm blue in the face about the tragedies of Your world. In the end, though, I can't help but fall in love with what I see.

Is it perfect? No. Yet it is blindingly captivating just the same.

Not just the clouds or the cars, but also the plants, the animals, and yes, the people.

I see in every human face a brother or a sister. And in every tree or dog, I see family too.

For all of the world's shortcomings, I love it just the same. I need only breathe Your air to remind myself of that.

CHAPTER 17

My Challenge

PLEASE LORD. SAVE ME from Your Followers.

It's kind of a catchy little saying isn't it? In one form or another, people have turned it into songs, T-Shirts, bumper stickers, you name it. And it certainly strikes a chord with me.

Who can deny that Your name has been invoked to justify starting needless wars? Or strip people of their rights? Or divide societies into "us" versus "them"? Or encourage young minds to devalue secular learning?

Please, Lord. Save me from all of that.

The thing is, though, it's not just "Your followers" I want to be saved from. It's Your enemies too—and I'm not so much concerned about the "New Atheists," who are still a pretty fringe group, but about the increasing number of people who get bored with even the briefest mention of Your name.

They remind me of the kids in a classroom who always seem to be yawning. They make the rest of us sleepy. And that's what's happening with You; You're becoming the subject of a class in which one student after another is tuning out. It doesn't matter if the teacher is dynamic and the lesson masterful. When we see other kids yawning, we lose interest. It's human nature.

Perhaps the problem is that for so many centuries, You were quite literally "the Man." We turned You into just another one of us, except that we were impotent and real and the god we created was omnipotent and mythical.

Then, our science and technology grew more advanced, and we became the gods of the earth. Obsessed as we were by our technological prowess, we lost the taste for mythology. And when our preachers continued to teach us mythology about You rather than literal truth, we began to treat You like an antique that has lost its original function.

Some people have come to leave Your name in their basements and only trot it out on special occasions. For others, Your name has become nothing more than an annoyance, a reminder that part of the reason why whole cultures refuse to enter the modern age is because of all the nonsense that's been said about You.

Either way, my society is now going through a transitional phase. We are overreacting to a time when Your name got in the way of our progress. And as long as we keep overreacting, we'll lose the chance to progress even further based on progressive religious principles.

I want to speed up that transition. My goal isn't to thin the herd of atheists, because I believe in free speech and ideological diversity. But I am tired of seeing You treated like a third wheel. I can't stand it when Your name is mentioned, and people just scoff, as if to say, "Wake me up when you want to talk about something that matters."

That's lousy enough conduct from a kid in a classroom. But when I contemplate millions of adults behaving that way, it feels like a bad dream.

↩

My challenge is clear:

- Avoid becoming one of those who gives religion a bad name.

- Help to usher in an era when we can talk about You at least as curiously as we could talk about, say, the stories in a newspaper.

- Convince skeptics that intelligent people can fall in love with You without compromising their integrity.

- Work to ensure that Your name is a force for unity and not division.

Unfortunately, I can't expect any supernatural help from You. I know this is a job for my fellow travelers and me to figure out on our own.

I only wish the job didn't seem so Herculean.

You see, a challenge like this only gets met when enough of us can agree on the goals, which is a tall order given how divisive Your name has become. When unified, my country used to win war after war. When divided, my planet can't even wage a battle against climate change.

But that fight must continue. And so will my fight to bring religion into the twenty-first century, where it belongs.

⭗

God, it looks like we've reached the point where it's time to end this monologue.

I have to speak directly to my own kind. But first, allow me one final moment with You.

A moment of silence. Void of ideas. Void of passion. Void of desire.

Just joy. Gratitude. And the feeling of being blessed. Eternally blessed.

PART III

GOD IN THE FIRST PERSON

So, are you persuaded yet that we can indeed have a meaningful relationship with God without fabricating the Divine in the image of man? I find it insulting both to God and humankind to suggest that we are only capable of worshipping a model of the human ideal. But I would concede that once we dislodge this idea, we threaten the foundation of the traditional Western faiths. It is no wonder that many defenders of those faiths fight hard to persuade the rest of us that their own model of God is the only one worthy of *The Name*.

The churchmen and women who teach that salvation can only come to those who view God in human-like terms are not without their ammunition. They are certainly correct that no language is as emotionally evocative as mythological language. Only those of us with the most stunted of imaginations do not love a good myth. Myths can open our eyes, broaden our minds, or moisten our tear ducts, and this applies whether their subject is a young lady, a swan, or the Deity of deities. But there is no justification for taking anthropomorphic myths about God and selling them as literal truths. Besides, we need our conception of God to pass the test of *ultimacy*, and when we look at the behavior of human beings over time, ultimacy would be the last word that comes to mind.

I would never contend that *The Ultimate Synthesis* is the "one true God," any more than I'd extend that description to the Lord of the Bible.

To me, all human characterizations of God inherently rest on some-what shaky grounds. How can any person—a mere creature living on a small planet for a limited amount of time—profess to have acquired indisputable answers about the ultimate questions of reality? Talk about chutzpah! What I was attempting to do in Part I was simply to describe one man's lifetime search for a conception of God that is both emotion-ally gratifying and intellectually honest. If that conception works for you, I am glad. If you can do better, I am even happier.

By the end of Part I, I had hoped to explain why I find *The Ultimate Synthesis* compelling on multiple levels as a conception of God. I tried to demonstrate its appeal to a seeker of truth. And I argued that despite all the claims of traditional theologians that only a human-like God can be meaningfully *encountered* as a Thou, *The Ultimate Synthesis* can satisfy us emotionally in many of the same ways as the Old God. The best way to make this latter point, however, isn't to argue it. I had to *show* you. That became the central goal of Part II of this book.

You will not see me claim that worshipping *The Ultimate Synthesis* should satisfy every human heart. We are too diverse a species for any-one to make such a claim about any conception of God. What I can say, though, is that my own relationship with *The Name*, which is so vital in providing meaning to my life, is only possible because I could ground it in what seems to be a reasonable religious philosophy. Otherwise, I may have given up on faith a long time ago. And while I may be more philosophical than most members of our text-messaging, multi-task-ing, video-gaming society, I fall within that ever-increasing group of people who respond with *extreme* skepticism towards grandiose claims, including the claims of religion. We have all heard too many ideologues of various stripes offer sweeping visions of reality that have turned out to be dangerous. As a result, when it comes to receiving religious mes-sages, we are shell-shocked. And this is why even non-philosophers are deciding that if religious claims are going to touch our hearts, they must first appeal to our heads. It is my hope that the idea of God as *The Ultimate Synthesis* can at least satisfy that criterion, and once it is entertained, can perhaps gratify some of our emotional needs as well.

That leaves us with one final "voice" to encounter. This is the voice that, from the standpoint of traditional religion, is nothing short of sacrilegious. From here on in, I will speak about God in the first person—specifically, in the first person *plural*. I will address you, my reader, as fellow parts or expressions of a panentheist God. No longer will I try to demonstrate that God appropriately can be conceived as *The Ultimate Synthesis*. For purposes of discussion, I will simply assume that you already buy into that belief and will turn our attention to exploring its ramifications. How might it affect the way we see ourselves as individuals and as members of the human family? How might it impact our views on human immortality? How might it influence the way we interact with other people who think about God differently, or not at all? And how might this conception of God impact our fundamental ethical values?

By exploring these questions, I hope to demonstrate what it means to take seriously a type of panentheism that honors not only God but also human beings. Let us begin by exploring how this philosophy develops our sense of self.

CHAPTER 18

Finding Our Own Place in God

WELCOME TO "GOD IN the first person," or, in other words, "God as We."

That may sound crazy to you, not to mention presumptuous, preposterous, conceited, and last but not least, blasphemous. Do you think you're reading the words of God? Do you feel like God today? What kind of god starts each day going to the bathroom?

One of the things I loved most about the children's book my aunt and uncle bought me roughly half a century ago is how it appeared to clarify our own place in the world relative to God's. I saw myself as Danny Spiro, a little Jewish boy from the suburbs. By contrast, God, the Most High, was aware of what was going on in my town and every other, even though He resided in heaven. There was nothing in that book that could possibly confuse such a message. God and I were fundamentally separate. Back when I was under the spell of that book, if someone had told me to think of God in the first person, I would have laughed.

I continue to maintain that we human beings, either as individuals or collectively, cannot be equated with God. But if I am correct that one way of viewing *The Name* is through the infinite forms that God expresses, we are obviously among those forms and can thus be viewed as divine expressions. Moreover, if another perspective on God is through the indivisible, inexhaustible, inscrutable Ground of Being—the power-generator that underlies all the world's forms—then yes, that power resides within and impels each of us. We both partake of God and are parts of God. In each of those senses, we are divine.

In fact, despite being limited forms, we play an integral role in the Divine. It is through us that God lives and breathes. It is through us that God loves and learns. And if indeed the core of God is pure power, do we not share in that too? Do we not summon incredible energy every instant that we take a step—or for that matter, every time we wake up and go to the bathroom?

Yes, my friends, there is no God except the one whose breath we breathe, whose laughter we laugh, whose tears we shed, and whose thoughts we think. That makes us divine beings.

It also makes us related to each other in the most intimate sense possible. I like to look at human beings as members of the same family, but truly, that doesn't do justice to our interrelationship. Do you view your own arms or legs as "members of the same family"? Is that the way you see the relationship between your own heart and your mind? Of course not, you see them as part of the same *person*. And from the standpoint of the eternal, the deepest standpoint of any, we are all just that—part of the same "person," which in this case, is God.

Traditionally, religious people have been moved to act altruistically because they've seen themselves as subjects of a great King who personifies the ideal of giving to others. This King is merciful, generous, just, compassionate, etc., and it is said to be our job to emulate him. By contrast, if we worship *The Ultimate Synthesis,* we are instead moved to act virtuously for an altogether selfish motive. We seek to help one another in the same way that our heart wishes to help our head and vice versa. We don't need to be admonished to "do unto others the way we would have them do unto us" because, from the deepest possible standpoint, there is no "other." There is only the God in which we and our fellow travelers find ourselves.

If we are all just worms in the same bloodstream, then why would we ever want to harm others? All that would accomplish is to harm our own bloodstream.

Here's the problem, though: that whole discussion takes place on a theoretical level. We need to be honest with ourselves. It is easy enough to acknowledge as a theoretical matter that God is in us, we are in God, and all other discrete forms of Being are part of this same divine bloodstream. But as a *practical* matter, that is hardly the standpoint that rules our day-to-day lives, now is it? It certainly is not the standpoint that holds sway in the good old US of A. As an American, I must say that any perspective that sees all discrete forms as part of the same "person" is completely alien to the way we are raised to think. We Americans pride ourselves on our sense of individuality. We separate ourselves from the "herd" at every turn, which is one reason why Nietzsche is so popular in our universities. We make movies about vigilante cops who don't play by the rules, lionize entrepreneurs who would rather strike out on their own than work for "the Man," customize our license plates (mine says "SPINOZA"), and tattoo our backsides. You could say that we don't mind feeling an ultimate sense of separation from other people or other things. In fact, we relish it.

The American in me will always look at people as separate forms who crave our own sense of individuality and define each other by the unique ways that we express ourselves. But the panentheist in me is duty bound to recognize that we are mere parts or expressions of God, and that is the sense in which we are as closely linked to each other as our heart is to our mind. Wisdom involves keeping both of these perspectives in our heads at the same time. We are separate in a very profound sense, and yet in an even deeper sense, we are one in God. So yes, it would be appropriate to say that the latter perspective points to our "greater" sense of self, and the other, more conventional, perspective points to our "lesser" sense of self. But the use of those terms must never prevent us from celebrating our divine status *as well as* our individuality.

Perhaps it is best to say that we should have two senses of self, one of which is deeper than the other, but neither of which is dispensable. We are unique beings, and we absolutely must nurture our uniqueness. And yet because we are also integral parts of the divine fabric and emanate from the divine source, we can legitimately think of ourselves as divine beings. The more we reflect on these two senses of self, the more we will see that rather than being inconsistent, they are quite complementary.

⊷

To begin the task of embracing these two perspectives, let us keep in mind that we are not just *any* form or expression of the divine power. As human beings, we are literally king-makers, slave-owners, climate-changers, and rocket-launchers. Our brains have enabled us to summon such incredible energy that we are largely capable either of wreaking chaos on an entire planet of organisms or of building a relatively harmonious world. That is another way of saying that while all discrete forms, organic and inorganic, are parts of God, we human beings are *especially important* parts of God. It is quite an honor, but it is also a source of responsibility.

As an example of how that status creates duties for humankind, consider our relationship with what we call the "environment." Thousands of years ago, my ancestors decided to characterize that relationship in a very bold way through the imprimatur of the Torah. It was said that this planet was donated by God to human beings, to serve not simply as its custodians, but rather as its rulers. Take the words of the psalmist: "The heavens belong to the Lord, but the earth He gave over to man" (Ps 115:16). Or better yet, start with Genesis: "And God said, 'Let us make man in our image, after our likeness. They shall rule the fish of the sea, the birds of the sky, the cattle, the whole earth, and all the creeping things that creep on earth'" (Gen 1:26). Spinoza, the renowned heretic, actually went still further in his chauvinism. He wrote that "whatsoever there is in Nature external to man, regard for our own advantage does not require us to preserve it, but teaches us to preserve or destroy it according to its varying usefulness, or to adapt it to our own use in whatever way we please."[1] That is what we lawyers call owning land in fee simple—meaning with an uncontested right to it, limited only by the powers of the government. In this case, though, we own every government.

Say what you want about the Bible, but when it comes to our species' rule over the environment, it has been prophetic. We have taken charge throughout the earth, both on land and in the sea. Even whales, which are believed to possess tremendous intelligence, live at our mercy. Recently, we discovered that we are doing considerable damage to our planet's climate, and yet we seem relatively unperturbed by that prospect. What modest concerns we do have only appear to involve our conduct's impact on future *human* beings. As to the impact of climate change on the earth's other animals or plants, we generally view that as a secondary concern at best.

If we take the Bible as the word of God, our attitude is perfectly understandable. One of the great things about ruling over land is that you can take liberties with it. We alone determine whether to concern ourselves with non-human beings; they don't get a vote.

Now, consider how our perspective changes once we start worshipping God as *The Ultimate Synthesis*. The lines of separation between ourselves and other earthly organisms fade more into the background, and the overarching unity takes center stage. At that point, our "fee simple" rights over the earth fall by the wayside.

1. Spinoza, "Ethics," Part IV, Appendix, #26, 361.

If, in fact, we bear more-than-just-familial ties to all the plants and animals we encounter, how can we be so indifferent to causing their suffering or death? That would be an attitude of absolute masochism, which is the height of insanity. In short, shouldn't we realize that rather than giving us carte blanche in our dealings with the environment, our ability to dominate the earth's other organisms morally compels us to serve them as holy *trustees*?

Some might claim that this kind of environmentalism threatens to sap us of our individual liberties—allegedly, it dampens the extent to which we can utilize the environment to "seize the day" for ourselves. But that is a shortsighted approach, for we need only to redefine what it means to seize the day. Rather than being seen as something we exploit, the environment becomes something we nurture, and it remains a source of challenges for us to meet *as individuals*. We simply ask ourselves different questions: not what can the environment do for us, but how can we serve the environment in a way that personally gives us joy? How can we utilize our own particular talents and interests to make a difference for individual plants and animals as well as for ecosystems? And how can we as individuals reach the minds of those fellow human beings who are most responsible for wreaking havoc on the environment in the name of the modern god known as the economy? Once we start asking ourselves these questions, it is clear that we can be both individualists and environmentalists without any cognitive dissonance whatsoever.

Seen from the perspective of the Old Time Religion, environmentalism is a "charitable" movement. Seen from the perspective of the philosophy advocated in this book, it is a religious imperative grounded in self-interest and sanity. By dishonoring that commandment we spurn the Divine, for we would have abused legions of God's other blessed earthly expressions, which are really just parts of our own greater self. Yes, we are more mentally powerful than many if not all of them, and in that sense, more "Godlike." But quite literally, we are all "in this" together—humankind, flora, and fauna.

To ignore the welfare of all non-human beings would make no more sense than to care deeply for our arms while paying no attention whatsoever to our legs. You don't have to be a doctor to know how ridiculous that is. To anyone who worships God as *The Ultimate Synthesis*, ignoring the interests of plants and animals is equally absurd. And irreligious.

꧐

To be a human being who worships *The Ultimate Synthesis* involves having not one but two healthy senses of self. And this is made possible by knowing the appropriate roles of humility and pride. Let us now turn our attention to these critical concepts.

In the first chapter of this book, we considered how the whole religious enterprise is antithetical to humility. It requires chutzpah, not humility, to even speculate about ultimacy, let alone to have faith in a particular conception of the *Ultimate*. Nevertheless, once we allow ourselves the freedom to develop convictions on this topic, humility becomes especially important. And indeed, it is considered to be at the heart of the Old Time Religion.

As central as humility is to the worship of the biblical God, however, I would argue that it lends itself even more to the worship of *The Ultimate Synthesis*. The secret as to why this is can be found in contemplating the profundity of the gulf between our "lesser" finite selves and our "greater" self (God). In learning to appreciate the nature and magnitude of that gulf, we gain a window on what it means to be humble and why it is so crucial to our spirituality.

In its own way, each of the faiths of Abraham places humility at the very top of its pantheon of principles. In Judaism, it is said that Moses was the greatest of prophets, not because he was the wisest or most courageous, but because he was the most humble. Christianity teaches that the "meek shall inherit the earth" and elevates to divine status a man who was humbled in the worst way possible—stretched out on a cross in agony. As for Islam, that word itself refers to submission or surrender. And in fact, five times every day, Muslims kneel and prostrate themselves on the ground before God. For all these faiths, the less humble you become, the less religious—at least in theory.

The fact remains, however, that many of the world's deepest problems can be laid at organized religion's door, and the direct cause has been the lack of humility among the faithful. It rings hollow to prostrate yourself one moment and then blow up a building the next, or to make the sign of the cross and then forcibly convert whoever doesn't join you.

I realize I'm preaching to the choir. Anyone reading this far into this book would surely decry religious intolerance or violence. But there is a broader point to be made involving the absurdity of calling ourselves humble when we use human features to depict the Lord of All Existence.

I'm not just talking about Christ's physical features; I'm also talking about the personality characteristics associated with Adonai and Allah (merciful, just, gentle, forgiving, generous, etc.). Yes, these traditions pay lip service to the idea that human beings are but tiny specks when compared to the divine glory. Yet in an attempt to make their faiths more accessible, traditionalists personalize God to the nth degree and utilize "his Word" to elevate the status of human beings as second only to God in the universe. Christianity, for example, conventionally uses the name of a flesh-and-blood human being to refer to the Son in the Holy Trinity, and Judaism teaches that because we have free will, we can rise to an even greater height than the angels. It is as if we are living in an aristocratic realm and have been tapped by the King of kings to be his dukes and duchesses.

The result is that religious traditionalists have commonly talked out of both sides of their mouths when it comes to the concept of humility. So why be surprised if, over the centuries and continuing today, so many people have invoked *The Name* to strip others of their human rights?

By contrast, the worship of *The Ultimate Synthesis* should never send such a blatantly mixed message when it comes to humility. While it is true that we can speak of God in the first person and assume the mantle of literally thinking God's thoughts and feeling God's feelings, let's not kid ourselves. When you contrast the status of *The Ultimate Synthesis* to that of the human being, what you get is day and night. Gone, in this philosophy, are the references to people being created in God's "image." Gone, too, are the suggestions that human beings occupy a penultimate place in the hierarchy of Being. In fact, our entire visible universe is treated as if it were merely one finite set of branches of an infinite and primarily mysterious tree.

Just consider the concepts that most readily come to mind when we conceive of *The Ultimate Synthesis*. Then consider what it means to be human. Do we really see ourselves as infinite, unlimited, or unbounded? Are those the characteristics to which we can aspire, like being merciful or generous? Of course not, and as we will discuss in the next chapter, this points to a bigger issue of how much more difficult it is to identify with *The Ultimate Synthesis* than with the Old God. But isn't that just as it should be? Do we really think we have much in common with the entirety of all existence or the force that powers it all? We tap into that divine Substance and occupy a tiny place in the whole. After that, the similarities end.

It is impossible to sincerely worship *The Ultimate Synthesis* and not be humbled by the experience. Not only is our personal sphere of influence seen as minute in relation to God, but all the dimensions of reality known to human beings are similarly conceived. Who are we to place ourselves at the center of the divine drama? The mere act of naming God is about as much hubris as we can proudly muster, and we do so mainly because we have become smitten with the idea of the *Ultimate*, not because of anything this God has said about us. Once we attempt to categorize or discuss God, as I have done in this book, we can't help but recognize that we're on shaky ground. And if anyone ever suggested that we should restrict other people's liberties because of God's verbal directives, we would have to respond, "That's your God, my friend. Not mine."

֎

The truth is that our humility should ultimately lead us not only to praise God, but also to nurture and respect ourselves as individuals. We must never forget that it's okay for a human being to be limited and flawed, for if we weren't, we'd be God. Oh, wait a minute; we are in God, so even God makes mistakes. And if that's the case, it surely must be okay to be human.

When it comes to respecting our individuality, however, the key isn't so much to maintain our humility, but to maintain its complement—our pride. Pride is generally considered in religious circles to be a vice. In Christianity, for example, it is said to be the worst of the seven deadly sins, for it is seen as the basis of the others. Simply consider the antithesis of the Christian God—the so-called "devil." What other characteristic do we possibly associate more with the devil than (false) pride?

Personally, I think of pride not as a vice, but a virtue. In fact, I see it as nearly as indispensable as humility for a healthy self-concept and a productive relationship with God. Maybe I have read too much Nietzsche, but the idea that the "meek shall inherit the earth" is, in my mind, neither accurate nor desirable.

That is not to deny, though, the depravity of excessive pride. Whenever it turns into arrogance, pomposity, or haughtiness, pride becomes worthy of its reputation. Nor is pride the best ambassador when it leads us to over-assess our own abilities. I'm reminded in this regard of the comments of that renowned, full-throated God-slayer, Richard Dawkins.

As part of his efforts to give pantheism its due, Dawkins quotes Einstein as follows: "To sense that behind anything that can be experienced there is something that our mind cannot grasp and whose beauty and sublimity reaches us only indirectly and as a feeble reflection, this is religiousness. In this sense I am religious."[2] To that Einstein quotation, Dawkins adds the following: "In this sense, I too am religious, with the reservation that 'cannot grasp' does not have to mean 'forever ungraspable.'"[3] By contrast, I have no trouble adopting Einstein's statement *without* Dawkins' reservation. For me, while human beings are parts of God, we are small enough parts that nearly all of our "greater self" must remain forever ungraspable. Anyone who honestly thinks that a human being could someday gain all of the secrets of the universe and beyond reminds me of the asylum resident who swears he's Napoleon.

I suppose we can all agree that if we must err, it is better to err on the side of humility than of pride. Then again, that's like saying that it is better to err on the side of caution; it doesn't mean that courage isn't a virtue simply because foolhardiness is a particularly dangerous vice. Just as we could generally use more courage, we could also generally use more pride. Everyone who seriously doubts whether pride is a virtue should ask herself the following question: Would you seriously want your daughter to marry someone who lacks an ample amount of pride? Only the most blatant religious hypocrite could possibly answer that question in the affirmative.

Why is pride so important to a healthy sense of self? Because without it, we lose the energy required to make an impact in a dynamic world. The "bubbling plenitude" is hardly a realm of ever-present harmony, and wherever we find conflicting interests, the meek shall inherit the hindmost. Thus, while it behooves us to be humble in relation to God, it is also appropriate to carry ourselves in human society with the proper sense of self-respect and dignity. Human beings who act like gods deserve our pity, not our servitude. And while it is important to work harmoniously within our society—which requires some degree of modesty—we each have a voice that needs to sing, and sometimes to sing loudly. If in the name of righteousness, that voice needs to clash with imperious or other self-important voices, so be it.

2. Dawkins, *God Delusion*, 19.
3. Ibid.

Moreover, even if we are not in conflict with anyone else, our pride is indispensable to summoning our full potential to achieve. It is pride that prevents us from giving in to weakness and impels us to explore our strengths; this isn't simply the pride in being "part of the divine whole" or "God's servant" but the pride in our own individuality. Even within a religious framework, that has an honored place at the table.

Still, just as it is indispensable in this philosophy to maintain a healthy sense of respect for ourselves in the narrow (or lesser) sense of the word self, so too is it important to be proud of our species and our planet. Consider the phrase "the world as we know it," and then reflect on just how rich that world is. The scientific discoveries? Ours. The technological advancements? Ours. The great musical and artistic compositions? Ours. The warm embraces between two consenting adults? Ours again. The other acts of human cooperation that we celebrate whenever we find them and often lament when we don't? Yes, they also resound to our credit. And if you ask me, the list is pretty darned impressive.

Of course, I cannot deny that in a very profound respect, we ultimately must attribute *all* of these accomplishments to God, but not in the sense that there must be an agency outside of us that willed us to have them, told us to have them, or even comprehends that we have them. We simply credit God in the sense that these accomplishments directly flowed from our hearts, minds, or hands, which are parts of God, and in the sense that God is the Ground of Being, including our own.

We can additionally take pride in the fact that human beings have been creators of meaning and morality. Those who worship the Lord of the Bible have celebrated the virtues associated with that Lord, like justice and mercy. We should all be proud of the extent to which human beings have taught one another to honor those biblical virtues. The system of morality developed by our ancient religions is nothing short of majestic. Indeed, the portrait of a super-human God in whom we have collected our most elevated hopes and dreams and who personifies the highest teachings of religious morality may well be our greatest creation as a species.

To the divine mystery, we owe the fact of existence, the hidden unity and power underlying existence, and an infinite number of things of which we know absolutely nothing and which, for the most part, shall forever remain ungraspable. To ourselves, we owe the thoughts, feelings, and deeds that make our lives meaningful and fulfilling and on which the fate of our planet largely rests. In other words, we must see ourselves and other human beings as potentially constructive and potentially destructive divine forms whose decisions matter profoundly, even to the health of God.

This all gets back to the Ken Wilber line about "giv[ing] to Caesar what is Caesar's, to Einstein what is Einstein's, to Picasso what is Picasso's, to Kant what is Kant's, and to Christ what is Christ's," only now we are making an even more fundamental point. We must give to our mysterious God everything, including what is ungraspable, and give to our humanity the responsibility for the world as we know it. As for those other things that Dawkins had in mind—that which we know nothing about but which our species will someday be able to understand and work with—we must accept whatever praise or blame is due when the time comes.

◈

Taking pride in our "lesser self" is important, as long as we are not deluded about the nature of our virtues and accomplishments. Yet it is also a blessing to be able to take pride—yes, pride—in our "greater self" (God). You might call that a panentheist's privilege. After all, we see ourselves as literally in God. Therefore, when we take note of the beauty of nature or of the infinite dimensions of mystery that transcend our perceptual world, we can't help but feel connected to such beauty, and that connection can be a source of pride.

From the standpoint of eternity, we may posit a perspective that is beyond time and in which everything is happening in the present. From that standpoint, the events of the world unfold just in the way they were meant to unfold, and we truly see ourselves merely as doing our part in a larger production—a part we could not help but play.

Such a perspective has given comfort to many, who might otherwise be inclined constantly to beat themselves up over their past (and likely future) mistakes. Yet the key to this perspective isn't to take on an attitude of fatalism, which is often used to justify a passive and unproductive lifestyle, but rather to rejoice in a largely mysterious God, the world as we know it and find it, and the unique roles that we each play in that world and in that God. The fatalist speaks as if human power is limited. But the person who rejoices in one's "greater self" celebrates human power and its intimate connection to the power of the Divine. Insofar as we partake in that power, we ourselves are infinitely great and must never forget that source of greatness, especially on those seemingly infinite number of occasions when our "lesser selves" let us down.

CHAPTER 19

Grappling with the Infinite
and Our Own Finitude

IF I EVER ENROLLED in a seminary, perhaps I could take a course called "How to Turn the Other Guy's Theology into a Strawman." Surely, I know one point that would be made on the first day of class: always contrast your theology with two other alternatives, present both of those alternatives as fundamentally imbalanced, and present your own as the golden mean. That's the way religious writers communicate. I must do it too. For some tragic reason, it seems to come with the territory.

Just this once, though, let me refrain from that sort of rhetoric and begin this chapter with a tribute to a theology that competes with my own. One reason why the traditional conception of God has dominated Western culture for so many centuries is because of how deftly it deals with the notions of finitude and infinity. That dichotomy, which poses such profound difficulties for my philosophy, is one of the calling cards of the Old Time Religion.

Let's begin with the way that the Abrahamic traditions speak about the human condition. One of the very first principles is to question our mortality. Yes, we are told that our bodies die, but we are also supposedly endowed with a "soul" that survives bodily death and that will be rewarded or punished based on our performance here on earth. That is a narrative with which anyone from a Jewish, Muslim, or Christian background is familiar. We Jews pride ourselves in being less afterlife-oriented than our Abrahamic cousins, but we can't deny that the closest thing our tradition has to an official canon—Maimonides' thirteen principles of faith—contains the following: "I believe with complete faith that the dead will be brought back to life when God wills it to happen."[1]

Immediately, the finitude of the human condition disappears. Whether or not we can trace the birth of our soul to a particular point in time, we are taught that the soul doesn't die but lives on forever. What's more, Muslims and Christians, and to a lesser extent, even Jews, are told that as long as we have lived in harmony with the directives of Scripture and its interpreters, that everlasting state should be a blissful one.

Once the Old Time Religion establishes our immortality, the traditional God becomes an easy character to identify with. For like us, he is both infinite in some respects and limited in others. We human beings would be seen as infinite in the respect that we live on forever—like a vector pointing forward in time and never reaching a terminus. And yet, we would be viewed as limited (and, in that sense, finite) insofar as our bodies occupy but a bounded space, and even our souls occupy a bounded amount of time, which began with the birth of our bodies. Similarly, the biblical God would be seen as infinite in the sense that the heavens are assumed to go on indefinitely, and he is said to exist throughout the past, present, and future. But yes, God would be also conceived as limited in that he is bounded by his creation, which is generally thought of as being outside of God. When traditionalists refer to the divine omnipresence, they mean that God's spirit can be found everywhere, not that God is composed of something as coarse as matter, which is clearly viewed as "beneath" the divine realm. What's more, to the extent people do terrible things, those offenses are traditionally attributed to them and *not* to God. He has made his divine bed in heaven; we are going to have to lie in ours here on earth.

Thus, much of the appeal of the Old Time Religion stems from the way that we share with God the status of being both infinite and yet limited. We have no trouble appreciating what it means when clerics praise God's infinite greatness, while at the same time absolving him of guilt— for it is easy enough to identify him only with the good and invoke his limitations to exclude him from the realm of evil. Further, we are able to view ourselves as the product of a God whose fundamental characteristics are mercy and charity precisely because he offers us the prize of infinite bliss if only we use our free will to follow the Scriptural code of conduct. So even though the traditional God is a transcendent God, he

1. Gurary, *Thirteen Principles*, 215.

bears profound similarities to the way we would imagine a super-human parent.

It should be obvious why this story has stood the test of time and is only recently being met with widespread skepticism. It is simple to understand, offers the greatest of possible rewards, and last but not least, doesn't introduce any characters to whom we have difficulty relating. Poifect!

By comparison, the philosophy espoused in this book must seem dreary. Allow me to summarize it in a relatively bleak form, as kind of a payback for any instances where I have inadvertently turned competing worldviews into a strawman.

God, under my philosophy, is not merely infinite but unbounded in all respects, whereas human beings are just the opposite. We are but finite expressions of an infinite God—limited presumably to a particular place and a particular time. Once we apply Occam's Razor, we feel compelled not to fabricate a "soul" that keeps us alive after our bodies die. Instead, we are faced with a reality in which absolute infinity pertains exclusively to the whole (God), and each human being is reduced to a miniscule morsel of that whole—"A poor player who struts and frets his hour upon the stage and then is heard no more," as Shakespeare might say.

Moreover, under my philosophy, all the things we hold dear—love, intelligence, will, desire—have been relegated to human beings and other limited expressions of God, rather than to the Ground of Being itself, which is the core of God. Thus, we have painted a picture in which the features of life that we have always deemed divine are, in fact, ephemeral, whereas that which is permanent refers to sheer, amoral energy. When considered at the greatest depths, God is like a functioning factory without any people in it. Perpetually active; perpetually soulless.

And it gets worse. This philosophy can be depicted not only as bleak, but also puzzling. For how do we explain the existence of an unbounded, soulless power-generator at the heart of the universe? Why is that more reasonable than envisioning that each person has an immortal soul? Are we not violating Occam's Razor in positing such a hidden, unifying force? Shouldn't we admit that all of our philosophizing has left us hopelessly confused, and leave it at that?

It is no wonder that the Old Time Religion has been around for thousands of years, and the perspective I am peddling remains—what is the euphemism?—*avant garde*.

෨

In coming to the idea of God as *The Ultimate Synthesis*, I deliberately strove to root out from my conception of the Divine traditional qualities that have been created in the human image. Obviously, that decision made God more difficult to identify with, but my voice of reason compelled it nonetheless. What's more, despite the recognition of the concrete element within *The Ultimate Synthesis*, this philosophy emphasizes at the core of the Divine the notion of mystery. For many, the centrality of this mystery is a source of frustration. But again, that was a price that our commitment to reason required us to pay. By contrast, for all its superficial appeal, the idea of the Old God is increasingly coming under attack as not merely unreasonable, but implausible.

Nietzsche misspoke when he said in the 1880s that he killed the Old God. But there are plenty of his fellow Europeans who would question whether that God survived another century. He was done in not by a philosopher with a pen, or by a small number of Nazis with their guns and gas chambers, but rather by the millions of Germans, Ukrainians, Poles, and other Europeans who, according to witnesses, went about their lives in the 1940s quite normally, seemingly unconcerned about the monstrous events taking place in their midst. Is it any wonder that so few Europeans today have kept the faith? Would you expect them to reflect on how so many of their own ancestors lived un-heroically through the Holocaust, and then subscribe to the heaven-and-hell narrative that was popular on their continent for so many centuries? And would you expect families like mine, who have lost large numbers of relatives in tragic fashion, to attribute genocides and other mass calamities to the will of a merciful God? Talk about implausible.

It is for reasons like these that I have searched for a philosophy more in keeping with our own experiences on this planet. And what I have found is a hard-headed philosophy that is arguably cold-hearted, in that its core consists of something mysterious, rather than a human-like figure. It might not be as gentle on the mind during funerals. But it does have its merits. And truly, as I hope you can see by now, its ramifications aren't as bleak as the above strawman would indicate.

To illustrate that point, let us address a topic that has been largely sidestepped until now: the question of whether we possess immortal souls. Some might proclaim that the Old Time Religion succeeds most where my philosophy succeeds least: in bestowing the joys of human immortality. Given the extent to which this topic has come to be associated with God and the relevance of religion generally, it is high time to address it head on.

If we refuse to assume that we each have individual, immortal "souls" because we lack any reason to infer such things, then yes, we would say from the perspective of our egos that our lives began with the birth of our bodies and will end when our bodies die. But again, that is the truth from a limited vantage point—one that is governed by a finite series of dimensions, including that of time.

Now, consider the same issue unburdened by human limitations. In other words, look at it from the standpoint of *The Ultimate Synthesis*. We now posit at the heart of reality a dynamic, transcendent unity. It exists in infinite dimensions that we cannot detect, as we are at the mercy of our limited perceptive apparatus. Through the benefit of language, members of our species have analyzed the dimensions of our world in various ways, but from the standpoint of the Divine, slicing and dicing misses the point. At the core of Being, all divisions are ultimately transcendable.

From this latter perspective, the "standpoint of eternity," there is more to existence than this visible universe, for Being exists in ways that are undetectable by our senses. And it is not unreasonable to assume that at some level, time itself can be transcended. From the standpoint of God, past, present, and future are a unity, together with space and all the other dimensions that are unknowable to human beings. In the words of Einstein, "People like us, who believe in physics, know that the distinction between past, present, and future is only a stubbornly persistent illusion."[2]

Considered, then, from the perspective of *The Ultimate Synthesis*, all of the divine forms, whether thoughts, bodies, or entities you and I cannot even begin to fathom, are forever being expressed in the eternal present. Far from being "mortal," each of us exists as integral parts of an eternal God. But just as we cannot imagine what it's like to exist outside of time, we cannot imagine what it means to have this type of immortality.

Yes, these are difficult concepts to grasp. Then again, that's the whole point. We are talking about the transcendent; if its secrets were easily grasped, it wouldn't be the transcendent. But the larger problem is that these are difficult concepts from which to derive emotional sustenance. And this is ultimately why the hard-headed rationalist, Spinoza, wrote

2. Albert Einstein, letter of condolence to Michele Besso's family, referenced in Dyson, *Disturbing the Universe*, 193.

that "A free man thinks of death least of all things; and his wisdom is a meditation of life, not of death."[3] The type of "immortality" we've discussed, if you want to call it that, pales in comparison with the portraits of the blessed hereafter that are set forth in Christian and Muslim literature.

Philosophies, as opposed to theologies, can be at their least comforting when they turn to the issue of death. The best they can offer is the unknown . . . and a vague sense that there are domains of reality that transcend the temporal and in which all of God's forms partake.

The good news, Spinoza would say, is that we're not required to think much about death. The blessedness offered by a philosopher is not a blissful afterlife, but rather the prospect of a fulfilling existence here on earth. Personally, I think this approach is the most compelling. In this book, I have espoused a philosophy that strips us of our faith in an eternal afterlife spent either luxuriating or burning, depending upon the will of a judging God, and leaves us instead with nothing but question marks. But it also beckons us to concentrate on what we *do* know a lot about—namely, how best to spend our living, breathing days in a righteous, fulfilling manner.

It may be impossible to "relate" to *The Ultimate Synthesis* in all the same ways that we can relate to the God-on-the-Cross or the God-who-parted-the-Sea. But that doesn't prevent panentheists from invoking *The Name* to forge a path on earth that is the opposite of bleak. In fact, at the point when our hearts are about to stop beating, we can legitimately rest content in the knowledge that we will have played a unique and constructive part in the great drama of divinity—the Play of Plays. Personally, that would give me more cause to smile than the promises of any paradise. Besides, I'd probably flunk out of paradise; there wouldn't be enough *Sturm und Drang* to keep me from being restless, and I'd be constantly admonished to stop complaining. I'll take my chances with the abyss.

3. Spinoza, "Ethics," Part IV, Prop. 67, 355.

CHAPTER 20

Bridging the Chasms by Embracing the Interfaith Movement

At bottom, I have argued, we are all in God, partaking in the mysterious divine power that underlies what is, was, and will be. This God isn't merely the One, but the One and Only. To the extent our senses point to a world of multiplicity—a "bubbling plenitude"—that is just the One God at work, expressing the divine power through infinite forms and dimensions. Ultimately, all is unity.

For me, religion is a vehicle to get in touch with that cosmic unity. You can imagine, then, just how frustrated I get when contemplating the divisive force that organized religion has become in our world. Even *The Name* has taken on divisive connotations. Various religious communities invoke it to explain how their own historical narrative, and no other, is the unvarnished truth. We hear them cite God as lawgiver, intervener in human history, and judge of the dead. Communities claim to possess his Word in its precise form. In fact, we are told that his Word can be expressed perfectly in one language, but not the others. (Traditional Jews say this about Hebrew, Muslims about Arabic.) And we have seen powerful groups engage in murderous "crusades," or crusades against the "Crusaders," all in God's name.

What in the name of hell has happened to us? I have tried to offer praise for our species as religious creatures—even suggesting that our portrait of the biblical God as an ethical role model is our single greatest feat. But look at the mess we've made of the Holy Name. We've turned lemonade into lemons!

This new millennium was ushered in by a monstrous act of religious-ly-inspired violence. Today, religious wars, whether they involve bombs, laws, or words alone, continue to captivate our attention. If you grow up today without the kind of book I received from my aunt and uncle, you might well decide to be done with the whole project of religion, lest it turn you into a Hatfield or a McCoy. I am reminded of an old Star Trek episode about a fictional character named Lazarus who was condemned to engage in hand-to-hand combat for all eternity with his twin from a parallel universe. How can I not think of Lazarus as a contemporary religious zealot? Are these zealots not eternally at war with one another? And do they not all bear a strong resemblance to one another, despite their differences in cultures and holy books?

Enough already. Those of us who care about God need to survey the war zone, take a breath, and devote ourselves to *unity*—not just in the Divine but in the domain of religion. I'm not advocating that we dissolve our religious communities and adopt a single religion. That's not throwing the baby out with the bathwater; that's replacing the bathwater with toilet water. Freedom requires religious diversity. But we must address the divisiveness just the same.

Earlier in this part of the book, I identified one powerful antidote: taking humility seriously. As soon as we realize that we are inherently ignorant when it comes to the deepest mysteries of God, religious dogmatism will wither away like Marx's communist state. And it is precisely such dogmatism that fuels the intolerance, fear, and hatred that has spread through the religious world like a cancer. If we were truly humble about our views, we would still engage in vigorous discussions, even disputes, but the wars of religion would end.

A second antidote, one that has become nearer and dearer to my heart during recent years, is the creation of a robust interfaith movement. I still consider myself Jewish; in fact, I routinely wear a yarmulke to all interfaith meetings, lest there be any question that I am coming (a) as a Jew and (b) as a religious Jew. Yet I no longer consider myself *just* a Jew. I am an *interfaith* Jew. Without that adjective, I would wonder if I were being part of the solution, or simply part of the scenery.

Those who are unfamiliar with the interfaith movement might not realize just how many bridges it is struggling to build. There are at present a variety of chasms that plague our ability to salvage *The Name* as a unifying force. We are divided between those who are religious and those who are not, between the "orthodox" and "progressive" members of each faith, and among adherents of different faiths. My Jewish-Islamic Dialogue Society has a number of atheist members; they come for secular reasons, such as the desire to see Jews and Arabs make peace with each other in the Middle East. I raise that example to show that interfaith activities can aspire to bridge various chasms, including some that are more political than religious in nature.

Truth be told, the interfaith movement is but a fledgling entity. The first significant ongoing interfaith activity occurred well into the twentieth century, for all previous attempts to gather representatives of different faiths never seemed to gather momentum. And even today, this movement remains but a small tributary off of the larger rivers of same-faith activity.

Professional clergy love to profess their support for the movement, yet when push comes to shove, their interfaith activities tend to be modest in relation to the time and energy they devote to "their own kind." That's quite understandable when you think about it. Clergy can expect considerable deference within their particular communities as a result of their superior knowledge base and their training in spiritual matters. By contrast, whenever they enter the interfaith arena, they lose control over the situation and become just like everyone else—crossing their fingers and hoping for the best. Plus, there is typically not a huge groundswell of demand for interfaith work on the part of the faithful. For most active congregants, religious activities are like comfort food. And whatever it is you can say on behalf of interfaith work—call it rewarding, stimulating, inspiring, challenging—comfort food, it's not.

Candor requires me to admit that interfaith dialogue can be frustrating for all concerned. It often takes place on the pablum level, where profound differences are whitewashed and the ideas presented are worthy of children, and not terribly bright children at that. Alternatively, the organizers might want to "keep it real," in which case they risk creating widespread animosity. Given the choice, I might actually prefer the combat to the Kumbaya. But you can see why many would opt for whatever is behind door number 3.

Still, despite the exasperations of interfaith work, I would argue that every person who cares about the scourge of religious divisiveness should seriously consider joining this movement. It is our best hope for creating a world in which the name of God will come to symbolize unity, and the domain of religion will come to symbolize tolerance. For me personally, participation in this movement is nothing short of an unwritten commandment.

⊕

When many people think about organized religion, pompous preaching immediately comes to mind. But the interfaith movement isn't centered on preaching of any kind. It isn't even centered on humble teaching. The focus instead is on listening—with an open mind and an open heart. As any interfaith practitioner can tell you, this is one context where it is far more appreciated to allow yourself to be moved by another faith than to wax eloquent about your own.

With that point in mind, I'd like to offer a midrash, or interpretation, of a Qur'anic parable that deeply moves me.[1] It is largely through this parable that I have come to appreciate the potential for members of different faiths to come together in a joint mission—to liberate the Holy Name. Whereas *the Name* is now commonly associated with a group of highly similar tribal Lords (those tribes are commonly known as "Jewish," "Christian," "Muslim," etc.), parables like this one can help us envision *the Name* as a symbol of the unity of all Being.

Hopefully, my midrash will give you an example of how we all can grow from a sincere effort to explore multiple religions. But more importantly, the substance of my interpretation should illustrate what has been missing in our religious life when God is viewed solely through a parochial, as opposed to a universalist, lens.

The parable comes from Surah (chapter) 24, and begins at verse 35:

> Allah is the Light of the heavens and the earth. The parable of His Light is as if there were a Niche and within it a Lamp. The Lamp enclosed in Glass. The glass as it were a brilliant star: lit from a blessed Tree, an Olive, neither of the East nor of the West, whose Oil is well-nigh luminous, though fire scarce touched it: Light upon Light! Allah doth guide whom He will to His light: Allah doth set forth Parables for men: and Allah doth know all things.

The parable contains three central symbols—the niche, the lamp, and the glass. The fourth, olive oil, is simply the beloved, universal

1. The commentary that has inspired my midrash can be found in Ali, *Meaning of the Holy Qur'an*, 876–77.

substance that fuels the lamp to make it the holy of holies, as we would say in Judaism.

Everyone has heard the word "niche," but many may not know that it literally denotes the small, shallow recess in a wall, such as the wall of a Middle-Eastern house. In the days before Edison, these houses needed niches—they would be placed high above the ground, and the lamp that would be inserted inside the niche would allow light to be diffused throughout the area below with a minimum of shadows.

In this parable, the light coming down through the niche connotes light of a *spiritual* nature. To find the source of that light, we must look "upward," with the aid of such Scriptures as the Torah, the Christian Bible, and the Qur'an.

As for the lamp, it contains the core of truth that beautifies and enlightens the world. And indeed, this core of truth is universal. The Qur'an teaches that the holy books of the Abrahamic faiths, at their core, convey the same fundamental teachings. They apply for all peoples and for all times—just as the mystical "olive tree" that fuels the lamp is supposed to be neither from the East nor the West, but from throughout the planet. This lamp of truth and the universal oil that fuels it are majestic beyond words and worthy of tremendous honor.

But there is a problem: we can't see the lamp directly in all of its splendor. We're only human. We live "down below" in the world, a world in which people's concerns are not always spiritual, and we are too limited intellectually and linguistically to grasp more than a superficial understanding of God and truth. We require a glass to enclose the lamp.

The glass is the transparent vehicle through which the light passes in both its physical and spiritual senses. It protects the lamp from invaders—wind, insects, or for that matter, human conduct. It also serves as a medium through which the spiritual light can be *filtered* so that people can comprehend it. Because both our minds and our language are incredibly limited in relation to reality as a whole, we need the filter of the glass in order to appreciate the lamp's transcendent light.

So there you have some mainstream Qur'anic commentary, with only slight embellishment on my part. After reading it, I realized that a progressive Jew like me has a lot to learn from that parable. Clearly, not all Muslims would gain precisely the same inspiration that I have from it, but then again, what makes the Abrahamic Scriptures great is that they can move different people in very different ways—they inspire progressive insights in progressive readers and traditional insights in traditional readers. So please allow me to add my own "progressive" midrash to the traditional commentary.

I take the above parable as a reminder that at the heart of all of the world's great religions are various common, fundamental principles. Such principles include, for example, the values of being trustworthy, avoiding violent impulses, feeling compassion for strangers and friends alike, and revering the awesome mystery that resides within Being itself. Consider these and other such fundamental principles, taken together, to represent what little we are able to discern from this magnificent lamp of truth. The wisest figures in each religion all seem to have internalized these principles and have bestowed upon us many ways to appreciate them. In fact, it is precisely because these people have so clearly devoted their lives to such principles that they are often viewed, both within their own community and outside of it, as holy.

You can find these universal principles either explicitly or implicitly in the Qur'an, the Christian Bible, and the Torah, among other Scriptures. But you can also find in these books detailed proscriptions and history lessons that go well beyond the fundamental principles expressed by the lamp. The ancient Scriptures preach ideas from a time when most people were illiterate, science was primitive, and philosophy reflected our primitive science. Admittedly, each pane of glass that emerged from these Scriptures was, in its day, an enlightened vehicle for filtering truth into the minds of our ancient ancestors. And even now, our limited minds require some sort of filter, for we are only human. Yet who can deny that our knowledge has progressed tremendously in the intervening centuries? So aren't we ready for a new medium, a new filter?

Just look at the way so many of our intelligent young minds are reacting to the glass, and consider the impact this is having on their access to the lamp. To them, religion, spirituality, and perhaps even social causes have become irrelevant to their daily concerns. It is incumbent on those of us who embrace those domains to learn how to make them resonate with more people. We can't simply assume that the disaffected among us will miraculously come to see the light. Nor can we assume that their attitude is exclusively *their* problem. This problem affects all of us. The question is how to address it.

First, I would make the following suggestion to the leaders of each of our great ancient faiths: *It's time to change the glass!* Whether we're talking about faiths or furnaces, even the best of filters need to be replaced periodically. And that takes nothing away from the beauty of our

Scriptures. As sources of prescriptions of how to live ethical lives, they serve us nearly as well as they've served our ancestors. These Scriptures also thrive as reminders of the divine lamp that lights our world—a lamp recognizable to all of our sages, whether they're Jewish, Muslim, Christian, Hindu, or Buddhist. But these Scriptures must not become nooses around our necks, precluding us from tapping into the scientific and philosophical insights of the past millennium.

I would never suggest replacing the glass with something altogether unrecognizable. If our traditions and rituals are comfort food, why would we want to rid ourselves of that? No, I'm thinking more in terms of replacing each glass with a modified version of its former self. We'd take a long look at the old practices and ideas and ask ourselves which ones have stood the test of time. Do they still speak to us? Or have they been undermined by the teachings of modern science or philosophy? Ultimately, we might want to make a compromise. Let's keep the familiar prayers, rituals, and holidays in each of our faiths—for that's the side of religion that so often comforts us. But let's also encourage our rabbis, priests, and imams not to mince words at the pulpit when it comes to confronting the antiquated ideas embedded in our traditions. Yes, that will create some cognitive dissonance, but it's a price we have to pay. Besides, there's nothing wrong with combining a comfortable place of worship with an intellectually lively and challenging place of study. Quite the contrary—when you combine what is comforting and traditional in religion with what is intellectually provocative, that's how you produce spirituality.

My second suggestion that stems from the above parable is directed to the interfaith movement as a whole, rather than to specific faith traditions. I have in mind a sustained, collective effort to confront, not just our respective panes of glass, but the one unique *lamp*. According to the parable, that lamp is the source of all spiritual light and universal truth. And residing within the lamp is the unified cosmic power. We have seen that religion has become engulfed by tragic divisiveness, so what better way is there to attack this problem than by collectively studying the lessons from the lamp that infuses our world with truth and beauty?

That lamp itself, not just its filters, needs to become a central focus of the interfaith movement. It is no longer adequate simply to assert that there exists a core of truth that underlies each of our faiths, or that this core is universal, applying for all peoples and all times. Now, we must insert meaningful *content* behind those truisms. *What is that universal core of truth?* Does it even exist? Is it broad in scope or is it tiny? How can anyone possibly find it amidst the discord that dominates organized religion today? And haven't we been fooling ourselves into proclaiming that religious people all think of God the same way when, in fact, a free and enlightened people is capable of holding a wide range of views on the topic? I would like to see the interfaith movement tackle each of these questions together. And when you focus on that last question, you'll see that what I have in mind would be anything but singing Kumbaya.

⋴⋵

Oh, I think those universal truths are out there. What's more, just as our species has been able to agree on various laws of nature (e.g., that there are reasons why airplanes fly and pigs don't), I bet that the rational members of our species can agree on some fundamental laws of the spirit. To do so, however, we need representatives of all the stakeholders at the table. We can't just ask the professionals—the ones in the "God business." Clergy *and* laypeople, practitioners of the Western *and* Eastern faiths, even folks representing secular, non-theistic schools of thought need to be included in the dialogue. If we who thirst for unity sincerely want to explore the universal lamp of truth, we need to hear from as broad a spectrum as possible.

In *The Creed Room*, I wrote about a fictional situation where a small, ideologically diverse group of strangers were thrown together into a chamber of an old Victorian home and were paid handsomely to formulate a new creed for humankind. Now, I'd like us to contemplate bringing together in a meeting hall a larger group of people. Together, they would collectively represent as many as possible of the world's most well-known belief systems, or non-belief systems. We'd task these people with the job of determining whether a core of universal, spiritual truths exist and, if so, of identifying it.

I suspect we all know that they would start their search with the realm of morality and would likely identify many of the same fundamental values. We'll explore these core values in greater depth in this book's next chapter. For now, let it suffice to say that the universality of these values becomes apparent whenever we examine the religious and secular myths that have been created by different cultures at different times, indicating just how remarkably similar our heroes and gods tend to be (not to mention our villains). In fact, the common values exemplified by those gods and heroes have proven to be as crucial to the survival of our species as the turtle's shell, the polar bear's color, or the porcupine's spines have been to theirs.

So yes, there is much that is universal about our core values. But what is especially interesting about the lamp is the question of whether anything can be said about it beyond these values and the civic virtues that spring from them. Can we identify any metaphysical beliefs that unify us? Does anything about the realm of the transcendent come to mind aside from the recognition of a realm of mystery that escapes human consciousness? What about the principles that God exists and is supremely worthy of our love and respect; are they included within the core universal truth that the author of the Qur'an had in mind? And if so, should they have been?

Clearly, the answer to that penultimate question is yes. But it is the final question that interests me. Let us imagine being in that meeting hall with a number of individuals representing a variety of communities. The suggestion is made to agree on the proposition "God exists" as a *universal* truth. And then, from the back of the room, none other than Richard Dawkins stands up and says, "Like hell it is!"

Now what?

If I were in that room and given the next opportunity to speak, this is what I would say:

"Professor Dawkins. Despite all your diatribes against religion, I've seen you try to be fair to the other side. You've actually acknowledged one way in which you view yourself to be religious. So let's see if we can all build from there.

"You've already adopted the idea that behind everything human beings have experienced, there is something our minds haven't grasped— something sublime, whose beauty reaches us only indirectly and as a feeble reflection. And you've admitted that this recognition makes you a religious man, at least in one sense of the term.

"Allow me, then, to suggest that there exists a realm of the transcendent—a realm beyond our comprehension, if only for the present. And allow me to suggest that this notion is an excellent example of a core universal truth.

"And let me also point out to you, sir, that in your seminal tract about the 'delusion' that is the supernatural God, you quoted Einstein in saying that he believes in a God 'who reveals himself in the orderly harmony of what exists,' and you never criticized that notion. Not once.

In fact, even though you generally enjoy ridiculing religion whenever given a chance, you said explicitly that 'There is nothing comical about Einstein's beliefs.'[2] I suspect, Professor Dawkins, that being a scientist in your own right, you can't help but be moved by the harmonies and patterns in nature—in other words, by her incredible unity. And I suspect you would agree that we human beings have an intuition that there is something mysterious that glues together all of nature's creatures and all of her non-organic objects as well.

"Now I'm not suggesting you believe that this mysterious glue is a supernatural mind. I know what you think about that idea. But can we not all agree that there appears to be an overarching unity in nature, and that we human beings have a deep appreciation for that cosmic unity, no less than we appreciate a hidden realm of the transcendent and sublime?"

(By this point, I would assume that the real Richard Dawkins would have interrupted me. But let's suspend disbelief on that point and pretend that I was allotted a specific amount of time during which he was forced to hear me out.)

"If we can include among our core beliefs the willingness to accept the existence of an overarching natural unity *and* a realm of the transcendent, we will have come a long way. But I'm not quite finished, sir. I ask that you also consider combining those concepts. Take what we earlier described as sublime and transcendent, and combine it with what we experience every day—the objects of our five senses and of our consciousness. Now, put it all together in a single overarching unity. What are you faced with? Call it 'Nature' if you like. I think you'd agree that the idea of this Unity beyond the multiplicity of the world as we know it takes on a majestic position in the mind of anyone who affirms it. Some call it the 'Creation' and attribute it to the will of a single Creator. Others say there is no such thing as a Creator; this universe is all there is. But I think we'd all agree that this majestic unity—this 'Nature with a capital N'—evokes more of a sense of ultimacy than any natural form or set of natural forms that we could ever encounter.

"Perhaps for you, Nature itself is the *Ultimate*. Perhaps for some of the priests here, the *Ultimate* is the Creator who they believe has manufactured Nature from the outside. I don't think we'll ever agree on our visions of the *Ultimate*. But can't we at least agree that for each of us there *is* an ultimate? And I don't just mean an ultimate concern; I mean an ultimate *unity*.

2. Dawkins, *God Delusion*, 19.

"Can't we also agree that over time, people have taken to using the word 'God' in the context of affirming an ultimate unity? Some use it as a name for Nature itself; they are the so-called 'pantheists.' Others use it to refer to a single Creator who they view as the sole source of Nature; they are the so-called 'theists.' In both cases, though, the *Ultimate* is associated with an overarching unity.

"And can't we agree that the word 'God' has incredible emotional power for pantheists and theists alike, and that adopting the use of that word can literally cause us to reorient the way we view our world and live our lives? And can't we additionally agree that just as the word 'God' has the capacity to confuse people if it is adopted by those like you who deny the supernatural, it also has the capacity to ennoble people? And in the case of Einstein and his mentor Spinoza, it did just that?

"In short, Mr. Dawkins, can't we please agree that part of our understanding of the core universal truth is that there is nothing inherently illegitimate about embracing the word 'God'? And that the vast majority of us can accept that there is an overarching unity in Nature, and that to those who don't believe in a supernatural Creator, Nature itself is truly *ultimate* and could aptly be called God? And that the only real problem with that idea is that the supernaturalists among us have come to monopolize that word because some of them have thrown their weight around over the centuries? And that it is the penchant on the part of many supernaturalists for coercing and power playing that we should call to task, not the word 'God'?"

My friends, if we all could agree to adopt these principles, I wonder just how many of us would eventually come to affirm *The Name*. I suspect the percentage of "believers" might even return to where it was in the days before Darwin, Marx, Nietzsche, and Hitler.

⊖

We started down this road because of one passage of the Qur'an. And my little monologue addressed to Dawkins has reminded me of another Qur'anic passage: "let there be no compulsion in religion" (2:256). While I doubt that Dawkins would accept everything I've said to him, he surely would agree that there is no legitimate place in religion for coercion. In fact, he would add that it's not enough to avoid coercion; we must take the next step of engaging in a free and open debate about religious ideas, for only then can we learn from outside of our own parochial communities.

As far as I'm concerned, if the devotees of our various faiths could take these principles to heart, perhaps they'd agree that different people are capable of seeing *The Ultimate* in different ways. Then, by basing our common notion of the Divine on the concept of ultimacy, rather than on the often anthropomorphic teachings of particular religious traditions, theists, and humanists alike may come to recognize common theological ground and to show greater acceptance of our differences. In fact, once we respect the notion that God may be conceived in a variety of ways, humanists may even feel less impelled to speak out against *The Name*. They could come to associate it with the never-ending search for a mysterious object (*The Ultimate*), and not with religious traditions that have acted intolerantly and, at times, even resorted to coercion.

I don't apologize for the shots that I have taken in this book against Dawkins. If anyone should have broad shoulders, it would be a deicide with a razor-sharp pen. But this much must be conceded: for all of Dawkins' hyperbole and sophomoric jabs, his intellect deserves our respect. As a scientist of some repute, Dawkins rightly appreciates clarity of thought and the elimination, where possible, of confusion. He is also undeniably correct in arguing that whenever panentheists or other pantheists invoke the name of God in a non-traditional way, they are inviting confusion. Just consider the old saw: "We all believe in the same God." Add Einstein and Spinoza to the mix, Dawkins could point out, and that statement has now been called into question.

Still, even a Richard Dawkins must appreciate that our species is not about to scrap spirituality root and branch. Nor are we all going to give up on the notions of cosmic unity, transcendence, and ultimacy. Finally, we're not universally going to jettison our love for *The Name*. If the author of *The God Delusion* truly thinks that's going to happen, he's the one who is most deluded.

So what do we do with all of this religion and spirituality that is surely here to stay? I think we have a fateful choice. We can build intergroup bridges and identify a core set of universal truths that can ground our ability to engage in collective action and avoid mutual destruction. Or, we can continue to pray exclusively in our separate churches, preach to our parochial choirs, and gradually replace the mythical Tower of Babel with a real one. Right now, we are walking down the latter path. We are constructing a tremendous edifice of mutual disrespect and polarization.

If only the name of God were its sole casualty.

CHAPTER 21

Honoring God in the Way
We Live Our Lives

VIEWING GOD IN THE first person is all about seeing connections wherever possible and building bridges wherever needed. In the last chapter, we spoke about the importance of building interpersonal bridges—such as those connecting religious and non-religious people, members of different faiths, and traditional and progressive members of each faith. But as we have previously noted, we can't expect to be constructive forces in the world without developing a healthy sense of self. If we don't balance the various impulses and goals within our own souls, we're likely only to make things worse when we try to interact with others. So that leads us to a fundamental question: can each of us identify an overarching purpose in life that will enable us to be a source of unity within our world and to attain harmony within our soul?

Once again, I won't propose that I have found the answer for everyone. But I can confidently assert that I have found it for myself. It lies not-so-deeply hidden within the structure of this book.

In Part I, God was the supreme "what" that we study. In Part II, God was the supreme "who" that we encounter. Now, God must be the supreme "self" that we *honor*. Optimally, our thoughts, feelings, and conduct would all be directed to that goal. The closer we come to this ideal, the easier it will be to develop the self-love and self-respect that each of us craves.

As lesser selves—combinations of limited bodies and egos—we are constantly letting ourselves down. We feel small and isolated to begin with. And when we add to those feelings the results of the bad decisions, poor habits, or sheer cluelessness that are an inevitable part of the human condition, we can easily enough come to see ourselves as relatively worthless.

That whole perspective changes when we see ourselves in God. Once we recognize ourselves as participants in the divine drama, we realize that we are eternal, so are our loved ones, and we each hold unique roles in the Play of Plays. But the question remains: what exactly is the nature of our involvement in this drama? As a passive witness, dreamer, or critic? Or dare we take on an active role—and if so, as what?

For me, there is but one satisfying response: we must identify our talents and interests and marshal them in a way that bestows honor on the Divine. Then, and only then, can we feel worthy of what it means to be human. Otherwise, we might as well have Stanley Kubrick in our ears saying "Cut! No, no, no, a thousand times no! We're going to need to do that scene again. Take two million and one."

⟨⊖⟩

Honoring God. Some people view those words as both the ultimate challenge and the ultimate privilege. For such people, to believe in God *as God* is to thirst to honor the Divine at all times and in every way possible. To live otherwise is to replace the Divine with different deities, like money, power, status, comfort, or whatever other goals drive secular society.

Still, there are plenty of people, including many who affirm God's existence, who see honoring God as a merely secondary goal. They might view this principle as too removed from what really matters to them—namely, the world around us. But what they might be missing is that you can't honor God without honoring our world. It is, after all, God's world too, and that can be said whether you are a pantheist or a theist. Either way, if you forsake the world, you spit on God.

Honoring God. In those two words, we who would affirm *The Name* can place all of our hopes, dreams, and exertions. Does that require us to be altruistic to the point that we invariably discount the needs of our "lesser" self? Hardly. To honor God requires us to think first and foremost about God—in other words, to reflect on the broadest possible view (the standpoint of eternity) before making our most critical decisions in life. Yet all sages, even universalistic ones, recognize that charity often begins at home. Consider the immortal words of the great Rabbi Hillel: "If I am not for myself, who will be? If I am only for myself, what am I? And if not now, when?" We alone may be the one person capable of advancing the welfare of our "lesser" self. Because we best understand our own unique bodies and minds, we are in the optimal position to do the job. Moreover, we are unusually well suited to care for other human beings who have come to be closely bound to us through blood, marriage, or friendship. If I am not for *them*, who will be? One person too few, that's who.

Honoring God. For many, that is associated above all else with offering prayers of gratitude and praise. As you well know by now, I deeply applaud those activities. And yet I must acknowledge that our prayers alone only scratch the surface of what is needed to meet our goal.

Offering prayers of gratitude and praise to God can inspire us to do all sorts of things for the world around us, not to mention for our (lesser) selves. Ironically, though, the one who does *not* benefit from such prayers is God, at least insofar as we are considering the most transcendent aspect of God, the Ground of Being. That core dimension of the Divine needs nothing, least of all our thanks and praise, and any suggestion to the contrary is probably a relic of the "jealous God" concept from the Old Time Religion. "Worship me! Don't worship them!" Maybe that made a lot of sense at a time when people built idols out of gold and knelt down to those false gods, but we've come a ways since then, don't you think? Once Shakespeare, in *The Merchant of Venice*, referred to jealousy as the "green-ey'd monster"; it stopped being tolerable to associate God with that same attribute.

If we don't honor God primarily through prayer, how do we? By hard work. If God is associated not merely with the *Ground* of Being but also with the fullest *life* of Being, which is manifested throughout our world and beyond, whenever we have the capacity to transform the world we impact the Divine. It is our greatest gift of all—the chance to *matter*, to look at life as we know it as an unwritten book that we individually and collectively can write.

On one level, I find it depressing that in the face of that opportunity, many religious people have adopted a fatalistic position and entrusted the future to centuries-old predictions about God. But from a traditionalist perspective, the faithful had no choice. As soon as such prophesy was proclaimed to be *the Word*, and as soon as their leaders taught them that to distrust that Word is to dishonor God, traditionalists were forced to accept prophesy about future events.

The truth is that the need to honor God has been the prime directive of organized religion for a long time. Yet this same fundamental objective can be derived from a *progressive* religious standpoint. So there you have it—a formula for some of the social unity we were talking about in the last chapter.

We religious progressives may or may not be able to persuade our traditionalist siblings and cousins to allow *The Name* to take on a wider array of connotations. But traditionalists and progressives alike should be able to reach a greater consensus on our basic vocation in life: to honor God. In other words, while we may diverge in our conceptions of God, we can at least recognize that it is our common mission to serve the One who is truly *ultimate*. Believe me, even if we only agree on that, we can accomplish a lot together.

⟜⟠

Honoring God—by offering praise, by expressing gratitude, and above all else, by beautifying the world. In that last respect, Goethe had his image of earthly beauty, and I have mine.

In his majestic *Faust*, Goethe's title character sold his soul to the devil for a wild ride on earth that he would willingly terminate once he experienced a moment truly worthy of eternity. Here was that moment:

> There is a swamp, skirting the base of the hills, a foul and filthy blot on all our work. If we could drain and cleanse this pestilence, it would crown everything we have achieved, opening up living space for many millions. Not safe from every hazard, but safe enough. Green fields and fruitful too for man and beast, both quickly domiciled on new-made land, all snug and settled under the mighty dune that many hands have built with fearless toil. Inside it life will be a paradise. Let the floods rage and mount to the dune's brink. No sooner will they nibble at it, threaten it, than all as one man run to stop the gap. Now I am wholly of this philosophy. This is the farthest human wisdom goes: The man who earns his freedom every day, alone deserves it, and no other does. And, in this sense, with dangers at our door, we all, young folk and old, shall live our lives. Oh how I'd love to see that lusty throng and stand on a free soil with a free people. Now I could almost say to the passing moment: Stay, oh stay a while, you are so beautiful. The mark of my endeavours will not fade. No, not

in ages, not in any time. Dreaming of this incomparable happiness, I now taste and enjoy the supreme moment.[1]

So, there you have a supreme vision of uplifting the world that is
worthy of its author, a literary giant. It is a vision of widespread freedom,
one of the greatest values known to humankind.

By contrast, my vision is more modest. And yet, I have felt it in my
bones ever since my father first lectured me on religious hypocrisy.

Goethe had his vision of supreme *freedom*. I have my vision of
supreme *piety*. It is inspired by Martin Luther King Jr.'s comment about
dreaming of a day when people are judged by the content of their character. For me, though, I am envisioning a day when people are judged
religious by the content of their work in perfecting the world. The more
driven they are by their commitment to social and environmental uplift,
the more pious they will be judged. Similarly, the more they treat other
people and other organisms with apathy or enmity, the less they'd be seen
as devout. As for their worshipfulness and their love for *The Name*, that
would be seen as a matter of personal preference and of little relevance to
how they are viewed in terms of their religious devotion.

That's right, *devotion*. In my vision, the pious ones, the "devoted"
ones, are the ones who tirelessly work to help their planet and their species. If they choose to live in that manner, it is assumed that they are devoted to the true God, regardless of whether they claim to be enamored
of the word "God."

In my vision, I see a woman accepting the Nobel Peace Prize. She
has become a living legend as a role model for religious people throughout the world, and yet she herself has never spoken publicly about "religion" or "God." The Nobel Committee honors her for a lifetime of work
engaged in, among other causes, eliminating poverty, bringing warring
peoples together, protecting endangered species, and stemming defor-
estation. In her acceptance speech, she humbly questions why she has
come to be viewed as an exemplar within the domain of spirituality. She
acknowledges her atheism matter-of-factly and non-confrontationally.
"I do not look down my nose on those who believe," she says, "but I've
always seen God as simply a figment of our imaginations." In my vision,
such comments raise eyebrows, but they don't tar the speaker's reputation
one whit. She is still universally beloved for being among the greatest
religious figures on the planet. You see, she has lived according to the

1. Goethe, "Faust," 1038–39.

highest ideals of religion—higher even than the love of *The Name*. She has honored the Divine by working relentlessly and effectively to perfect God's world.

That's my vision. I am well aware of one respect in which it differs from those of Goethe and King. Theirs would be universally appreciated, whereas mine would be viewed as perverse, if not crazy, by many traditionalists, who view atheists as the opposite of religious.

I can assure you that in my own heart, I cannot imagine abandoning my faith or erasing the relationship between religious belief and spirituality. All that has been said above about the *power* of belief I still believe with every fiber of my being. And all that I have said in praise of *The Name*—not only the Divine per se but also the word "God"—has been said with sincerity. In the present context, however, those earlier comments would be missing a larger point.

We as a society, and especially our religious communities, have gotten our means and our ends completely reversed. Belief is important *as a means*. Prayer is important *as a means*. But the supreme religious *end*, honoring God, is first and foremost about deeds—noble, constructive, non-reckless deeds. Such deeds are designed to identify who is suffering, who is impaired, what is lacking, and what is excessive and return them all to a healthy state of balance. Through these deeds, we transform the world. We beautify it, we enliven it, and, yes, we honor it. And in so doing, we honor God.

Truly, whether you are a traditional theist or a panentheist, there is no better way to honor God than to perfect that which we most closely associate with the Divine. Call it the world, call it creation, call it nature, call it the forms-of-God, call it the concrete element of *The Ultimate Synthesis*, call it what you will. It is our most complete vista onto the unity of the *Ultimate*. And that is why, for all the ugliness it includes, it remains dearer than the holy Torah, Gospels, Qur'an, and Upanishads combined.

⟡

Traditionally, religious people speak about honoring God "through his commandments." But it is incumbent upon us, if we wish to honor God as profoundly as possible, to go well beyond identifying specific "do"s and "don't"s. We must identify the fundamental, overarching values that will guide us in the way we live our lives. We must remain loyal to these values, respecting them even when it may not appear expedient to do so. And we must work relentlessly to see these values realized in our communities and in our world. However we conceive of God, this becomes a moral imperative.

Will the overarching values we identify be the same for all people? Not necessarily, but I think you will find them to be more similar than they are different. Where the major differences lie will not be in the values themselves, but in the content that we assign to them. And that is where the differences in our religious beliefs come into play. Even though you and I may identify the same set of fundamental values, depending on how we conceive of God specifically or faith generally our understanding of those values may diverge sharply, and our efforts to uphold them may be in out-and-out conflict.

In short, we might begin with the same goal (honoring God, accomplished primarily by beautifying God's world), agree upon the overarching means of reaching this goal (by devoting ourselves to the same basic set of values), and still end up fighting tooth and nail. But if religious progressives and traditionalists alike can agree upon an ultimate goal and a fundamental set of values, we would at least have identified the perfect foundation for a robust dialogue. And given that we have been spending generation after generation fearing, ridiculing, and at times killing each other, a robust dialogue would be a huge step in the right direction.

So what do you say we put some meat on the bones? I'm going to identify a set of five values that I trust most of us would agree are fundamental. In each case, I'll also explain how the philosophy of God promoted in this book influences my understanding of these values and the best way to uphold them. But as you will see, the process works both ways—whether we like it or not, we tend to choose our philosophies of God in part because of how we understand these fundamental values. They are that important to us.

The first value is *truth*. If we once again invoke the metaphor of a journey, the truth must be our means of orientation. When we wake up in the morning, it is the truth that we must first consult. When we go to bed at night, we must turn to the truth in taking stock of the day. And at all times, we must strive never to lie to ourselves and rarely to lie to others. In fact, I would go further and say that while being honest is a virtue, being generally candid (within limits) is both a rarer and greater one.

You sometimes hear people say that the truth is in their hearts. Not for me. I view the truth as something that is in my mind, at least if I am fortunate. Just as I see God as the grand totality—*The Ultimate Synthesis* of the Ground of Being and the sum of all beings—I consider the truth to be a synthesis in its own right. John Stuart Mill hit the nail on the head when he said that "It might be plausibly maintained that in almost every one of the leading controversies, past or present, in social philosophy, both sides were in the right in what they affirmed, though wrong in what they denied."[2] As we say in the legal profession, even the thinnest of pancakes has two sides. To find the truth, you must have the courage to identify multiple sides and entertain them. One might be stronger than another, but if you have the luxury of incorporating lessons from the weaker sides as well as the stronger, you will be thinking with the greatest possible depth.

Spinoza's notion of looking at the world from the "standpoint of eternity" is a wonderful vehicle for identifying truth. To be a disciple of Spinoza is to explore, for every topic, both the causes of our own idiosyncratic biases and the broadest perspective imaginable. Goethe identifies the "utter disinterestedness which shone forth in [Spinoza's] every sentence" as that which "especially riveted me to him."[3] This, I am quite sure, was what Freud was referring to when he said that "I readily admit my dependence on Spinoza's doctrine," not because of the study of Spinoza's work, but because of "the atmosphere created by him."[4] It is the atmosphere of opening one's mind to the truth without fear of what one might find. It is the atmosphere of treating all accepted dogma as icons, rather than the word of God. Parochialism is truth's greatest enemy; universalism, its dearest friend.

Clearly, in order to adopt this perspective on truth, it helps to disbelieve that we know of precise ideas that God has communicated to human messengers. Once we take a religious text to be the work of God, whether it is given by him word-for-word or otherwise, the total disinterestedness referenced by Goethe is gone. And this is why a powerful argument can be made that we would have been better off if Scripture had never been reduced to writing so that it could not strangle our ability to think freely. I have even seen that argument made by otherwise traditionalist rabbis.

Religious people tend to agree on the centrality of truth as among the highest of goals. Where we differ is in how we find the truth. If "truth"

2. Mill, "Coleridge," 123.
3. Goethe, *Auto-Biography*, 26.
4. Yovel, *Spinoza and Other Heretics*, 139.

comes from an ancient text, as confirmed by the teachings of scholars who can verify the text's divine origin, we must orient ourselves in one way. If "truth" comes from whatever belief comports with our desires, whatever they may be, we will orient ourselves differently. And if "truth" comes from our most clear and convincing ideas, as informed by observations and logical inferences, we will orient ourselves in still another way.

While I try to opt for the last of these three approaches, I realize that this is more of an aspiration than a reality. That second approach—the one about believing what we want to believe simply because it makes us feel better—is insidious and can affect every one of us, sage or simpleton. But if we all can at least remind ourselves of the dangers of allowing our hearts to control our minds, this will go a long way to uplifting our world. I am not denigrating the heart. I am merely asking us to make room for the mind. It deserves its own honored place at the table.

The second fundamental value I'd like to discuss is *justice*. As the value to which I have devoted my professional life, it is dear to my heart. But you hardly have to fight corporate fraud for a living to pursue this value. My colleagues and I are joined, for example, by anyone in the private or public sectors—or, for that matter, people who are outside of the labor force altogether—who fight to right wrongs or to ensure that we all obtain the privileges that are due to us.

Clearly, any determination of what each of us deserves is a function of how we perceive one another, and this is where our religious philosophy comes into play. In my case, I have envisioned a God-centered universe in which human beings cannot claim to be God's "chosen" species, and all concrete forms (whether human or non-human, organic or inorganic) are seen as expressions of the Divine. As Spinoza would say, we are all but worms in a cosmic bloodstream. As such, the difference between people and other organisms is quantitative, not qualitative; we may possess either more or less power than they do, but we are all cut from the same cloth. While that might give us a legitimate claim to take our needs into account above theirs, it precludes us from neglecting their interests altogether. I have already discussed our obligation to treat this planet as if we were its custodians and not its rulers. That obligation is grounded in the value of justice.

Leaving aside the rights of animals or plants, we routinely face issues regarding our obligations to other people. Some are more book smart than others, some have more street smarts, some are more physically

gifted, some have more artistic talent, some are more driven to work hard
. . . and some don't especially excel in any of these respects. Even if we
completely equalized opportunity, certain people will be more economi-
cally productive than others. And that raises the question, how much
does justice require us to equalize wealth within a society despite the differences in productivity among its members?

Unfortunately, I am unable do that question "justice" in this book.
But please allow me a limited response. Our answer cannot help but be
influenced by a philosophy that regards human beings as finite expressions or fragments of a divine unity whose mysterious nature shapes not
only our respective talents but also the way we exercise our wills. This
perspective will lead us to see one another essentially as equals regarding
our right to live free and happy lives. It will also encourage us to organize
our societies in ways that produce the best results for all concerned and
does not merely cater to the most productive members. In other words,
this philosophy assumes that law-abiding citizens are all equally deserv-
ing of happiness and recognizes that once inequalities of wealth become
sharp enough, we are infringing on what Jefferson called the inalienable
right to the pursuit of happiness.

Thus, for example, our willingness to provide added rewards to
incentivize superior production would be less a matter of justice than
a means of maximizing overall utility. (Any corporate CEO who really thinks he "deserves" to earn three hundred times the income of his
secretary has an altogether different worldview.) If that means that this
religious philosophy tends to produce what is commonly known as a
"progressive" approach to political-economic issues, so be it.

Similarly, just as differences in how we view individuals can affect
our view of justice, so too can the differences in how we view *peoples*.
Zionism, which is near and dear to my heart, is largely grounded in a
sense of justice for the Jewish people, who feel that we deserve our own
"peace of oith" no less than the French, Italians, and Japanese. Similarly,
the Palestinians' claim that they have the "right" to return to the Israeli-
occupied land that was seized from their families in 1948 is also grounded
in a sense of justice.

Again, this isn't a book to fully explore those competing claims. But
what I can say is that those of us Jews who don't view the land grants
in the Torah as divine donations tend to be willing to compromise on
the issue of how much of the "Holy Land" should belong to the Jews, as
opposed to Palestinian Arabs. As for the Palestinians, I submit that they

would be well advised not only to embrace the idea of "two states for two peoples," but to publicly acknowledge that *both* of these peoples hold legitimate claims to the same land. The more the Palestinians use rhetoric that denies the Jewish claim to a state in the Middle East, the less likely the Israelis will be to trust the Palestinians as state-owning neighbors.

Let's turn now to our third fundamental value, *peace*. In a philosophy that affirms not simply the One God but the unity of all existence *as* God, peace necessarily takes center stage. For if God is the *Ultimate Unity*, and if we all reside within that unity, gratuitous violence must be seen as deicidal.

One of the most common questions I get asked in life is why I eat a vegan diet. My deepest answer is that I am trying to eradicate the fruits of gratuitous violence from my life. No, I don't take this ethic as far as some people, who even restrict the plant life that they eat. But we can eat just fine without having to consume animal products, and by eating vegan, we don't incentivize anyone to kill or mistreat animals for the sake of our own luxuriating.

Does that make all meat-eaters "deicides" or "murderers"? Only in the ridiculously silly sense in which all of us who has ever been drunk on alcohol is a deicide or a murderer, since we've all killed brain cells. Clearly, extremist rhetoric on behalf of veganism or vegetarianism serves primarily to antagonize people and does animals no favors. There is a difference between a human being and the kinds of animals people eat, and no vegan should deny it. But that having been said, none of us can deny the importance of working into our lifestyles different reminders that we in our hearts must affirmatively strive for peace; it means more than the mere cessation of violence. Moreover, like any other virtue, peacefulness takes discipline to develop, and an especially challenging type of discipline at that. For we in the Western world are accustomed to building our skills through exertion and aggression, whereas peace-seekers must develop themselves non-aggressively and yet effectively. It's not a simple trick to pull off.

Just turn on your television and watch the local news. Gentleness is hardly something we can take for granted. Clearly, we are hard-wired for violence. So, in the pursuit of peace, our work is cut out for us. Whether we are coping with our own aggressive instincts as individuals, working to resolve impassioned conflicts among nations or groups, or reading in Scriptures that God takes sides between warring parties, making peace can feel less natural than making war.

We mustn't kid ourselves. Just because we as individuals may not have engaged in any acts of criminal violence doesn't mean we don't have a violence problem. To be human is to be descended from far more killers than Christs and far more gunners than Gandhis. Never is discipline more needed than if you want to be a disciple of peace.

So, do you want some concrete suggestions as to how to make peace possible? How about taking steps both to confront our epidemic of violence and to bolster our affirmative love for peace? With respect to the former, we need the progressives and conservatives to unite. Until now, the progressives have been calling for stricter gun laws, like requiring background checks or banning assault weapons, whereas the conservatives have supported waging a cultural war against excessive violence in movies, video games, and popular music. I say, why not fight for both? Those who are serious about the scourge of violence need to call for boycotts—against stores, for example, that sell assault weapons or against Hollywood studios that produce violence-glorifying movies. In fact, I would argue that if more than ten people die in a film and it isn't a war movie set well in the past, it's time to start looking at the film for what it is: pornography. A society with an epidemic of violence can't afford a more "tolerant" attitude.

As for how to develop an affirmative love for peace, I can think of a number of vehicles at our disposal, but one strikes me as the most effective, and it is one that I have spoken about before: join the interfaith movement. Devoted interfaith activists can't help but begin to see *the other* as family, and this change allows us to *crave* peace among nations and even individuals. You see, for those who are committed to experiencing the world from an interfaith standpoint, wars and violence epidemics anywhere in the world become horrors that we ourselves take to heart.

The fourth fundamental value I must address is *freedom*. This one may not be on every person's list, but it sure might be on every American's. We have geography largely to thank for making us the "land of the free," for few things are as conducive to freedom as the wide open spaces my country has enjoyed since its inception. And while our love for justice has not been sufficient to extend the right of freedom to all Americans, at least this remains a common source of shame.

The philosophy embraced in this book underscores freedom's importance. If the divine power is seen as unfolding naturally through an infinite array of self-expressions, it only stands to reason that we would come to appreciate the importance of self-expression at the human level.

It becomes our sacred obligation to cultivate this world so as to foster self-expression as broadly as possible. Only then can those of us who share the earth begin to reach our potential as manifestations of God.

Similarly, by cultivating freedom, we also foster diversity, another characteristic that is associated with *The Ultimate Synthesis*. As the Ground of Being, God is absolute, indivisible unity—the hidden force that powers us all. But as the fullest life of Being, God is absolute diversity—the manifestation of that unity through infinite forms and infinite dimensions. If we are to take this latter perspective on God seriously, how can we not revere the variety in even the finite number of divine forms that are known to us? How can we not attempt to cultivate such variety here on earth? Accordingly, we must work to preserve endangered species even in the face of opposition from industrialists. And we must strive to cultivate diversity within human society. That entails more than just looking past a person's race, gender, or religion in making hiring decisions. It requires us to encourage individuality in all of its manifestations by allowing people to determine for themselves how to dress, whom to love, and what to do with their own bodies.

Of course, we can take that encouragement too far. We can embrace anarchism and allow people to run amuck, all in the name of liberty. But note what would happen: we would usher in an era of injustice and war, and thereby create conflict with some of the other values discussed above. If we hope to honor God, it is not enough for us simply to identify and flesh out the most fundamental values that must be affirmed. We must find a place for each value that gives the others their due.

In my opinion, our freedoms should cease whenever justice or peace is threatened. But that does not make freedom a secondary value. Indeed, if we wish to model God in the clearest way possible (by fostering self-expression) and honor God's most visible characteristic (the beauty of variety), we must never ignore the centrality of freedom.

As an analogy, consider that justice and peace would together form the foundation of a house. You absolutely need them to function or the whole thing will collapse. But the real beauty in the house is in its rooms. And in this case, the "rooms" are the product of our freedom.

So, there you have four of the five values that I would identify as most fundamental for changing the world in a constructive direction. I have deliberately saved for last my number one choice: *love*.

An argument can be made that love is the pre-eminent value in Judaism. Jews are directed to "love thy neighbor as thyself" (Lev 19:18), a verse in the Torah that the great Rabbi Akiva singled out for its importance. And we are told that "hatred stirs up strife, but love covers up all faults" (Prov 10:12). Moreover, while the God of the Jewish Bible is clearly willing to send his chosen people into battle, I have never found support for Matthew's comment that, according to Judaism, "Love your neighbor and hate your enemy" (Matt 5:43). Quite the contrary, Jews are told that "When you encounter your enemy's ox or ass wandering, you must take it back to him" (Exod 23:4).

The sincere Jew is indeed a loving soul. And so is the sincere Muslim. Yet if I were forced to single out only one of the faiths of Abraham in terms of the importance it places on love, that faith would be Christianity. Neither in the Torah nor the Qur'an do we find the statement "God is love," which is stated explicitly in the Christian Bible (1 John 4:8). And I know of no other scriptural tribute to love that is nearly as eloquent as the lengthy passage in the First Corinthians that culminates with "And now these three remain: faith, hope and love. But the greatest of these is love" (1 Cor 13:13).

Unfortunately, it is one thing to praise love in the abstract and quite another to practice what is preached. In each of the great religions, we can find plenty of examples of people who extol love as a virtue but fail to implement that teaching in day-to-day life. Surely, it is hard to imagine anything more difficult than loving all of your neighbors as you love yourself. Well, okay, I can imagine something even harder—loving all of your *enemies* as you love yourself. And what if your enemy is a rapist or a con man, and he has victimized a member of your family? Exactly how are we supposed to muster affection for him?

Prayer would help; I have no doubt about that. But so, too, would adopting a religious philosophy that ties us to our enemy in the closest bond imaginable. According to Matthew, in making the argument to "love your enemies," Jesus explained that in this way "you may be sons of your Father in heaven. He causes his sun to rise on the evil and the good, and sends rain on the righteous and the unrighteous" (Matt 5:44–45). I deeply appreciate the point of that passage. Unfortunately, though, it maintains the conventional view that each of us is an ultimately isolated actor—whether we're talking about people or God. Moreover, Matthew's statement permits us to divide one another fundamentally into the categories of "good" and "bad" people, which hardly inculcates a love-your-enemies attitude.

By contrast, those who contemplate God as *The Ultimate Synthesis* should find such an attitude considerably easier to adopt. Suddenly, we stop perceiving people primarily as "good" or "bad," "honest" or "dishonest," "sinful" or "saintly." We also stop holding them at arm's length from ourselves. Instead, we see us and them linked together in the same cosmic bloodstream and begin to elevate "saint" and "sinner" alike as parts of our greater self. In other words, we perceive them not simply as isolated individuals but as eternal portions of the divine collective in which we reside.

Moreover, recall that in the philosophy espoused in this book, when we perceive one another from the standpoint of eternity, we come to think of each other as the expressions of a God who is understood as acting *naturally* rather than willfully. As a result, we focus less on our own "good" will or our enemy's "evil" will and consider instead that we all do what we do because of our *natures*, which fit together in a single divine unity. This gets back to the idea that we are each fated to play unique roles in the ultimate drama—or, as we have characterized it before, "the fullest life of Being." From this perspective, hating another human being, even an enemy, seems petty. It makes little more sense than hating a deer that jumps onto a road and causes an accident or a man who has a seizure behind a wheel and accomplishes the same result. In these cases, no less than in the case of the drunk driver, the ones who cause injuries wouldn't be seen as "bad" creatures claimed by the devil but rather as authentic expressions of the divine nature who were "just being themselves." To hate that person or deer would involve hating part of God's very fabric. What's the point of doing that?

I am not suggesting that the perspective on God espoused in this book must invariably impel us to "turn the other cheek," for surely we have every right to fight to protect our own rights and those of others in the face of an attack. Yet there is rarely a justification for hatred and always some cause for compassion. If nothing else is possible, we can at least try to treat others with the respect that they deserve as human beings despite whatever shortcomings they may exhibit.

Finally, please recall that we went down this road because we were talking about the obligation of obligations: to *honor God*. And we decided that this is best accomplished by uplifting the world, including treating people with respect. Somehow, though, when I contemplate such lofty goals, treating people with respect doesn't seem sufficient—necessary yes, but not sufficient. Justice requires that we treat people with respect and affirm their dignity. But to honor God, we must move beyond the requirements of justice. We must take seriously the beckoning of love. That entails treating one another warmly and compassionately. In short, it requires us to *treat one another with honor*. If, indeed, each of us partakes in God's being and is truly one of God's manifestations, how else can we honor our God except by honoring each other? And how better can we bestow such honor than with our love?

That is what makes this value supreme.

⊖

I often think of my religious philosophy as heretical largely because it posits no separation between the "Creator" and the "creation" and also because it doesn't view God as acting in accordance with a human-like will. And yet, what I love most about being human is precisely our willing faculty.

For all of our faults and limitations as creatures, the human condition is an elevated one. Arguably, it is the most elevated condition we are capable of imagining. If you consider the Divine insofar as God is the Ground of Being, we are left to imagine nothing at all—that perspective on the Divine is purely mysterious and evocative of the infinite abyss. By contrast, to be human is to be an inventor of *meaning and morality*. It is to seize the chance to decide for ourselves the principles and values to which we will devote our lives.

Personally, I welcome the fact that we all are able to make these moral decisions for ourselves and fully accept that we will come up with different answers. Regardless of whether from the standpoint of eternity we are fated to make the decisions we make, the fact is that we make them—and the result can be a thing of beauty. It heartens me that despite my heretical beliefs, when asked to identify my mission in life I can come to a very traditional answer: our job, above all else, is to *honor God*. It also pleases me that when I try to put a little flesh on that principle, I must first begin with an idea that is also hardly without precedent in the traditional faiths: *we best honor God by honoring one another throughout our lives.*

This is fully compatible with the teachings of the great modern thinkers. It is what Buber was talking about when he preached the value of treating *the other* as a "Thou" and not an "It." It is what Levinas was referring to when he said that to recognize *the other* is to give, and give as if the one you encounter approaches you "in a dimension of height."

And it is what Heschel had in mind when he said that we should view one another not merely as people, but as God's "partners"—indeed, as "divine needs."

In my opinion, any philosophy that fails to make room for the importance of human beings is not worth adopting. We deserve better than that. But let us never put ourselves on the same pedestal as God. Let us remember that God possesses all that we possess and infinitely more. And in that regard, we must acknowledge what every Muslim says several times a day: that God is greatest.

Ultimately, we honor God above all else not because it serves our interests to do so. We honor God because the One and Only deserves nothing less.

Conclusion

It had been my goal when beginning this writing project not only to teach about God but also to learn about God. I see now, though, that what I have largely learned about are my own idiosyncrasies.

The study of "God" is a grand topic. It invites us to reach inwardly and outwardly for the *Ultimate*. And it dares us to approach our task with the same "boundless disinterestedness" that we attribute to our greatest philosophical heroes. I, too, have my heroes. But, as suggested above, I don't buy for a second that they are without biases or blind spots. Whether they write in musical notes, poetry, or prose, if they have walked this earth, they can't possibly have approached the *One* in an unbiased, disinterested way. No matter who we are, we are destined to encounter the Divine with hopes, fears, aversions, sympathies, and a whole lot of ignorance. And yet, many of us have the chutzpah to address the Most High in an intimate way and even to preach to others about the God we intend to serve. In other words, we proclaim our own humble devotion at the same time we manifest our conceit. Such is the fate of any mortal who dares to enter the public discourse about religion.

In the last chapter, I praised the importance of love above all other values as a means of honoring God through the uplifting of this world. If forced to praise another value as penultimate, I would need to choose truth. As a student of philosophy, I have at times even flattered myself by considering the attainment of truth to be the primary aim of my own personal search, the one that led to the commencement of this book.

But now I must confess that I am no exemplar of love. Lovers par excellence do not become professional litigators—or at least not lifelong practitioners of that vulgar occupation. Nor am I the most devoted servant of truth. Truth's greatest disciples spend their lives in sober, tireless reflection, whereas I have come to be ruled largely by my passions. It was precisely those passions, and not just the inquiries of my mind, that led me to God.

The reality is that what fuels my flame above all else isn't love, it is hatred—and not hatred of falsity but of injustice. Perhaps, when you're the only child of two leftist Jews who grew up poor during the Great Depression, and you yourself grew up a few miles from politics-obsessed Washington, DC, you've got little choice in the matter. Practically from the womb, you're exposed to the plethora of devils that we associate with injustice and unfairness, rather than to the "one God." If you eventually find it in your heart to worship God, perhaps that is because you found in religion an antidote to those devils.

A lover of truth might become fascinated by the study of quarks, mitochondria, sea otters, weather patterns, or computer chips. I became fascinated by the study of God and of morality. It mattered not that my favorite subject as a schoolboy was math, or that math is so commonly associated with the sciences and technology; there was something about the study of those "hard-headed" disciplines that I found profoundly wanting. They didn't impact directly enough on the notion of injustice and the opportunity to right wrongs. I have known for decades that this would become the focal point of my career—not using the law to play word games or make millions of dollars, but rather to use the judicial system against those who abuse the rights of others. Only now, however, have I realized that my interest in religious philosophy arises from the same roots. I became fascinated by the profound ignorance in our society on matters of religious philosophy less because it offended my love of truth than because it sparked my passion to fight injustice.

We have discussed in the Introduction the way many traditionalists have attempted over the centuries to monopolize what is meant by the Divine and how their efforts are now being furthered by, of all people, outspoken atheists. Both of these groups have created a forced dichotomy between two and only two choices: either you adopt the traditional view of God (call it the Nurturing God or the Planning God, depending on whether you are a child or an adult) or you forsake religion altogether. There is no third alternative. That was my perspective when growing up. It is not surprising that for many of those years, I viewed myself as a merely cultural Jew and an atheist.

The forced dichotomy between religious traditionalism and athe-ism/secularism stultifies our intellectual growth and thereby foments ignorance. But worse yet, it just isn't fair!

It isn't fair to those of our ancestors who worked hard to develop the great systems of faith. Assuming Karen Armstrong is correct, they wouldn't want us to take their words as literal, immutable doctrines, and yet that is precisely what we have done. As a result, the more educated we are, the more likely we are to ignore those majestic words altogether.

This forced dichotomy also isn't fair to those of our contemporaries who would be inspired by non-traditional approaches to religion gener-ally and God in particular if only they were exposed to these approaches. At the same time that we challenge our children to study such complex disciplines as calculus and physics, we assume that they're unable to con-template the Divine in any manner other than as a projection of human ideals. As a result, our kids grow up in a world where scientific, historical, and economic knowledge can progress, but religious knowledge largely stagnates.

It has been over three centuries since Spinoza joked that if a triangle could speak it would call God's nature triangular, and a circle would refer to God as circular. Is it fair to condemn a species like ours that *can* speak to serve forever as the punch line of that joke?

In addition, the forced dichotomy isn't fair to God or to the divine name. *The Name* should signify such words as ultimacy, unity, infinity, and mystery, but instead, we are attempting to possess it for ourselves by clothing it in human-like attributes. Who are we to appropriate *The Name*? How is such conduct any more just or fair than stealing from a store or robbing a bank?

So, if we wish to be fair to ourselves and others, we must (a) encour-age the flowering of religious ideas from both traditional and non-tradi-tional sources, (b) treat religious learning with at least as much respect as we extend to secular learning, and (c) recognize that the real enemy here, the real source of injustice, isn't the fact that different people view God differently, but that so many people—atheists as well as believers—want to claim that *The Name* can only legitimately refer to the most traditional conceptions of God.

Perhaps the Jealous God was very protective of the way his name was used. But that God has had his day, and that day has passed. Not only does the mixture of worship and dogmatism conflict with the value of humility, but it is splitting our world into pieces and turning *The Name* into an object of disdain. Just as God deserves better, so do we.

Truth be told, people's conceptions of God shouldn't all be the same, just as our notions of ultimacy aren't always the same. For some, what is ultimate is human excellence—both in terms of what our greatest heroes have achieved and in terms of what we are capable of achieving in an idealized future. For such people, it makes sense to join faith systems that elevate human beings to divine status and to worship a God who is known through recognizable emotional faculties. For others, including myself, that type of God won't work. It doesn't ring true. People like me are searching for that which is more mysterious, and yet whose presence is closer to us than our jugular veins. We are able and willing to address this God, but we won't expect to hear any message in return—or at least not any clear, verbal message. We might, in fact, view *every* lesson learned in life as coming from God. But that doesn't mean we will attribute those lessons to the motivations of a divine will. We prefer instead to think of God as acting supra-consciously—as expressing the divine nature through an infinite number of forms, extending over an infinite number of dimensions, and transcending time as we know it. As to *why* things work that way, we have no answer, nor do we feel the need for one.

We have come to a point where it is time to recognize, individually, the two heroes of this book: God (meaning the true God, or the Divine) and *"The Name"* (meaning any linguistic expression that purports to refer specifically to God). As I have suggested above, it is critical never to conflate these two heroes, for each is vastly different from the other.

When I have spoken about God or the Divine and was not describing other people's theology, the core of what I have been referring to is a boundless mystery—not merely a process, the sum total of beings, or even Being itself, but a combination of these. Anyone who tries to hold on to this "God" will grasp at air. We don't hold on to God; God holds on to us, and metaphorically at that.

Then there is *The Name*. *The Name* is a powerful tool that we can hold on to—at least in our minds. We can invoke it as a force of unity, or to command armies whose aim is conversion or death. We can invoke it to convince others to blow up buildings in its honor, or to convince ourselves to devote our lives to serving the disadvantaged. For that matter, we can invoke it as part of a plan to escape from our society altogether so that we can contemplate it every minute of every hour of every day.

For centuries, nothing in this world seemed more powerful than *The Name*. Appearances were deceiving, of course. There was something more powerful: namely, God. But when you're blinded by the power of *The Name*, it is easy to forget the distinction between the two. It is easy to forget that there exists a God beyond *The Name*.

Our priests have become so facile in the way they throw around *The Name* that their flock tends to confuse what the priests are talking about with the true God. The difference, of course, is that there is so little that we can say about the essence of the true God compared to what we cannot even begin to fathom. Sure, you can open your mind, heart, and eyes and soak in as much as possible, and everything you learn about will shed light on God. But what you'll be soaking in is less than one googolplexth of the true God. By contrast, when a priest begins to tell stories about *The Name*—when he explains how "God" has shaped the destiny of world history, what exactly "he" wants from us, and what we are commanded to avoid—we feel in control of the amulet of amulets. Even some of my fellow heretics who have resisted the hypnotic power of the priests have been mesmerized by the power of *The Name*. As Voltaire said, in what was as much a reference to *The Name* as to God, "If God did not exist we should have to invent him."[1] Who couldn't use such an incredible power source?

Imagine a thought experiment in which two passionate and intellectually curious college students walk into a professor's office after taking the same four-year course of study in science and philosophy. Assume that they share identical views about the fundamental philosophical issues as well as the basic teachings of science. And let us also posit that while they both subscribe to the notions that there is ultimate unity in Being and that Being itself is infinite, neither student would have claimed to have believed in God when entering the professor's office. Now, assume that the professor requests that for a period of two years both students contemplate the infinite, ultimate unity in which they have come to believe. The professor then directs one of the students invariably to refer to that unity as "God," and the other to refer to that unity as "Nature." Both students would be asked, if possible, to feel affection for this cosmic

1. Voltaire, *Epistle to the Author of the Book: The Three Imposters*, as referenced in Cliteur, *Secular Outlook*, 73.

unity (as, for example, Nietzsche did, even though he rejected the word "God"). The professor is candid about the purpose of the exercise—to evaluate the importance of *The Name* itself as a life-changing device. He requests that these students return in two years and report on how the use of the word "God," in the case of the first student, and "Nature," in the case of the second, has influenced their lives.

While I have never conducted that experiment, I am confident that the student who adopts the word "God" instead of "Nature" would find life more meaningful, enchanting, demanding . . . I can go on, but if you have read this far, perhaps you can fill in your own words. That's how powerful *The Name* can be, whether it is embraced by a traditional theist, pantheist, or other type of believer.

Still, for all its potential power, *The Name* is hardly being universally embraced in the contemporary world. What is happening these days throughout Europe and Japan, and in much of coastal America, is not a revolt against God, but against *The Name*. I have trouble believing that hundreds of millions of people have lost their faith in something/some-one/some process that transcends our self-important little planet. But I don't doubt for a second that they have lost faith in our species' ability to speak constructively about the true God. Stated differently, many people have reached the point that whenever they hear *The Name* invoked, they expect it will be used to oppress others or express ignorance, rather than to free or enlighten.

In Voltaire's day, even the heretics were believers—they just called themselves names like "deists." But that was the eighteenth century. By the late nineteenth century, Nietzsche could joyously proclaim that "God is dead," and the Marxists and many of the Darwinians were right there with him. The irony, though, is that Nietzsche appears to have been at least as spiritual a person as Voltaire, if not more so. He claimed to have a problem with God, but really, he had a problem with *The Name*—in particular, with the way the priests had invoked it as a tool of social domination.

Today, to be a progressive—even a religious one—is to appreciate Nietzsche's broader point. Legions of powerful people in government and in the media don't think twice about invoking *The Name* as a means to restrict liberty or put a brake on common sense. It is no wonder that so many residents of the twenty-first century have had it up to their ears with *The Name*.

I can't totally blame those who are fed up with religion. But you'll forgive me if I fight them just the same. You see, apes aren't the only ones who can evolve. People can too, and that includes our attitudes about *The Name*. We need to reclaim religion from those who would assert a monopoly over the divine name and from those who would invoke *The Name* as a means to stifle freedom of thought and worship rather than to unleash it. But at the same time, we should recognize that there is no need to reclaim God. God was never the problem. We were.

Our challenge, then, is cut out for us. And we must meet it both as individuals and as members of communities. Part of the challenge is to ensure that *The Name* stops being used as a tool of divisiveness and ignorance. Yet we must also ensure that *The Name* never stops being used altogether.

If we go back to Faust's dream of standing "on a free soil with a free people," what do we see but a cornucopia of intellectual and religious diversity? Some will be proclaiming *The Name* theistically, others panentheistically, and still others will be bored with religion and unlikely to proclaim *The Name* at all. But everyone will be treating each other with respect and dignity, and will show at least some modicum of appreciation for the fact that we are able to choose for ourselves what to do with this potentially powerful object.

To be free and enlightened is to realize that *The Name* may not be embraced by everyone, and that for those who ignore it, no hell awaits. But freedom and enlightenment also teaches us that *The Name* can matter deeply to those who affirm it, and it can just as easily be a source of social good as it can be a source of oppression.

Most importantly, to be free and enlightened is to realize that *The Name* isn't God. It is an object in our heads—a mere word. *The Name* has a clear denotation that most of us tend to accept (the *Ultimate*). But, for each of us as an individual, it will also come to have a connotation that we can fill in over the course of our lives with narratives, concepts, feelings, or all sorts of other means.

As for God, the Divine is replete with an infinite number of thoughts and creatures, and we ourselves can play an important role within this realm. But in an even deeper realm, the Divine is a mystery. We can love this mystery with the greatest of intensity, but when we try to name the mystery, we must do so with the utmost humility imaginable. And whereof one cannot speak, thereof one must be silent.

⊕

Before I leave you completely to your own thoughts, I want to share a lengthy passage from an autobiography of yet another disciple of Spinoza—George Santayana. A philosopher who lived from 1863 to 1952, Santayana is claimed by the atheist movement as one of their own—much like such other Spinozists as Einstein and Nietzsche. But in the passage I would like to cite, Santayana reflects on a trip he took to the south of Italy and expresses just how distasteful it is to be exposed to people who are not merely revolting against a certain type of faith but against *The Name* itself.

More specifically, Santayana presents an actual dialogue between two people, and then he responds to the dialogue with his own commentary. It is not hard to imagine that the dialogue Santayana witnessed could have taken place today in any affluent world metropolis. One of these speakers is depicted as a post-religious, self-satisfied bore. The other is his child—naïve, curious, open-minded, and thus an easy prey to all adults, whether they speak for or against religion, who have cast out any sense of doubt and humility from their encounters with *The Name*. To me, this passage is about as powerful an indictment of contemporary atheism as you can find.

> At Paestum there was only the railway station and no hotel. . . . I was waiting at the station for the train to Naples. The only other persons on the platform were a short fat middle-aged man and a little girl. . . . The child was asking questions about the railway buildings, the rails and the switches. "Where does that other line go?" she asked . . . "Oh, you can see," the father replied, slightly bored. "It runs into that warehouse." "It doesn't go beyond?" "No. It stops there." "And where does this line go?" "To Naples." "And does it end there?" "No, it never ends. It goes on forever." "*Non finisce mai?*" the girl repeated in a changed voice. "*Allora Iddio l'ha fatto?*" "No," said the father dryly, "God didn't make it. It was made by the hand of man. *Le braccia dell'uomo l'hanno fatto.*" And he puffed his cigar with a defiant resentful self-satisfaction as if he were addressing a meeting of conspirators.
>
> I could understand the irritation of this vulgarian. . . . The child must have known that the earth is round, and that the continents are surrounded by water. The railways must stop at the sea, or come round in a circle. But the poor little girl's imagination had been excited and deranged by religious fables. When would such follies die out?

... [S]omehow this little scene shocked me. I saw the claw of Satan strike that child's soul and try to kill the idea of God in it. Why should I mind that? Was the idea of God alive at all in me? No: if you mean the traditional idea. But that was a symbol, vague, variable, mythical, anthropomorphic; the symbol for an overwhelming reality [i.e., what truly is *Ultimate*], a symbol that named and unified in human speech the incalculable powers on which our destiny depends. To observe, record and measure the method by which these powers operate is not to banish the idea of God; it is what the Hebrews called meditating on his ways. The modern hatred of religion is not, like that of the Greek philosophers, a hatred of poetry, for which they wished to substitute cosmology, mathematics or dialectic, still maintaining the reverence of man for what is superhuman. The modern hatred of religion is hatred . . . of all sublimity, hatred of the laughter of the gods. . . . Here, then, . . . at the railway station returning from Paestum, where I had been admiring the courage and the dignity with which the Dorians recognized their place in nature, and filled it to perfection, I found the brutal expression of the opposite mood, the mood of impatience, conceit, low-minded ambition, mechanical inflation, and the worship of material comforts.[2]

Do you recognize the author of that story? I couldn't blame you if you didn't, because he's hard to find in our society. Oh, we have plenty of anti-religious people who dislike traditional religion, freely label it fundamentalism in whatever guise they find it, and look down on anyone— Jew, Christian, or Muslim—who practices such a faith. Similarly, we have plenty of traditional religious people who dislike contemporary society, label it secularism run amok, and look down on anyone who isn't a member of a traditional religious community and who thus must be "Godless." The author of that diatribe falls into neither of those groups. Santayana, the Spinozist, surely would be called "Godless" by many religious people today, but in this passage, he is speaking in support of God—the sublime, mysterious deity who pervades the All—and against those who in the name of progress are waging a war against God, transcendence, and spirituality . . . in other words, the baby, as well as the bathwater.

In the above passage, Santayana is taking on some of the same people who drive me to distraction. His battle, and mine, is against those who find something they don't like (religious fundamentalism) and use

2. Santayana, *Persons and Places*, 452–53.

it to justify giving up on an entire domain of human existence. Whether it is thought of as an object of study, a source of hope, a foundation for meaning in life, or the springboard for an affair with the Most Beloved, religion has been at the forefront of our ancestors' hearts and minds for all of recorded history. To wage a war against that entire realm, root and branch, is one of the most arrogant and reckless pursuits I can imagine.

Unfortunately, the real tragedy revealed by Santayana's statement isn't the existence of men, like the father in the railroad station, who affirmatively scoff at religion and God. No, the tragedy is that for every such individual, there are scores of others who just don't give a damn, for they have fallen prey to a new "god" that the modern world has to offer. Santayana's reflections on his trip to Paestum were written prior to the advent of oral contraceptives, video games, CD players, home computers, and iPhones. If people in his day were worshipping their "material comforts," I suspect that such worship is even more intense now.

The domain of religion is at its most ennobling when it inspires wrestling with the big questions and the greatest challenges. In other words, the religious life in its purest form is inherently hard work. If we are so exhausted by our day jobs that the only thing we have left is the desire to relax, we might as well give up the fight.

Yet that wouldn't be respectful to our ancestors, who put so much effort into all this "God" business. It wouldn't be respectful to ourselves, whose minds are capable of asking the most profound questions and of at least gaining the wisdom captured by Socrates—that humility is the key to enlightenment. It wouldn't be respectful to our descendants, whose happiness requires us to put aside our differences and unite over the holy obligation to serve as trustees over their precious planet. And it wouldn't be respectful to the One who truly is the *Ultimate*.

Besides, do we really want to go through life as laziness-inspired deicides? Is that the best we can do?

American society is at a crossroads today when it comes to God. And leading the way to this crossroads are the young people who do not identify with any traditional faith community and who are part of the reason why "none of the above" has become America's fastest growing religion.

The members of this vanguard need to ask themselves a number of questions. Do they wish to emulate the father in Santayana's story? Do they see the worship of God as being in competition with the betterment of humankind? Do they find religion to be a distraction—an antiquated discipline, like astrology, that is unworthy of contemporary minds? Are they willing to snuff out our sense of the transcendent or of the unity beyond the multiplicity? Or are they challenged by the prospect of finding a new sense of the Divine that speaks to them—one that provides joy and meaning, just like the Old Time Religion, but without the associations of God as a strict father whose morality was mired in millennia-old ideas?

The more that I ask those questions, the more skeptical I become. It is harder to see us embracing that type of challenge than it is to imagine us washing our hands of the entire religious project. That is, after all, the easy way out of the predicament.

But just once, let's say "Hell, no!" to the easy path.

Instead of burying *The Name* because it has often been misused in the past, let's figure out how best to use it in the future. What do you say we each honor the God who we believe is worthy of *The Name*, and not worry so much about all the gods who are not?

Take it from an iconoclast and a believer—as fun as it is to identify the false gods of the world, it is even more satisfying to search for the One who isn't false. We will never truly find that God. Then again, we will never embark on a more ennobling journey. I wish you all the best with yours.

Bibliography

Al-Badawi, Mostafa. *Man & The Universe*. Amman, Jordan: Wakeel, 2002.

Ali, Abdullah Yusuf. *The Meaning of the Holy Qur'an*. Beltsville, MD: Amana, 1989.

Armstrong, Karen. *The Case for God*. New York: Knopf, 2009.

Beiser, Frederick C., ed. *The Cambridge Companion to Hegel*. Cambridge: Cambridge University Press, 1998.

Birnbaum, Philip. *Daily Prayer Book*. New York: Hebrew, 1949.

Bradley, Bill. "Speech by Senator Bill Bradley on the Rodney King Verdict." April 30, 1992. No pages. Online: http://www.billbradley.com/assets/PDF/920430_rodneyKing_speech.pdf.

Buber, Martin. *I and Thou*. Translated by Walter Kaufmann. New York: Touchstone, 1996.

————. *On Judaism*. Edited by Nahum Glatzer. New York: Schocken, 1973.

————. "Spinoza, Sabbattai Zevi and the Baal-Shem." In *The Origin and Meaning of Hasidism*, translated by Maurice Friedman, 89–112. New York: Horizon, 1960.

Cliteur, Paul. *The Secular Outlook: In Defense of Moral and Political Secularism*. New Brunswick, NJ: Rutgers University Press, 2010.

Cooper, David A. *God is a Verb: Kabbalah and the Practice of Mystical Judaism*. New York: Riverhead, 1997.

Dawkins, Richard. *The God Delusion*. Boston: Houghton Mifflin, 2006.

Dyson, Freeman J. *Disturbing the Universe*. New York: Basic, 1979.

Friedman, Maurice S. *Martin Buber: The Life of Dialogue*. London: Routledge, 2002.

Goethe, Johann Wolfgang von. *The Auto-Biography of Goethe*. Translated by A. J. W. Morrison. London: Bohn, 1849.

————. "Faust." In *J. W. von Goethe: Selected Works*, 747–1049. Translated by Barker Fairley. New York: Knopf, 2000.

————. *Wilhelm Meister's Apprenticeship*. Translated by Eric A. Blackall. Princeton: Princeton University Press, 1995.

Green, Darrell. Pro Football Hall of Fame Enshrinement Speech. No pages. Online: http://www.profootballhof.com/hof/member.aspx?PlayerId=273&tab=Speech.

Gullan-Whur, Margaret. *Within Reason: A Life of Spinoza*. New York: St. Martin's, 1998.

Gurary, Noson. *The Thirteen Principles of Faith*. Northvale, NJ: Aronson, 1996.

Heidegger, Martin. *Identity and Difference*. Translated by Joan Stambaugh. 1969. Reprint. Chicago: University of Chicago Press, 2002.

Heschel, Abraham Joshua. "A Conversation with Doctor Abraham Joshua Heschel." Interview with Carl Stern. *The Eternal Light*. NBC. February 4, 1973. Television. Reprinted as "Carl Stern's Interview with Dr. Heschel." In *Moral Grandeur and Spiritual Audacity*, edited by Susannah Heschel, 395–412. New York: Farrar, Straus & Giroux, 1996.

———. *The Prophets*. New York: Harper Torchbooks, 1962.

James, William. *A Pluralistic Universe*. Lincoln, NE: University of Nebraska Press, 1996.

Johnston, Mark. *Saving God: Religion after Idolatry*. Princeton, NJ: Princeton University Press, 2009.

Kant, Immanuel. *Groundwork for the Metaphysics of Morals*. Translated by Allen W. Wood. New Haven, CT: Yale University, 2002.

Kenny, Anthony. *The Wittgenstein Reader*. 2nd ed. Malden, MA: Blackwell, 2006.

King, Martin Luther, Jr. *The Papers of Martin Luther King Jr.* Berkeley, CA: University of California Press, 1994.

Levinas, Emmanuel. *Of God Who Comes to Mind*. Translated by Bettina Bergo. Stanford, CA: Stanford University Press, 1998.

———. *Totality and Infinity: An Essay on Exteriority*. Translated by Alphonso Lingis. Dordrecht, The Netherlands: Kluwer Academic, 1991.

Marx, Karl. "Toward the Critique of Hegel's Philosophy of Law: Introduction." In *Writings of the Young Marx on Philosophy and Society*, translated by Lloyd David Easton and Kurt H. Guddat, 249–64. Indianapolis: Hackett, 1997.

Michaelson, Jay. *Everything is God: The Radical Path of Nondual Judaism*. Boston: Trumpeter, 2009.

Mill, John Stuart. "Coleridge." In *The Collected Works of John Stuart Mill, Volume X: Essays on Ethics, Religion, and Society*, edited by John M. Robson, 117–64. London: Routledge & Kegan Paul, 1985.

Moreau, Pierre-Francois. "Spinoza's Reception and Influence." In *The Cambridge Companion to Spinoza*, edited by Don Garrett, 408–33. Cambridge: Cambridge University Press, 1996.

Nadler, Steven. *Spinoza: A Life*. Cambridge: Cambridge University Press, 1999.

Nietzsche, Friedrich. *Beyond Good and Evil*. Translated by R. J. Hollingdale. Harmondsworth, UK: Penguin, 1977.

———. *The Gay Science*. Translated by Josefine Nauckhoff and Adrian Del Caro. Cambridge: Cambridge University Press, 2001.

———. *Twilight of the Idols and The Anti-Christ*. Translated by R. J. Hollingdale. Harmondsworth, UK: Penguin, 1979.

The Pew Global Attitudes Project. "Among Wealthy Nations, U.S. Stands Alone in Its Embrace of Religion." December 19, 2002. No pages. Online: http://people-press. org/.

Plato. *Selected Dialogues of Plato: The Benjamin Jowett Translation*. New York: Modern Library, 2000.

Rosenzweig, Franz. *The Star of Redemption*. Translated by William Hallo. Notre Dame, IN: University of Notre Dame Press, 2002.

Samuels, Ruth. *Bible Stories for Jewish Children*. New York: Ktav, 1954.

Santayana, George. *Persons and Places*. Cambridge, MA: MIT, 1987.

Schacter-Shalomi, Zalman. *Wrapped in a Holy Flame: Teachings and Tales of the Hasidic Masters*. San Francisco: Jossey-Bass, 2003.

Spinoza, Baruch. "Ethics." In *Spinoza: Complete Works*, translated by Samuel Shirley, 213–382. Indianapolis: Hackett, 2002.

———. "The Letters." In *Spinoza: Complete Works*, translated by Samuel Shirley, 755–959. Indianapolis: Hackett, 2002.

———. "Treatise on the Emendation of the Intellect." In *Spinoza: Complete Works*, translated by Samuel Shirley, 1–30. Indianapolis: Hackett, 2002.

Tillich, Paul. *Systematic Theology: Volume One*. Chicago: University of Chicago Press, 1951.

Unamuno, Miguel de. *Tragic Sense of Life*. Translated by J. E. Crawford Flitch. New York: Dover, 1954.

Unitarian Universalist Association of Congregations. "Hospitality and Marketing Outreach Resources: The Uncommon Denomination SM." No pages. Online: http://www.uua.org/growth/marketing/uncommondenomination/

Webster's New World College Dictionary. 4th ed. Foster City, CA: IDG Books Worldwide, 2001.

Wilber, Ken. *Integral Spirituality*. Boston: Integral, 2007.

World Committee for the Victims of German Fascism. *The Brown Book of the Hitler Terror and the Burning of the Reichstag*. New York: Knopf, 1933.

Yovel, Yirmiyahu. *Spinoza and Other Heretics: The Adventures of Immanence*. Princeton: Princeton University Press, 1989.

General Index

deicide/God-slayer, 45–47, 49, 51,
    80, 172, 194, 205, 222
Deism/Deists, 9, 218
determinism, *see* free will and
    determinism
Deleuze, Gilles, 67
devotion, *see* piety
diversity, *see* multiplicity/diversity
divine drama, the, 133, 172, 175,
    182, 196, 209
Dixon, Frank, 70
doubt, 1–3, 35, 220, *see* humility
Ein Sof, 74–77, 108
Einstein, Albert, 49–50, 69, 136,
    138, 173, 191–94, 220
enchantment, sense of, 26–27, 36,
    55–56, 80, 130–33, 153, 218
Enlightenment, era of, 9, 31, 42, 114
environmental concerns, 167–69,
    203, 207
Ethics of the Fathers, *see* Talmud
fatalism, 44, 175, 197
Fiddler on the Roof, 106
finitude, 76, 108, 177–82
Frank, Anne, 66
free will and determinism, 37–38,
    46, 69, 115–16, 171, 178
freedom, 46–47, 53, 83, 105, 105,
    115–16, 118, 170, 184, 198–
    99, 206–7, 219
    as a fundamental value, 206–7
Freud, Sigmund, 48, 202
Friedman, Maurice, 86
Fulghum, Robert, 19, 23
fundamentalism, 4, 8, 11–12, 62,
    136–37, 149, 221
Ginsberg, Alan, 66
God,
    as the Absolute Other, 88
    as the Absolute Person, 86,
        91–92
    as acting supra-consciously, 216
    as Adonai, 20, 70, 75, 88–89,
        106, 171
    as Allah, 20, 33–34, 72, 77,
        93–94, 100, 105–6, 112, 117,
        171, 186

    as beloved, 24, 60, 104, 106, 122,
        132, 153–56, 222
    as benefactor, 118, 125–29, 140
    as closer to us than our jugular
        veins, 34, 66, 105, 118, 216
    as commander, 19, 22, 25–27,
        31, 46, 97–98, 104, 117–18,
        148–52, 169, 185–86, 200,
        216–17
    as the Consciousness of the
        Universe, 72, 95, 98, 155
    as the Cosmic Santa Claus, 26,
        29, 58, 72, 92, 155
    as the Cosmic/Divine
        Superman, 13, 31, 41, 98,
        178–79
    as the Creator of the universe,
        20, 40, 73, 178, 192–93, 210
    as cruel/wrathful, 21, 29
    as an ethical role model, 174,
        183
    as the Ein Sof, *see* Ein Sof
    as the Eternal, 5, 32, 70, 73–74,
        87, 89, 93, 100, 112, 115–16,
        181, 196
    as the Eternal Thou, 2, 13, 79,
        82, 86–87, 90, 94–95, 132,
        135
    as flawed/imperfect (from a
        human perspective), 116,
        128, 172
    as friend, 144–47
    as God the Father, 95, 109–10,
        208, as father or parent
        generally, 41, 179, 223
    as the Ground (or Source) of
        Being, 70, 81, 94, 104–5,
        108, 110–12, 114–16, 118,
        130, 138, 140, 142, 165, 174,
        179, 197, 202, 207, 210
    as Hashem, 117, 129, 146–47
    as the Infinite, 10, 38, 69–76, 80,
        88–89, 94, 107–8, 111–17,
        128, 131–32, 140, 146, 148–
        49, 165, 171, 174–81, 183,
        206–7, 210–11, 215–17, 219

Scripture Index